NAFTA, WTO and Global Business Strategy

NAFTA, WTO and Global Business Strategy

How AIDS, Trade and Terrorism Affect Our Economic Future

Bradly J. Condon

QUORUM BOOKS
Westport, Connecticut ▪ London

Library of Congress Cataloging-in-Publication Data

Condon, Bradly J.
    NAFTA, WTO and global business strategy : how AIDS, trade and terrorism affect our economic future / Bradly J. Condon.
      p. cm.
    Includes bibliographical references and index.
    ISBN 1–56720–549–6 (alk. paper)
    1. Free trade. 2. Free trade—Environmental aspects. 3. Free trade—Social aspects.
4. Free trade—North America. 5. International business enterprises—Management.
6. Business planning. 7. Canada. Treaties, etc. 1992 Oct. 7. 8. World Trade
Organization. I. Title.
    HF1713.C627 2002
    382′.71—dc21   2002023040

British Library Cataloguing in Publication Data is available.

Library of Congress Catalog Card Number: 2002023040
ISBN: 1–56720–549–6

First published in 2002

Quorum Books, 88 Post Road West, Westport, CT 06881
An imprint of Greenwood Publishing Group, Inc.
www.quorumbooks.com

Printed in the United States of America

The paper used in this book complies with the
Permanent Paper Standard issued by the National
Information Standards Organization (Z39.48–1984).

10 9 8 7 6 5 4 3 2 1

Dedicated to my Mom and Dad, Cathy and Kip Condon

Contents

Tables

Preface

Over the last few years, clashes between police and protesters have become fixtures at international meetings where government leaders gather to discuss political, legal and economic aspects of globalization, particularly trade agreements. Beginning with the World Trade Organization (WTO) meeting in Seattle in 1999, "globophobics" have gathered to protest efforts to achieve the integration of the global economy. In these battles, international trade agreements and global corporations are cast by their opponents as the enemies of humankind. What do these trade agreements contain? What is the strategy of global corporations? This book examines trade agreements in detail and their relation to global business strategy.

At the same time, the world has witnessed the onset of global environmental threats, the rapid spread of the AIDS epidemic, and the start of a global war on terrorism. None of these issues can be separated from the globalization of trade and business. This book examines these issues and shows how they interact with the North American Free Trade Agreement (NAFTA), WTO and global business strategy.

The World Trade Organization administers a variety of agreements, covering among other things trade in goods, trade in services, foreign investment, government procurement and intellectual property. Regional trade agreements, such as the North American Free Trade Agreement, interact with the global regime in ways that can make or break a firm's business strategy. Moreover, regional trade agreements can offer clues as to the directions in which global agreements may be headed.

A firm's strategy needs to take into account both the impact of today's rules of international trade and investment and how progressive stages of trade and investment liberalization will affect strategies in the future. Firms also need strategies for influencing the negotiation of future agreements. Most importantly, firms need to know how these agreements can be used to support their global business strategy.

This book explains key aspects of the two major trade agreements that apply in North America. It uses cases to illustrate how these agreements work and how they interact with firm strategy. In each of these cases, trade rules affect crucial business interests. Whether doing business within the NAFTA region, into the NAFTA countries or from the NAFTA countries to the rest of the world, business people will want to consult this book when formulating strategies.

This book is intended primarily for students, policy makers, lawyers and business people who want to understand what international trade agreements contain, how they work, and how they affect business. In my experience teaching undergraduate and graduate business students, and in conducting seminars for business executives and government policy makers, I have observed that most nonlawyers want to learn about trade agreements in greater detail. This book can be used not only in courses but as a reference source, to be taken off the shelf and consulted regularly by anyone involved in international business.

However, this book is about more than just business. The intersection of regional and global trade rules with global business strategy has major implications for global prosperity and security. It will therefore be of interest to anyone who wants to understand how what is happening in the world today will affect their economic future.

In the writing of this book, I received the help and support of many friends and colleagues. As in all my endeavors, my parents, Kip and Cathy Condon, have offered constant encouragement. Alice DuBose has provided invaluable feedback throughout the writing process. María de la Luz S. de Uriarte has provided constant *apoyo*. My colleague at the Instituto Tecnológico Autónomo de México (ITAM), Dr. Tapen Sinha, has been a guiding light, in addition to contributing to the writing of some of the cases in this book and providing insightful comments on earlier drafts. I would like to thank him also for his contributions to part of chapter 7.

I am grateful to the hundreds of students who have taught me over the years about the importance of trade agreements to business people. I thank ITAM for providing me a place to hang my hat in Mexico. I am particularly grateful to Dr. Carlos Alcérreca for sparking my interest in the topic of global business strategy.

I am grateful to Jim Dunton of Quorum Books for seeing the value in this topic and shepherding my work through the proposal process. Lynn Zelem, Senior Production Editor at Greenwood Publishing Group, and copy editor Pelham Boyer did a superb job of editing the manuscript, which immensely improved the final product.

Chapters 1 and 2 are based on materials I developed for courses at Simon Fraser University and ITAM. In chapter 3, the opening case was developed as an article (with Tapen Sinha) that was published by the *Estey Journal for Law and Economics in International Trade*. The analysis of the impact of WTO and NAFTA rules on financial services was developed in the following articles, in which I analyze the provisions affecting the insurance industry:

Tapen Sinha and Bradly Condon, "The Mexican Insurance Sector under the Shadow of the North American Free Trade Agreement (NAFTA)," *Journal of Insurance Regulation* 20, no. 2 (2001), 207–19.

Bradly Condon, "Smoke and Mirrors: A Comparative Analysis of WTO and NAFTA Provisions Affecting the International Expansion of Insurance Firms in North America," *Connecticut Insurance Law Journal* 8 (2001), 97–130.

Bradly Condon and Tapen Sinha, "Digesting the Regulatory Layer Cake in the North American Insurance Market: Integrating Trade Agreements in the International Expansion Plans of Insurance and Reinsurance Companies," *Global Reinsurance* (2001).

The last article won a Lumina Award for Pioneering Research. I am grateful to my coauthor, Tapen Sinha, as well as the editors of these journals, whose assistance in developing my ideas was invaluable.

Abbreviations

ABT	(WTO) Agreement on Basic Telecommunications
ADD	antidumping duty
APEC	Asia Pacific Economic Co-operation
ATC	(WTO) Agreement on Textiles and Clothing
BCSC	Supreme Court of British Columbia
BIT	bilateral investment treaty
CITES	Convention on International Trade in Endangered Species
CUSFTA	Canada-United States Free Trade Agreement
CVC	(WTO) customs valuation code
CVD	countervailing duties
DSB	Dispute Settlement Body
FDI	foreign direct investment
FIL	(Mexican) Foreign Investment Law
FSA	(WTO) Agreement on Trade in Financial Services
FTAA	Free Trade Agreement of the Americas
GATT	General Agreement on Tariffs and Trade
GPA	(WTO) Agreement on Government Procurement
HS	Harmonized Commodity Description and Coding System
ICC	(U.S.) Interstate Commerce Commission
ICJ	International Court of Justice
ICSID	(World Bank) International Center for the Settlement of Investment Disputes

IJC	International Joint Commission
IMF	International Monetary Fund
ITA	information technology agreement
ITC	(U.S.) International Trade Commission
MAI	(OECD) Multilateral Agreement on Investment
MEUFTA	Mexico-EU Free Trade Agreement
MFN	most-favored nation
MNE	multinational enterprise
MOU	memorandum of understanding
NAFTA	North American Free Trade Agreement
NTB	nontariff barrier to trade
OECD	Organization for Economic Co-operation and Development
TRIMS	(WTO) Agreement on Trade-Related Investment Measures
TRIPS	(WTO) Agreement on Trade-Related Aspects of Intellectual Property Rights
USTR	U.S. trade representative
WB	World Bank
WTO	World Trade Organization

Chapter 1

The Global Trading System and International Business Strategy

INTRODUCTION

Canada, Mexico and the United States are all members of both the North American Free Trade Agreement (NAFTA) and the World Trade Organization (WTO). As a result, the governments of all three countries are subject to the obligations of both agreements. In most respects, NAFTA is more advanced than WTO. The intersection of the two agreements affects trade policy and business strategy in many ways. Business people need to understand the relationship between these agreements, whether they are doing business within the NAFTA region, expanding from the NAFTA region to other parts of the world, or expanding into the NAFTA region from elsewhere.

The goal of business strategy is to allow the firm to achieve its goals in an unpredictable environment. International trade agreements seek to eliminate some of the uncertainty of the legal environment, by establishing boundaries for the trade-related laws of their members. The reduction and elimination of barriers to the movement of goods, services and people, along with laws protecting investments (including investments in intellectual property), expand the strategic options available to firms. However, many barriers remain. Global free trade is a long-term project.

Firms can help to shape the rules that are negotiated in trade agreements by lobbying their own governments to take specific negotiating positions. They can also play a role in the enforcement of trade agreements that have been reached. It is important for business to be involved in the trade liberalization process.

To be involved in this process, business strategists need to understand what trade agreements contain and how they work. As the labyrinth of

international agreements grows, creating what some call "treaty conges-
tion," this task becomes more complex.[1] Access to major markets affects
the success of multinational enterprises (MNEs). International trade and
investment agreements determine the kinds of access that are available.

Regional trade and investment agreements, such as the European Union
(EU) and NAFTA, have reinforced the organization of business at the re-
gional level. Rugman argues that failures in multilateral efforts to liberalize trade and investment globally—such as the inability to launch the
WTO Millennium Round in Seattle, and the abortive Organization for
Economic Co-operation and Development (OECD) negotiations on multilateral investment—have hampered the efforts of multinational enterprises
(MNEs) to organize their activities on a global basis.[2] However, at Doha,
WTO members succeeded in a launching a new round of global trade
negotiations. The agenda includes the key issues of services, investment
and trade remedy laws.

This book begins with an overview of the context in which trade negotiations take place. It then compares the progress made by WTO and
NAFTA on goods, services, investment, intellectual property and dispute
settlement and how these agreements affect global business strategy. An
examination of current trends then provides a basis for predicting what
the future may hold for NAFTA, WTO and global business strategy.

The intersection of regional and global trade rules and global business
strategy has major implications for the prosperity and security of the
world. Global security issues such as environmental protection, AIDS, and
terrorism interact to affect the outcome of trade negotiations. In turn, trade
affects the manner in which global security issues are handled. Thus, the
detailed rules of NAFTA and WTO must be viewed as part of a bigger
picture.

THE ECONOMIC RATIONALE FOR FREE TRADE

Over the past three centuries, there has been a gradual evolution of economic theories on international trade. The theory of comparative advantage explains how international trade increases wealth. However, many
governments continue to pursue protectionist trade policies that are more
closely aligned with mercantilism.

Mercantilism and the Balance of Payments

In the seventeenth and eighteenth centuries, mercantilism argued that
the goal of national trade policy was to maintain a surplus in the balance
of payments by having more exports than imports. Although later developments in economic theory showed that this is an unrealistic goal over

the long term, the trade policy of many nations is still influenced by this notion.

In 1752 David Hume developed a theory that international trade maintains equilibrium in the trade balance. This theory explains why mercantilism does not work in the long run. There are two market adjustment mechanisms that operate to bring a country's trade balance surplus or deficit back into equilibrium. The *internal market adjustment* refers to the movement of prices and incomes within the country in response to the state of the trade balance. The *external market adjustment* refers to fluctuations in the value of the country's currency with respect to the currencies of other countries—that is, exchange rate fluctuations.

The Internal Market Adjustment

When a country exports more than it imports, the result is a surplus in its trade balance. Its internal money supply grows as the residents of the country receive more payments from foreigners for the goods and services sold and the foreign investments made. Regardless of where these payments or investments are deposited, they become assets of the country's residents.

As the money supply increases, the residents spend more and domestic prices rise—that is, inflation occurs. Increases in domestic prices make foreign goods relatively cheaper, and the residents import more goods from abroad. The increase in imports corrects the surplus and brings the trade balance back into equilibrium. The reverse analysis applies in the case of a country with a trade deficit.

The External Market Adjustment

When a country exports more than it imports, another result is an increase in demand for the currency of the nation. Foreigners must buy more of the currency to pay for the goods and services of the country. At the same time, there is relatively less demand for foreign currency on the part of the domestic residents, because they are buying fewer imports relative to exports. The increase in demand for the currency causes it to appreciate in value with respect to foreign currency. This makes the country's exports more expensive for foreigners, causing them to buy fewer goods and services and shrinking the surplus.

Other factors may affect the equilibrium of the trade balance and thus maintain a country's surplus for an extended period of time. For example, foreign consumers may prefer the country's goods to those of other countries notwithstanding the higher cost generated by currency appreciation. Luxury goods, such as Mercedes and BMWs, would fall into this category. In other words, some consumers do not care what they pay for certain products. On the other hand, the exporters of the country may decide to absorb the cost of the currency appreciation rather than pass it on to foreign customers, where the product is more price sensitive. Finally, the value of the currency itself will be influenced by more than just the state of the current account. Currency markets also respond to such factors as the size of government deficits and the political stability of the country.

The Theory of Absolute Advantage

In 1776, Adam Smith's theory of absolute advantage argued that countries should engage in free trade. In this view, a country should specialize in the production of goods in which it enjoys an absolute advantage—that is, goods that it can produce more efficiently than its trade partner. Such trade would increase wealth in both trade partners and could even increase wealth in a country that chooses the path of unilateral trade liberalization. With specialization, total production increases using the same amount of resources, thereby increasing overall wealth.

However, for the two countries to experience gains from trade, their advantages need to be complementary. Moreover, inside each country there will be winners and losers, since the distribution of the gains from specialization would be unequal. Those who win will be in favor of free trade, while those who lose will oppose it.

In practice, it is difficult for one country to maintain an absolute advantage in a product. Moreover, a country that has no absolute advantage in any product would, in theory, be ruined by international competition.

The Theory of Comparative Advantage

In 1817, David Ricardo's theory of comparative advantage filled in the gaps left by the theory of absolute advantage. He argued that, given two countries trading two products, free trade brings mutual advantage even where one nation has an absolute advantage in both products. In his now famous example, England can produce cloth with a hundred units of labor and wine with 120 units. Portugal enjoys an absolute advantage in both goods, producing cloth with ninety units and wine with eighty units. If each specializes in the production of the good in which it enjoys a comparative advantage, England gets wine for the equivalent of a hundred units (by trading cloth for it), and Portugal gets cloth for the equivalent of eighty (in exchange for wine); both are better off. Each country increases production by specializing in the product it can produce relatively more efficiently—that is, the product in which it has a comparative advantage. Through specialization, there is an increase in production using the same amount of resources.

Critics of this theory argue that it assumes that capital and labor are not mobile and that it therefore no longer applies in a world where capital moves freely and production can be moved to countries with lower labor costs. Notwithstanding, and though it has been further refined over time, the theory of comparative advantage still forms the basis of free trade policy.

In the 1920s, Heckscher and Ohlin's "factor proportions hypothesis" argued that countries enjoy a comparative advantage in goods that use their more abundant factors of production, such as capital, land or labor, more intensively. Countries should therefore export goods that use abundant factors in exchange for imports that use scarce factors. A simple example would be that a country with plenty of capital but little arable land should export capital-intensive goods and import agricultural ones.

In the 1960s, Vernon's "product cycle theory" argued that countries with vast financial capital and highly specialized human capital enjoy a comparative advantage in the research and development stage of product innovation. However, once the innovation becomes widely diffused and its cost of production goes down, the comparative advantage shifts to countries that can produce the product at lower cost. For example, Japan might enjoy an advantage in developing the videocassette recorder, because it has the capital to invest in research and the scientists to do the research. Later, however, countries with lower manufacturing costs, such as China, would be able to produce VCRs more cheaply.

Since the 1980s, global mobility of factors of production and increased sophistication in governmental industrial policies have led to a greater effort on the part of governments to shape comparative advantages. Advances in communications and transportation have increased the mobility of financial capital, technology, human capital, and labor. Specialization and comparative advantage are influenced by savings rates, which increase the availability of investment capital. Governments can increase savings and direct the investment of savings through such mechanisms as tax incentives.

Government investment in human capital—for example, education and research—helps to shape comparative advantage in knowledge-intensive industries. Investments in public infrastructure, such as transportation and communication systems, can make a country more attractive as a location for industries that require the infrastructure. Tax incentives and other policies can promote the growth of specific industries in which a country enjoys a comparative advantage. Michael Porter's "theory of competitive advantage" has further shaped the kinds of policies governments adopt to promote industries that can compete globally.

HOW TRADE AGREEMENTS WORK

The globalization of the world economy is characterized by increasing flows of international trade in goods, services and foreign investment.

Evidence of the economic benefits of trade and investment liberalization has led many governments to open their economies to trade and investment. In recent years there has been a proliferation of international trade-and-investment agreements at the bilateral, regional and global level. WTO membership has increased dramatically. With the entry of China and Taiwan at the WTO's Doha meeting in 2001, membership stood at 144 countries, with twenty-eight more waiting for their memberships to be approved. Governments now recognize the importance of capturing a share of global trade and investment flows if they are to achieve economic growth. Rather than discourage foreign investment, most governments now actively seek it out, though barriers remain in some industries. In short, most countries now seek to capture the benefits of globalization.

A larger and more diverse WTO membership and the increased complexity of the global economy have expanded the range of policies and laws governed by global trade agreements. Trade agreements facilitate international business. Nevertheless, domestic politics still influence the choices governments make. Special interest groups seek to shape trade policies to suit their specific agendas.

Regulating the Regulators

Governments pass many laws and regulations governing business. Some are designed to favor certain business interests over others. Often, domestic business interests are favored over foreign business interests. Free trade generates winners and losers. The losers oppose free trade and lobby for regulations that protect them from foreign competition. Such regulations are the focus of trade agreements.

Of course, governments pass other kinds of regulations whose purpose is something other than to play favorites among various business interests. Criminal law seeks to constrain actions that spring from the darker side of the human soul. Environmental law seeks to preserve a healthy, balanced environment in which to live. Contract law makes people honor their commitments. Consumer protection law tries to keep gullible people from getting swindled. Tort law tries to constrain incompetence, by making the negligent pay for mistakes that cause harm to others. Constitutional law places limits in the authority of governments to interfere in the lives of their citizens. Privacy laws make busybodies mind their own business. The list goes on. What these kinds of laws have in common is that they are not regulated by trade agreements, except when they embody regulations whose true purpose is to restrict trade.

Trade agreements establish limits on the kinds of regulations its members may use to regulate international business. They are contracts between countries, contracts that establish regulatory boundaries. The rules contained in trade agreements are not dictated by some global parliament;

the countries themselves agree on the rules after lengthy negotiations. Trade agreements regulate the regulators, much like the constitutions of many countries.

The basic structure of trade agreements consists of general rules, general exceptions, narrow exceptions (known as *reservations*), and dispute-settlement mechanisms. The most important general rules prohibit discrimination. The "national treatment rule" prohibits discrimination between nationals and foreigners. The "most-favored-nation rule" prohibits discrimination between different foreigners. Both rules apply to a broad range of matters, including goods, services, intellectual property rights and investments. National laws that violate either of these nondiscrimination rules may be challenged before arbitration panels, subject to exceptions.

General exceptions exempt specific categories of law from the application of the trade rules. The main objective is to ensure that trade law does not impinge upon the right of member countries to maintain independent policies on nontrade issues that affect the welfare of their citizens. Some of the most important general exceptions cover environmental protection, health, safety, and national security. A national law that violates a general rule may nevertheless be maintained if it fits a general exception.

Countries may negotiate exemptions for certain industries to protect them from foreign competition. Exemptions are listed as reservations in the agreements. Reservations provide a means to accommodate specific issues that otherwise could be deal breakers. Reservations are often of limited duration or subject to future negotiation. When they expire, the laws in question must be amended to comply with the general rules or fit under general exceptions.

Key Matters Governed by Modern Trade Agreements

Modern trade agreements regulate far more than just trade. The General Agreement on Tariffs and Trade (GATT) has substantially reduced tariffs on goods over the past fifty years. As tariffs have been eliminated or reduced, GATT members have turned their attention to nontariff barriers to trade in goods, such as standards and customs procedures.

NAFTA expanded the scope of trade rules far beyond merchandise trade. It contains chapters on foreign investment, trade in services, temporary entry of business people, standards, government procurement, competition law and intellectual property, in addition to provisions relating to trade in goods. Side agreements on environmental cooperation and labor rights link these issues to trade and investment in the free trade area.

The conclusion of the Uruguay Round of GATT negotiations followed the implementation of NAFTA. In addition to creating the WTO, the Uruguay Round expanded the scope of WTO rules beyond merchandise trade. Many of the topics covered by WTO agreements echo those of NAFTA. However, many WTO agreements have less depth than equivalent NAFTA provisions. The comparative lack of depth in some WTO agreements reflects the compromises that had to be made to achieve agreement among over one hundred countries that ranged from the most advanced economies to the least developed.

A BRIEF HISTORY OF TRADE AGREEMENTS

International trade is not a recent phenomenon. Peoples have traded goods for millennia. The Aztecs of the central Mexican highlands traded with the tribes of the coastal plains. Ancient Greeks, Romans and others conducted a flourishing trade around the Mediterranean. The search for better trade routes motivated Marco Polo to travel to China and Christopher Columbus to sail to America. People have always traded to gain access to goods that others produced and to find buyers for their own.

Not surprisingly, international rules governing trade go far back in history too. The Roman Empire created the *lex mercatoria*. The Aztecs also had rules governing trade relations between the Aztec traders and others: if an Aztec trader were cheated, the penalty for the cheater was death; if an Aztec trader were killed, the killer's people would be enslaved. Modern trade agreements take a less drastic approach.

The World Trade Organization: Better Late than Never

In 1947, twenty-two countries signed a "provisional" agreement to reduce tariffs on goods and begin eliminating other barriers to trade in goods. The agreement, GATT, became the primary vehicle for international trade liberalization when negotiations to create a permanent "International Trade Organization" (ITO) failed. The ITO was meant to be one of the three pillars of postwar peace and prosperity, together with the International Monetary Fund (IMF) and the World Bank.

After World War II, policy makers realized that protectionism, in the form of increasingly higher tariffs and other trade barriers, had contributed to the severity of the global depression of the 1930s. The depression, in turn, had contributed to the rise of fascism and the war. They reasoned that countries that were prosperous and linked by international trade would be less likely to engage in war. The goal of the three institutions was therefore to raise living standards and form stronger links between member economies.

Over the years, successive rounds of negotiations added more members to GATT, continued tariff reductions and created a series of related agreements. In 1968 GATT members negotiated the Anti-Dumping Code to regulate the use of antidumping duties. In 1973, the Multi-Fiber Arrangement created a specific set of rules for trade in clothing and textiles. In 1979 GATT members added a Subsidies Code, a Standards Code and a Customs Valuation Code. However, GATT members could pick and choose which agreements they signed.

The most ambitious round of negotiations, the Uruguay Round, took place between 1986 and 1993. The Uruguay Round created the WTO. It linked most of the agreements together; membership in the WTO required acceptance of almost all of the agreements that were negotiated. One hundred nineteen countries became members of WTO at the end of the Uruguay Round.

The main achievements of the negotiations were to reduce the average tariff on goods to 6 percent; to apply the general rules of GATT to agriculture, textiles, services and intellectual property; and to improve the dispute-settlement system. Previously, each member country had effectively had a veto in votes on whether to adopt the decisions of arbitration panels. The new agreement eliminated the veto and created a permanent appeal court for decisions of panels.

After the formal conclusion of the Uruguay Round, the WTO itself oversaw negotiations in unresolved areas. For example, negotiations have created several sectoral agreements in such markets as telecommunication services, computers, financial services, and textiles and clothing.

In 1999, the WTO met in Seattle to begin a new round of negotiations to liberalize global trade further; it was to have been called the Millennium Round. However, a split between developing and developed countries caused the talks to fail, and no new round of negotiations was launched. The meeting was marred by violent protests, which became known as the "Battle in Seattle." The Seattle protests marked the beginning of a pattern in which violent protests accompany meetings held anywhere in the world by government leaders to address international economic issues. The term "globophobes" has since been coined to refer to the loose coalition of labor, environmental, anarchist and other groups who participate in the protests.

In November 2001, WTO members met in Doha, Qatar. This time, the protesters were kept away from the meeting, security for which had been heightened because of the terrorist attacks of September 11 and the war in Afghanistan. Once again, the divide between developed and developing countries threatened to derail the talks. However, members agreed on a negotiating agenda and launched a new round, scheduled to take place from January 2002 to January 2005.

The European Union: The Seeds of NAFTA's Future?

A provision of GATT permits members to form free trade areas and customs unions that liberalize trade to a greater extent than GATT does.

A customs area goes farther than a free trade area in integrating the economies of its members. Members of a customs union adopt a common trade policy with respect to nonmembers; once goods from nonmembers enter, they move freely throughout the customs union. In a free trade area, members maintain independent trade policies with respect to nonmembers; thus, each member maintains its own customs controls to regulate the flow of goods across its borders.

The process of economic integration in Europe began with the creation in 1951 of the European Coal and Steel Community. The motivation was similar to the reasons for the creation of the IMF, WB and ITO/WTO. Having suffered through two world wars, European leaders began the process of economic integration by pooling resources that were essential to warfare.

In 1957, six nations signed the Treaty of Rome to form the European Community. From 1958 to 1985 membership grew from six to ten members. From 1987 to 1992, the members negotiated the Single Europe Act, which provided for the harmonization of standards and the mutual recognition of certificates. It also changed the decision-making system from one of consensus to majority voting in the Council of Ministers on "single market" issues.

In 1994, the Maastricht Treaty of European Union scheduled the creation of a common currency. The "euro" was launched January 1, 1999; notes and coins changed on 1 January 2002. The political purpose of the common currency was to encourage further European integration and to provide a counterweight to the negotiating power of the United States. The economic purpose was to reduce transaction costs associated with currency exchange, to coordinate fiscal and economic policies, and to reduce interest rates.

The process of European integration has moved well beyond a customs union, but not without resistance to deeper integration. The division of power between national governments and supranational institutions has been a difficult issue. The EU has several supranational institutions to deal with political, economic and legal affairs. The European Council is made up of heads of state, plus the president of the European Commission. The European Commission, legislators located in Brussels, consists of twenty commissioners appointed for four-year terms. The United Kingdom, France, Germany, Italy, Spain each appoint two, while the remaining members appoint one each. The Council of Ministers must approve EU laws. The European Parliament is directly elected, but its role is more consultative than legislative. The European Court of Justice has one judge per member country, and is the supreme court of EU law. A European Central Bank oversees monetary policy. Some members have proposed further movement in the direction of political union.

North Americans sometimes see the EU as an example of where NAFTA may be headed. However, historical, political and economic differences between Europe and North America should be taken into account when considering whether to move in the same direction. Europe's history of devastating wars gave an urgency to economic and political integration that does not exist in North America. However, September 11 has made integration of border security operations an urgent matter among the NAFTA countries. Political and economic power is more evenly distributed among the members of the EU than among NAFTA countries. In Europe, no one country dwarfs the others the way U.S. economic and political influence dominates that of Canada and Mexico.

NAFTA: The Politics of Being Neighborly

NAFTA started out as a bilateral free trade agreement between Canada and the United States; it came into effect January 1, 1989. Canada had sought the negotiations in response to rising protectionist pressures in the U.S. Congress. For many years the Canadian government, led by Prime Minister Pierre Trudeau, had tried to lessen Canada's economic dependence on the United States through efforts to diversify its own trade relations. In the 1980s, the government of Prime Minister Brian Mulroney recognized that geography was working against those efforts and that secure access to the U.S. market had to be an essential element of Canada's trade policy.

The proposed free trade agreement generated heated political debate in Canada and became the central issue in the national election of 1988. The incumbent Progressive Conservative government championed the agreement, while the opposition Liberal and New Democratic parties were vehemently opposed. The opposition parties split the anti–free trade vote between them, allowing the Conservatives to win reelection and proceed with the implementation of the Canada–United States Free Trade Agreement (CUSFTA). The issues raised in the debate foreshadowed the globalization debate that would surface at the end of the 1990s.

Opponents argued that CUSFTA would cause job losses and depress wages in Canada. Proponents responded that this might happen in non-competitive sectors but the net effect on the economy would be positive. The evolution of the economy would cause job displacement in any event; in the long run, Canada would benefit from the elimination of non-competitive industries. Moreover, the national government could ease the pain of the transition with social programs for those who lost out.

Opponents argued that CUSFTA would degrade social programs. In order to compete with the United States, Canada would have to reduce its generous safety social net to the level of that of the United States.

Proponents argued that wealth creation must precede redistribution and that CUSFTA would create the wealth needed to sustain Canada's social security system. Moreover, they urged, trade liberalization is not inconsistent with redistributional social policies, such as government spending on education, health and welfare. In any event, decades of poor financial management on the part of Canadian governments had created huge deficits and a large debt that left less to spend on social programs.

Another great fear of the opponents was that CUSFTA would lead to cultural homogenization, causing Canada to lose its cultural identity. This fear highlighted the cultural insecurity of English Canadians, most of whom have an unclear vision of what makes Canadians different from Americans. Opponents of CUSFTA feared that it would force Canada to abandon state-sponsored cultural programs and allow the country to be taken over by the commercialized culture of the United States. Proponents argued that interaction between cultures leads to new perspectives that strengthen a nation's culture, and that cultural isolation had become almost impossible in any case, with the advent of modern communications and transportation. Moreover, they argued, cultural isolationism leads to intolerance, arrested development and censorship, none of which are desirable.

The rallying cry of the CUSFTA opponents was that free trade would lead to the loss of Canada's sovereignty. The country would lose its independence and be forced to adopt a wide range of policies that mirrored those of the United States. Nothing less than the country's existence, they warned, was at stake. Proponents argued that the economic benefits would outweigh the constraints on domestic policy options. They argued further that smaller, trade-dependent nations such as Canada were better off with a rules-based system of dispute resolution than a power-based system that would leave the country vulnerable to economic blackmail. Finally, many of the rules in CUSFTA mirrored those of GATT, which had already reduced trade barriers between the two countries. However, CUSFTA extended those rules into new areas, such as services, intellectual property law, investment and energy trade, that reflected the direction in which the Uruguay Round negotiations were headed.

In the end, the economic arguments won out. Better access to the U.S. market would permit expanded production that would in turn allow Canadian industry to achieve greater economies of scale. Greater competition would enhance productivity and efficiency, making Canadian business more competitive worldwide. The costs of adjustment to greater competition, such as job losses in noncompetitive industries, would be compensated by job creation in competitive industries. While greater dependence on the U.S. market might make Canada more vulnerable to downturns in the American economy, Canada would benefit when it was doing well. The reality was that this was the largest trade relationship in the world, and the two countries were each other's number-one trade partners. However, Canada was more dependent on the United States than was the United States on Canada. With roughly 80 percent of Canada's exports going to the United States, the American market had become more important than the domestic market for many Canadian manufacturers. The trade relationships of the United States were, and still are, more diversified than Canada's.

The NAFTA Debate

While the CUSFTA debate made for high drama in Canada, the negotiation and passage of the agreement was barely noticed in the United States. The same cannot be said for the NAFTA debate in the United States, where opponents took up the same arguments that the Canadian anti–free trade forces had used five years earlier. The fear that lower environmental and labor standards in Mexico would lead to a "race to the bottom" became a central issue in the U.S. debate.

The Canadian fear of job losses and wage depression was translated into the same fear in the United States, expressed by presidential candidate Ross Perot as the "giant sucking sound" Americans would hear as manufacturing jobs were moved to lower-wage Mexico. However, being more confident than Canadians, Americans had no fear of a loss of sovereignty or cultural identity.

In Canada, as in the United States, the NAFTA debate coincided with an election year; in both countries NAFTA became an election issue. In both elections, the governments that had negotiated the agreement lost, and new governments would have to implement NAFTA. In Mexico, in contrast, President Carlos Salinas was in power during both the negotiations and the implementation of the agreement.

Canada's Motives

For Canada, CUSFTA had been proof of the special relationship it enjoyed with the United States. CUSFTA had given Canadian business preferential access to the U.S. market and an advantage over other countries' firms. When Mexico entered free trade negotiations with the United States, Canada was like the wife who has just learned of a mistress.

Canada pushed to be involved in the negotiations and to negotiate a trilateral agreement, rather than two bilateral agreements. As much as possible, Canada wanted to preserve its CUSFTA gains and to make sure that Mexico did not get a better deal than Canada. Moreover, to be able to influence the negotiations, Canada had to be at the table. Almost as an afterthought, Canada sought to enhance its access to the Mexican market (the destination of about 1 percent of Canadian exports at the time) and to promote Mexico as a gateway to Latin America for Canadian business.

However, the most important reason Canada pushed for a trilateral agreement was to avoid a hub-and-spoke situation that could have a negative impact on Canada's ability to attract foreign direct investment (FDI). With two bilateral agreements, the United States would become the hub and Mexico and Canada the spokes. The United States, as the only one enjoying free trade with everyone involved, would be a more attractive location than either Canada or Mexico for FDI, because firms located in the United States would have equal access to the entire market. This would have put Canada and Mexico at a disadvantage in attracting FDI.

Mexico's Motives

Mexico's motives for seeking the free trade agreement were similar to those that had motivated Canada to negotiate CUSFTA: increased access to the U.S. market; more secure access to the U.S. market; a larger market that would allow Mexico-based firms to expand production and achieve economies of scale; greater competition to enhance productivity and efficiency; and a trade relationship based on rules, not power.

President Salinas's slogan was that Mexico wanted to export goods, not people. Free trade would promote economic growth, modernize Mexican industry, and attract more FDI, creating more and higher-paying jobs. With better jobs at home, fewer Mexicans would have to risk illegal migration to the United States in search of work. Finally, NAFTA would entrench the economic reforms put in place by Salinas, reducing the risk that later governments might roll back the clock on what was known as "Salinastroika."

U.S. Motives

The immigration issue was also a major motivation for the United States, as was the economic and political stability of its southern neighbor. A prosperous, free-trading Mexico would be less likely to erupt in political violence or suffer economic disintegration, either of which could send floods of economic and political refugees fleeing north. In terms of its economic interests, the United States wanted to enhance its access to Mexican market, use Mexico as gateway to Latin America, and protect U.S. FDI in Mexico.

Another Reason for NAFTA

As members of GATT, all three countries were simultaneously involved in the Uruguay Round negotiations. NAFTA negotiations could move more quickly than GATT negotiations, because fewer countries were involved. At the time NAFTA was negotiated, it was by no means certain that the Uruguay Round would reach a successful conclusion. NAFTA would provide insurance against a failed Uruguay Round, creating a "Fortress North America" that could compete against a "Fortress Europe."

On a more positive note, the successful conclusion of NAFTA would set an example and provide a precedent for the agreements being negotiated under the Uruguay Round.

THE GLOBALIZATION DEBATE: CRASHING THE PARTY

Economic globalization takes the form of ever-increasing flows of international trade and foreign direct investment. The globalization of financial markets has made currency exchange rates more volatile and has opened up stock markets around the world to portfolio investment from almost anywhere. Together, these economic and financial trends have increased the interdependence of the nations of the world. The 1997 economic crisis in Asia lowered commodity prices by lowering world demand, in turn lowering the value of the Canadian dollar, whose value was linked to commodity prices. The strength of the U.S. economy in the 1990s was echoed in the economic growth experienced in Canada and Mexico. The slowing of the U.S. economy in 2000 lowered the prospects of global economic growth, and the terrorist attacks of 2001 damaged the economic prospects of nations around the world.

The globalization of business has made competition, innovation, and business strategy global issues. Rugman defines globalization, from a business perspective, as "the activities of multinational enterprises engaged in foreign direct investment and the development of business networks to create value across national borders."[3] He refers to the standard definition of economic globalization as "the worldwide production and marketing of goods and services by multinational enterprises."[4] According to Rugman, FDI by MNEs drives international business, and 90 percent of FDI (as well as over half of world trade) is dominated by the five hundred largest MNEs. Most of that trade and investment occurs between firms and is regionally based. More than 90 percent of MNE manufacturing is regional rather than global (with notable exceptions, such as consumer electronics); in services, over 95 percent of employees are local, not global (again, with notable exceptions in certain industries and professions). Rugman thus concludes that "operating globally for an MNE really means operating regionally."[5]

The international strategies adopted by business can be either facilitated or impeded by national trade and investment policies. The formation of regional trade and investment blocs helps to explain the regional orientation of global MNEs. At the same time, the globalization of some industries has coincided with global liberalization agreements under the WTO. For example, the WTO Agreement on Financial Services has coincided with a wave of mergers and acquisitions in insurance and banking, at both the regional and the global level.

The globalization of law takes the form of numerous international agreements under which countries agree to harmonize their laws to a certain extent, primarily through trade and investment agreements. However, legal globalization is not limited to economic matters. International environmental agreements have led most nations of the world to adopt uniform laws on global environmental issues, from the use of ozone-depleting chemicals to the commercial use of endangered species.

Economic and legal globalization in turn accelerates the globalization of politics. The political positions that governments adopt are implemented using economic and legal instruments. Global war-crimes tribunals seek to punish crimes against humanity wherever they take place. Economic interdependence facilitated the use of trade sanctions to bring about an end to apartheid in South Africa. Global political activism is now pushing the United Nations, WTO members, and global pharmaceutical companies to address the AIDS crisis.

The globalization of communications and transportation technologies plays a crucial role in all other aspects of globalization. Modern communications technology facilitates the globalization of production and the creation of global markets. Modern transportation processes facilitate the transportation of inputs and finished goods, as well as people.

Opposition to free trade has created a global coalition of interest groups and "globophobic" protesters. At the heart of the protests are labor and environmental groups who oppose free trade, for different reasons. Theirs is what Bruce Yandle calls "a coalition of Baptists and bootleggers." Baptists and bootleggers in the 1920s both supported the prohibition of alcohol in the United States, but for different reasons. The Baptists wanted to stop alcohol consumption, whereas the bootleggers wanted to maintain sales of illicit alcohol. Nevertheless, having a common goal, it was in their interest to cooperate in achieving that goal.

Organized labor fears that free trade will lessen the bargaining power of unions by creating a world in which moving a factory to a lower-wage country becomes a credible threat in labor negotiations. Moreover, increased international competition may motivate companies to seek greater flexibility in the deployment of labor or to contract out certain aspects of production. Both strategies may conflict with the workplace rules sought by unions. Workers in uncompetitive industries that are threatened by free trade blame globalization when they have to look for a new job.

Some environmentalists oppose free trade agreements because they do not allow the use of trade sanctions to force developing countries to adopt the environmental standards of developed countries. Other environmentalists view economic growth and international transportation as inherently harmful to the environment. Extremist environmental groups see human activity of any kind as harmful to the planet.

The protesters have raised valid points regarding the need for greater transparency at the WTO and the need to address the concerns of developing countries. Indeed, the WTO has responded by using its Web site to enhance public access to information. With respect to developing countries, the WTO has expanded programs to better prepare their trade negotiators to pursue their interests in WTO negotiations.

BUSINESS STRATEGY AND THE RULES OF INTERNATIONAL TRADE

In business, as in life, change is the norm. Successful firms create change rather than react to it. The goal of business strategy is to allow the firm to achieve its goals in an unpredictable environment.

International trade agreements seek to eliminate some of the uncertainty of the legal environment by limiting the ability of members to enact trade-restrictive laws. The agreements add a degree of predictability to the laws member nations impose on foreign firms. The reduction and elimination of barriers to the movement of goods, services and people, along with laws protecting investments (including investments in intellectual property), expand the strategic options available to firms. However, global free trade is a long-term project.

Theodore Levitt at the start of the 1980s provocatively presented the notion that the globalization of markets required global business strategies.[6] He argued that the emergence of global markets for standardized consumer products would require companies to operate as if the world were one large market, not a series of regional and national markets. However, while firms can achieve economies of scale through standardized products and uniform marketing, a global strategy is not appropriate in many industries.

Both formal and informal barriers prevent MNEs from applying standardized global strategies. Formal barriers include trade and investment restrictions, while informal barriers include structural and competitive differences between markets, as well as internal difficulties in managing the relationship between headquarters and subsidiaries. Moreover, the introduction of flexible manufacturing has allowed firms to maintain low production costs while simultaneously adapting products to local consumer preferences. Despite the popular notion that MNEs homogenize consumer tastes and threaten national sovereignty, most continue to struggle to accommodate variations in consumer preferences and differences in national policies.[7] Even where national governments enter international agreements to remove barriers to trade and investment, regional and municipal governments may pursue different policies.

Global sourcing and manufacturing strategies are influenced by the barriers that impede the movement of goods. Global pricing strategies are influenced by laws on dumping (selling a product in a foreign market for less than the home market price). Market entry strategies are influenced by foreign investment restrictions, trade barriers and the ability to transfer personnel between countries. Intellectual property laws may influence the kind of technology a firm chooses to bring to a foreign operation.

Large industries with political influence can help to shape the rules that are negotiated in trade agreements, by lobbying their respective governments to take specific negotiating positions. They can also play a role in the enforcement of trade agreements. The financial services industry of the United States, through the U.S. trade representative (USTR), played a strong role behind the scenes in the WTO financial-services negotiations. The pharmaceutical industry lobbies for strong protection for patent rights, pushing the USTR to challenge intellectual-property laws of WTO members that provide inadequate protection for drug patents. The trucking and insurance industries of the United States have influenced the way the U.S. government implements its NAFTA obligations to open the American market to Mexican trucking companies.

It is important for business to be involved in the trade liberalization process. Therefore, business strategists need to understand what trade agreements contain and how they work. They must also understand the political, historical, legal and economic context in which trade agreements are negotiated and implemented. This context has been the focus of this chapter.

CONCLUSION

Most people enjoy being able to choose from among a wide range of good quality, competitively priced products and services when they go to the market. Most people want to enjoy higher standards of living and good rates of return on their savings. However, most people also fear change.

Global competition between firms leads to innovative products and higher quality at a lower price. However, it also drives firms that produce inferior products out of business. Globally competitive firms seek to eliminate barriers to international trade and investment. Uncompetitive firms seek to create such barriers.

The book next examines NAFTA and WTO rules affecting trade in goods and trade in services, as well as foreign investment and intellectual property. Each of these chapters begins with a case that shows how trade agreements work in practice and how they affect firm strategy. This is followed by a comparative analysis of NAFTA and WTO rules. This comparison will show that NAFTA has made more significant progress in most areas, but not all. The analysis of the agreements is followed by a discussion of specific business strategies that may be affected by the rules. Each of these chapters ends with a closing case that further illustrates how the agreements work in practice. These chapters are followed by an examination of firm strategy in the enforcement of trade agreements and by predictions as to what the future may hold for NAFTA and WTO.

NOTES

1. Daniel Schwanen, "Investment and the Global Economy: Key Issues in Rulemaking," in Pierre Sauvé and Daniel Schwanen, eds., *Investment Rules for the Global Economy: Enhancing Access to Markets,* 7 (Toronto: C.D. Howe Institute, 1996).

2. Alan Rugman, *The End of Globalization: Why Global Strategy is a Myth and How to Profit from the Realities of Regional Markets* (New York: Amacom, 2001).

3. Ibid., 4.

4. Ibid.

5. Ibid.

6. Theodore Levitt, "The Globalization of Markets," *Harvard Business Review* 3 (1983), 92–102.

7. Preet S. Aulakh and Michael G. Schecter, "The Multidimensionality of Globalization: A Critical Perspective," in Aulakh and Schecter, eds., *Rethinking Globalization(s): From Corporate Transnationalism to Local Interventions* (New York: St. Martin's Press, 2000), 1–10.

Chapter 2

International Trade in Goods

OPENING CASE: THE U.S. EMBARGO AGAINST SHRIMP IMPORTS

In the process of catching shrimp, sea turtles may be accidentally killed. Environmentalists in the United States lobbied their government to regulate shrimping methods to reduce the killing of the turtles. The United States enacted a law that applied to American fisherman and U.S. territorial waters, and it introduced trade restrictions to compel shrimp fishermen from other countries operating outside U.S. territorial waters to comply with the American shrimping standards.[1]

Background

The United States banned shrimp imports from World Trade Organization members that did not comply with U.S. legal requirements regarding the protection of sea turtles from incidental death in the shrimp harvesting process. The countries that were subject to the trade ban were all developing countries. The United States negotiated and concluded a regional international agreement on sea turtle protection and conservation with some countries but not with others that were affected by the trade ban.

The United States gave some countries three years to introduce "turtle exclusion devices" (TEDs), while others were given only four months. All species of turtles involved were listed in the Convention on International Trade in Endangered Species (CITES) as being under threat of extinction,[2] and all occurred in U.S. territorial waters, which were on their migratory routes.

India, Malaysia, Pakistan and Thailand complained to the WTO that the U.S. measures violated the General Agreement on Tariffs and Trade.[3] A WTO panel found that the measure violated the general rule against import bans (article XI:1) and did not fit within the scope of the general exception for the conservation of exhaustible natural resources (article XX[g]). On appeal, the WTO Appellate Body held there was a sufficient nexus between the endangered, migratory marine populations involved and the United States for the purposes of article XX(g), because all of the species occur in waters over which the United States has jurisdiction, even though they migrate across national borders and international waters. The Appellate Body recognized that a country has a legitimate interest in the protection of migratory species that occur within its territory.

International law regarding territorial limits effectively prevents a country from taking unilateral measures to conserve natural resources outside its own territory. However, in the case of endangered migratory species, such as the turtles, failure to act would threaten the ecosystem inside U.S. territory by permitting the destruction of the species during the portion of its migration outside the territorial limits. The Appellate Body appears to have solved this quandary by granting the U.S. jurisdiction over the species, if not over extraterritorial waters.

However, the Appellate Body also implied that jurisdiction over the turtle was shared by other nations. While it recognized the U.S. policy goal as legitimate, it decided that the unilateral method chosen for achieving that goal was not. In an effort to balance the need to conserve the species against the need to respect the legal rights of other nations, the panel ruled that "the Inter-American Convention . . . provides a convincing demonstration that an alternative course of action was reasonably open to the United States for securing the legitimate policy goal of its measure, a course of action other than the unilateral and non-consensual procedures of the import prohibition." The appellate body concluded that the U.S. measure could therefore not be justified under the resource conservation exception.

Key Points Raised by the Case

International trade in goods among WTO members is governed by the basic rules of GATT and by a series of additional agreements negotiated in successive rounds of GATT negotiations. This case provides a good example of the interplay between the general rules and the general exceptions of GATT. In this case, the United States violated the basic rule against trade bans and sought to justify its violation under the general exception relating to the conservation of exhaustible natural resources.

This case also demonstrates how the basic principles of international law relate to international trade agreements. As a sovereign nation, the

United States can make laws governing activities inside its territorial limits and governing the activities of its own citizens. However, the United States has no jurisdiction under international law to regulate the actions of noncitizens outside U.S. territory. Had the United States not agreed to abide by GATT rules, it would be free to ban all imports if it so desired. However, having agreed to follow GATT rules, it may ban imports only if its trade ban can be justified under a GATT exception. However, GATT exceptions must be interpreted in accordance with international law. As a result, the exception allowing measures relating to resource conservation has been interpreted to apply only to the resources inside the territorial limits of the country invoking the exception.

This case also raised the issue of the relationship between different international treaties. In this case, the international trade agreement, GATT, prohibits trade bans as a general rule. The international environmental agreement, CITES, requires signatories to impose trade bans to protect endangered species. However, CITES bans only trade in endangered species themselves. Thus, the United States could have banned imports of sea turtles, which are endangered, but not shrimp, which are not endangered.

The case sheds light on the reasons why environmental groups are upset about the WTO. Environmentalists, principally in developed countries, want to use trade restrictions to compel foreign governments to raise their environmental standards. However, the WTO is not the problem. The problem lies in the principles of international law that govern relations between sovereign nations. If one nation wants to tell another how to govern its internal affairs, in principle the same nation must subject itself to the dictates of others regarding its own internal affairs as well. That is an unworkable state of affairs. Sovereign nations can either negotiate international agreements in which they agree how they will regulate certain matters or maintain their independence by refusing to enter such agreements. There is no alternative that respects the principle of national sovereignty, and we have yet to discover an alternative method of regulating relations between nations.

INTRODUCTION

GATT began the process of liberalizing trade in goods more than fifty years ago. The main focus was to achieve agreement among members to eliminate barriers to trade in goods and gradually to reduce tariffs, in a series of negotiating "rounds." These negotiation rounds are generally named after the place where they were launched (for example, the Tokyo Round and the Uruguay Round) or after leaders who were instrumental in them (such as the Kennedy Round). As the most obvious trade barriers were dealt with in the rules, negotiations increasingly focused on less obvious "nontariff" barriers to trade, such as standards and customs procedures. The result is an extensive body of rules governing a wide range of issues.

Certain sectors have proved more difficult to liberalize than others, particularly agricultural products and clothing. Under the Uruguay Round, some progress was made in these sectors. At the Doha meeting of WTO ministers in 2001, however, the difficulty of negotiating trade liberalization in these sectors remained. The political clout of domestic lobby groups in these sectors continues to make it difficult for developed countries to reduce trade protection for their domestic textile and apparel industries and to decrease subsidies for agricultural producers. Thus, trade in these sectors is still not based on the comparative advantage of nations.

This chapter begins with an examination of the principles of international law that apply to international agreements in general. It then examines NAFTA and WTO rules that apply to trade in goods. Many of these rules are similar. However, sometimes NAFTA governs matters that are not covered in WTO, and vice versa. NAFTA covers different matters in separate chapters, while WTO governs distinct issues in separate agreements. It is beyond the scope of this book to address every rule in every agreement; therefore, this chapter focuses on the most important rules and agreements. The closing case examines how law, politics and economic issues have affected the Canada–United States lumber trade.

Rules mean little without enforcement mechanisms. There are essentially three venues for enforcing the rules discussed in this chapter. General rules of international law have the weakest enforcement system, and only governments can enforce them. In disputes between countries, governments must agree to submit to the jurisdiction of the International Court of Justice (ICJ), which is located in The Hague, the Netherlands. Unless all governments involved submit to ICJ jurisdiction, cases cannot proceed; when they cannot, the disputes can be resolved only through negotiation.

The rules set out in NAFTA and WTO relating to trade in goods, similarly, can be enforced only by governments, using the dispute settlement systems of each agreement. However, governments usually seek enforcement of these rules for the benefit of their firms. Business people therefore have at least indirect access to enforcement venues through their government. For this reason, it is important for business people to know what the rules are and how they work so that they can recognize situations in which they should lobby government to enforce the rules to break down barriers to trade.

Customs rules and procedures in NAFTA countries provide business people with direct access to dispute-settlement mechanisms in domestic courts and administrative tribunals. They also provide business people with opportunities to seek advance rulings on customs decisions. It is important for business people to know what the rules are and to take advantage of advance rulings and appeals to protect their interests in customs matters.

With respect to customs, the major issues facing firms are to minimize duties and ensure predictability in how imports and exports will be treated. Firms understand the need to minimize taxes. Duties are a form of tax and also need to be minimized. Duties increase manufacturing costs when materials must be imported. Duties also increase the cost of products in export markets. They thus have a direct impact on the price competitiveness of a firm's products. This in turn affects decisions regarding the location of manufacturing facilities and the choice of export markets. Prediction of what duties will be imposed on a given shipment of goods is an essential part of the business planning process, particularly with respect to setting prices.

While NAFTA and WTO have made considerable progress in breaking down barriers to trade in goods, the process is far from complete. Firms still have many opportunities to use trade barriers to protect their home markets against foreign competitors. Barriers to trade in goods therefore continue to affect the international competitive position of firms.

BASIC PRINCIPLES OF INTERNATIONAL LAW

International trade agreements are treaties. As such, they form part of the system of international law and must be interpreted in accordance with the principles of international law. In spite of the escalating pace of global integration, sovereign nations still form the backbone of the legal system, and international law remains in its infancy. The globalization debate, in particular criticisms aimed at WTO, frequently reveals profound ignorance of the rules of international law. International organizations do not rule the world—national governments do. What follows is a brief explanation of the basic principles that govern the creation of international law by national governments.

General Principles of Public International Law

There are two principal sources of international law. *Customary international law* arises from the customary practices of countries, which are referred to as "states" in international legal parlance. *Treaties* are the other major source of international law. However, as agreements between countries, treaties are like contracts and can bind only the parties that sign them. Where no treaty governs a particular subject matter or the country in question has not signed a treaty, disputes between countries are governed by principles of customary international law.

The principle of *state sovereignty* is the linchpin of customary international law. State sovereignty empowers countries to enter into agreements (treaties) with other countries. Except for some international organizations, only a sovereign nation may enter into treaties with other sovereign nations. Conversely, states (that is, like those of the United States or Australia), provinces and colonies do not enjoy this status under international law. This principle gives countries authority to regulate the acts of persons inside their territory and the acts of their citizens. It gives countries the right to exploit their own resources as they wish, along with the responsibility to ensure that activities inside their borders do not cause damage to the environment outside their borders (in other countries or in international areas). In short, sovereignty gives the national government jurisdiction over the nation's territory and people.

When actions inside one country cause harm in the territory of a neighbor, the neighbor is technically entitled to sue for damages at the ICJ. However, both countries must agree to submit to the jurisdiction of the ICJ. The classic case in this area is the Cominco dispute, which involved Canada and the United States. Cominco, a Canadian mining company, operated a smelter in the Canadian province of British Columbia. Its operations polluted a river valley in the state of Washington. The United States sued Canada for the damage that the pollution caused in the United States; both countries agreed to accept the jurisdiction of the IJC to settle the matter. The IJC ruled in favor of the United States, thereby confirming the responsibility of Canada in international law to ensure that activities in its territory did not cause harm outside its territory.

The flip side of sovereignty is the principle of *nonintervention,* which limits the ability of one nation to interfere in the internal affairs of another. This restricts the ability of all nations to regulate acts outside their territorial limits. *Extraterritorial laws* (laws applied to persons, acts or property outside the country's borders) are invalid under international law. Thus, in the Cominco case, the United States could not regulate the actions of Cominco in Canada but could only file a claim against Canada for failure to regulate the firm in a way that prevented the damage to the United States.

One way to conceptualize these principles is to think of the nations of the world as neighbors in a condominium complex. Each neighbor is entitled to determine what goes on inside his condominium, but no neighbor is entitled to tell others how to carry on their lives inside their private spaces. In other words, busybodies need not be tolerated. The only limit on each neighbor is that his enjoyment of his personal freedom ends where it impinges on the freedom of his neighbor to enjoy his own private space, such as when music is played too loudly. Only where the neighbors enter into an agreement in which they voluntarily agree to accept restrictions on this freedom do the neighbors have a say in what goes on in each other's private lives.

If countries do not sign trade agreements with other countries, they have no obligation to permit trade with those countries. They remain free to regulate imports and exports as they see fit. They can ban imports or exports and raise or lower tariffs as they wish. However, once they enter a trade agreement, they assume obligations that they are bound to fulfill with respect to all other signatories of the agreement. That is, they voluntarily limit their freedom to regulate international trade as they wish. They maintain absolute freedom over trade policy only with countries that are not parties to the trade agreement.

Returning to the condominium analogy, it is fairly clear how the principles of sovereignty and nonintervention apply to what goes on in each neighbor's space. Sometimes, however, jurisdictions of regulation can overlap. For example, country A may regulate the acts of persons inside its territory and the acts of its citizens wherever they may be. Therefore, when the citizens of country A are in the territory of country B, they may be subject to the laws of both A and B. By analogy, when neighbor A's children visit neighbor B, the visiting children's behavior is subject to the rules imposed by their own parents and also, as long as they are inside neighbor B's space, by the rules imposed by neighbor B. Since the rules of A and B may differ, conflicts can arise. Generally, however, the actions of individuals are governed by the laws of the territory in which they find themselves.

For example, citizens of the United States are required to file income tax returns regardless of where they reside. An American who works and resides in Canada must also file a tax return in Canada, which taxes people on the basis of residence rather than citizenship. Should this individual choose to disobey the law of the United States and not file a tax return there, the United States can do nothing to enforce its law as long as the person remains outside its territory, unless Canada agrees to help out. In the absence of an agreement, Canada would have no obligation to arrest or extradite the U.S. citizen. However, should the person choose to return to the United States, he would be subject to arrest there. In this instance, in practice, there is no conflict; Canada and the United States have signed agreements, such as treaties regarding extradition and the avoidance of double taxation, to resolve matters like this.

Another important question that arises in the condominium complex is how rules are made in the metaphorical hallway and other common areas. In other words, who regulates international spaces that do not fall inside any nation's territory, such as international waters and international airspace? Each country's authority to pass laws ends at its territorial limits, which include a two-hundred-mile strip of coastal waters. Therefore, no single country can regulate the common areas of the world. If laws are to exist in the common areas, they must arise through the customary practice of the nations of the world or through agreement by all interested nations. Where there is no agreement or customary practice, there is no clear rule. Even where an agreement exists, a country that refuses to participate in it is not bound by its rules.

When no country has jurisdiction, and thus no responsibility, what often occurs is the "tragedy of the commons." This term comes from an essay that described how common pastures in England were overgrazed when no one enjoyed their exclusive use and no agreements were reached to limit use by everyone. Shared resources tend to be overexploited. A modern-day example occurs, on a grander scale, with respect to overfishing in international waters.

For centuries, the fishing nations of the North Atlantic have exploited the extraordinary abundance of fish in the waters of the Grand Banks off Newfoundland. Codfish were particularly numerous. Early European explorers recorded that the waters were so thick with codfish that it seemed one could walk upon the water on the backs of the cod. However, modern fishing technology has allowed fishermen to harvest more fish than the cod stocks can tolerate, and their numbers have declined.

The members of the North Atlantic Fisheries Organization (NAFO) agreed to limit the quantity of fish that each fishing nation could take each year, in order to preserve the resource for all. All fishing nations agreed to annual quotas that limited the catch of their fishermen and agreed to enforce those quotas against their citizens—all except Spain. Spain would not agree to limit the number of fish its fleet could catch in international waters. With cod stocks dropping to precarious levels, the fishermen of Canada (the nation closest to the Grand Banks) were losing their livelihoods. Legally, nothing could be done to force the Spaniards to comply. Nevertheless, Canada chose to seize a Spanish vessel that was fishing in international waters, arrest her crew, and seize the catch.

Spain accused Canada of violating international law. Canada replied that it had acted out of necessity, given the Spanish refusal to limit its catch. The matter was ultimately settled by negotiation, but the incident demonstrates the limits of international law in regulating the global commons. Without legal obligations or economic incentives, the nations of the world are likely to exploit international resources in an unsustainable manner. Where there is potential or actual economic gain at stake, countries may be unwilling to enter into agreements governing the activities of their citizens in international waters.

One way to provide countries with economic incentives to regulate such activities is to impose trade restrictions in important markets for the products which are thereby produced. The United States is an important market for the products of many countries but is home to a politically influential environmental lobby. More than once, this lobby has produced trade embargoes against seafood caught in international waters in an environmentally unfriendly manner.

In the 1980s, the United States banned imports of tuna from nations whose fishermen used tuna-fishing methods that killed dolphins. In the 1990s, as noted in the opening case, the United States banned imports of shrimp when fishing methods killed sea turtles. Had the United States not signed trade agreements in which it agreed not to ban imports from other signatories, these actions would have been perfectly legal. Alternatively, had those trade agreements contained exceptions that allowed such trade bans, the U.S. trade embargoes would have been allowed. In fact, however, the United States is a party to trade agreements that forbid environmental trade embargoes unless they are necessary to protect the environment inside the territory of the United States. In other words, according to the interpretations of international trade panels, it may not use trade restrictions to regulate indirectly the actions of other countries' citizens that occur outside the territory of the United States.

Since trade agreements create international legal obligations, they generally require that their provisions be interpreted in accordance with international law. NAFTA requires that its provisions be interpreted "in accordance with applicable rules of international law." [4] Similarly, the WTO dispute-settlement system "serves to preserve the rights and obligations of Members under the covered agreements, and to clarify the existing provisions of those agreements in accordance with customary rules of interpretation of public international law."[5] The Vienna Convention on the Law of Treaties (the Vienna Convention),[6] which entered into force on January 27, 1980, codifies the rules of treaty interpretation and is the most important source of international law used to interpret trade agreements.

Interpretation of Treaties

Treaties are agreements between countries. If the same countries enter into more than one treaty, a conflict may arise. There are three ways to resolve such conflicts. The simplest way is to insert in a new treaty a *conflicts clause* that determines which prior treaty prevails in case of a conflict.

Where there is no conflicts clause, there is a presumption that a later treaty prevails over an earlier treaty on the same subject. The presumption flows from the idea that the countries would be aware of the earlier treaty when they created the later treaty and that their intention would therefore be to have the later treaty take precedence in the event of any inconsistency. However, another presumption is that the more specific treaty is intended to prevail over the more general one. For example, the Canada and the United States agreed to restrict trade in endangered species under CITES before they agreed to a general rule against import and export restrictions under NAFTA; the logical presumption, in that view, is that the specific trade restrictions in CITES were intended to prevail over the general rule prohibiting trade restrictions.

The Vienna Convention codifies these rules of international law on the interpretation of treaties and applies to international trade agreements.[7] Some of the other key rules of interpretation are:

Article 31(1): "A treaty is to be interpreted in good faith in accordance with the ordinary meaning to be given to the terms of the treaty in their context and in the light of its object and purpose."

Article 31(3)(b): "There shall be taken into account, together with the context[,] . . . any subsequent practice in the application of the treaty which establishes the agreement of the parties regarding its interpretation."

Article 32: "Recourse may be had to supplementary means of interpretation, including the preparatory work of the treaty and the circumstances of its conclusion, in order to confirm the meaning when the interpretation according to Article 31 leaves the meaning ambiguous or obscure; or leads to a result which is manifestly absurd or unreasonable."

These rules of interpretation, together with the general principles of international law, should be kept in mind as specific provisions of trade agreements are analyzed in the rest of the book.

NAFTA AND WTO AGREEMENTS ON TRADE IN GOODS

NAFTA and WTO use the same basic set of principles to regulate national trade rules. This section begins with a look at these general principles and at the most important general rules. It then compares the rules that apply to trade in goods under NAFTA and WTO. GATT is the central WTO agreement on trade in goods, but there are several others that deal with specific technical issues, such as product standards and customs valuation. In addition, there are WTO agreements that deal with specific sectors of goods, such as textiles and clothing.

General Procedural Principles

Transparency is a procedural principle that requires countries ensure that their laws and administrative practices are accessible. They must publish laws and regulations so that they may be located easily. They must accept comments from trade partners on proposed changes to laws that will affect the rights of trade partners. They must make administrative decision making "transparent" by ensuring decisions are based on recorded evidence and arguments, not corruption or nepotism. For this reason, transparency is also known as the "sunshine" principle—when government affairs must be conducted in the light of day, for all to see, certain practices that might have occurred in the shadows happen less frequently.

Reciprocity is another procedural principle. The principle of reciprocity means that countries are to endeavor to make equivalent concessions in trade negotiations and may take equivalent retaliation against other countries' trade barriers. In both NAFTA and WTO dispute-settlement systems, where a country fails to remove a trade barrier that has been ruled inconsistent with its trade obligations by an arbitration panel, the complaining party may be authorized to retaliate with trade sanctions. In principle, preference will be given for sanctions for an equivalent amount of trade in the same type of goods or services. For example, in the dispute between the United States and the European Union over the failure of the latter to remove its ban on imports of hormone-treated beef, the United States was authorized to retaliate against imports of European agricultural products.

National Treatment

The *national treatment* principle prohibits discrimination between domestic products and imports. This requires domestic laws, regulations and procedures to treat imported goods no less favorably than "like goods" produced domestically. In other words, imported apples must be treated no worse than domestic apples. However, imported oranges can be treated differently than domestic apples, because they are not "like goods."

The national treatment principle requires countries to refrain from using *internal* taxes and other regulations to discriminate against imports. GATT article III(4) provides: "The products of . . . any . . . party imported into the territory of and other . . . party shall be accorded treatment no less favorable than that accorded to like products of national origin in respect to all laws, regulations, and requirements affecting their internal sale, . . . purchase, transportation, distribution or use." NAFTA article 301 incorporates national treatment for trade in goods and extends its application to provincial and state measures. The treatment by provinces and states of goods from outside the country must be no worse than of goods from other states or provinces within the country.

Most-Favored Nation

The *most-favored nation* (MFN) principle prohibits discrimination between the products of trade partners. It prohibits favoring the imports from one trade partner over those of another. That is, MFN does not allow a country to *have* a "most-favored nation." If a country provides preferential treatment for one member of a trade agreement, the same treatment must immediately be extended to all other members of the same trade agreement.

The MFN principle is set out in GATT article I:1, as follows: "With respect to customs duties and charges of any kind imposed on . . . importation or exportation or . . . the international transfer of payments . . . and all rules and formalities[,] . . . any advantage . . . granted . . . to any product [of one country] . . . shall be accorded . . . to the like product . . . of all other contracting parties." NAFTA applies the MFN principle between NAFTA members.

There are some important exceptions to the MFN rule. GATT article XXIV permits WTO members to create free trade areas (such as NAFTA) or customs unions (such as MERCOSUR, the common market of the Southern Cone of South America) within which members are given better treatment than nonmembers. In addition, the GATT "generalized system of preferences" (GSP) allows developed countries to grant preferential market access to developing-country products.

Import and Export Restrictions

There is a general prohibition against import and export restrictions or quotas, prohibiting restrictions on the volume or value of particular goods. This rule includes the prohibition of outright bans on trade in a given product. Traditionally, the principal exceptions have been in specific sectors (such as textiles, clothing and agricultural products) where countries have been permitted to maintain limits on the volume or value of imports. Such import quotas are being phased out under WTO—for example, in the WTO Agreement on Textiles and Clothing (ATC). In addition, trade partners have often avoided the application of this rule through bilateral agreements (so-called voluntary export restraints). In this scenario, in order to settle or avoid a trade dispute, the exporting country "voluntarily" places export restrictions on the quantity or value of a given product. While this violates the rule against export restrictions, the rule is not enforced in such situations, by agreement between the affected countries.

The ATC is a sectoral agreement negotiated after the conclusion of the Uruguay Round. World trade in textiles and clothing in 1995 was worth U.S.$311 billion and accounted for 6.3 percent of world merchandise trade. Prior to the ATC, WTO members imposed quotas on the volume of imports they allowed in this sector. Generally, developed countries imposed quotas to protect their domestic producers from competition from developing countries. The ATC removes these quotas under a ten-year transitional program that began on January 1, 1995. As of January 1, 2002, 51 percent of each country's total volume of 1990 imports entered free of quotas. Quotas on the remainder must be eliminated by January 1, 2005, at which point the ATC will no longer apply, and this sector will be fully regulated by GATT.

The ATC contains special safeguard provisions that allow import restrictions on specific products from specific countries where surging imports cause or threaten serious damage to the domestic industry of the importing country. In 1995, the United States invoked this safeguard provision twenty-four times against fourteen developing countries. This provides some indication of the power of the American domestic industry lobby in Washington. At the Doha meeting, developing countries sought to accelerate the ATC schedule but did not succeed, due to opposition from the United States.

General Exceptions

NAFTA and WTO both contain general exceptions whose purpose is to allow members to maintain independent social, environmental and other nontrade policies that may have the effect of restricting trade. Other important exceptions allow temporary restrictions on trade to safeguard a country's balance of payments and safeguard measures affording emergency protection against injury to domestic industry from surges in imports. One of the broadest exceptions permits measures to protect national security.

GATT article XX sets out a list of exceptions to the general rules, a list that has been incorporated, by reference, into NAFTA. For example, one allows measures relating to conservation of exhaustible natural resources (article XX[g]); another allows measures necessary to protect human, animal or plant life or health (article XX[b]). However, the use of such measures, where they restrict trade or otherwise violate the general rules, must not constitute arbitrary or unjustifiable discrimination. These latter provisions have been interpreted to require members to use the least trade restrictive measure available to achieve their safety and environmental goals.

Due to the nature of national security, the relevant GATT exception permits each member to determine what actions it considers necessary to protect its security interests and to determine what information it is able to disclose. This language makes the exception very broad and means that such measures are difficult to arbitrate in the event of a dispute. The preparatory work relating to the GATT article XXI security exception is the only source of guidance in this regard, because the provision has not been interpreted by any panels. One of the drafters of the original draft charter stated: "We gave a good deal of thought to the question of the security exception. . . . It is really a question of balance. . . . We cannot make it too tight, because we cannot prohibit measures which are needed purely for security reasons. On the other hand, we cannot make it so broad that, under the guise of security, countries will put on measures which really have a commercial purpose."[8] The NAFTA security exception mirrors that of GATT.

Tariffs

Tariffs are import duties of general application, as opposed to anti-dumping and countervailing duties, which apply only to dumped or subsidized imports. Thus, a country may eliminate tariffs on a particular product but still impose antidumping and countervailing duties on the same product. A good example is Canadian lumber exports to the United States. The United States imposes no tariff on Canadian lumber but has frequently imposed countervailing duties, effectively rendering moot the absence of a tariff.

Trade agreements generally favor the use of tariffs over other methods of restricting trade, referred to as *nontariff barriers* (NTBs). NTBs include such measures as import and export license requirement, customs user fees, and customs valuation methods. Where licenses are required, they may be denied, which has the same effect as a trade ban. Customs user fees can be used to replace tariffs that have been lowered or eliminated under a trade agreement. Similarly, since tariffs are normally based on a percentage of the value of a good, customs valuation methods that artificially inflate the value of a good will also drive up the payable tariff. All of these methods of erecting barriers to trade are less transparent than tariffs and are therefore more difficult to detect and eliminate in trade negotiations.

Tariff negotiations are obviously more complex under GATT than under NAFTA, due to the number of countries involved. Tariff rates vary enormously, depending on the product and the country that is applying the tariff. However, once a WTO member reduces or eliminates a tariff for one WTO member, the same must be applied to all WTO members, under the MFN rule. These tariff rates are therefore referred to as *MFN duty rates*. The reduction or elimination of tariffs has been a perennial issue on the negotiating agendas of successive rounds of trade negotiations under GATT. The ultimate goal is to eliminate tariffs between WTO members.

Following the end of the Uruguay Round negotiations, the WTO negotiated the Information Technology Agreement (ITA), in order to speed up tariff elimination in this particular sector. The ITA covers computers (including scanners, printers, monitors, hard-disk drives, power supplies); telecommunications products (including telephone sets, fax machines, modems, pagers); semiconductors (chips and wafers); semiconductor manufacturing equipment; software (such as diskettes and CD-ROMs); scientific equipment; cash registers, computer networks equipment; and certain photocopiers. However, electronic consumer goods are excluded. The ITA eliminated customs duties on these products on January 1, 2000.

However, not all WTO members participated in the ITA negotiations. Nevertheless, the forty participating members[9] account for over 92 percent of world trade in this sector. The tariff reductions made by these countries apply to all WTO members, by virtue of the MFN rule.

NAFTA eliminates tariffs over a fifteen-year transition period. As with GATT, once tariffs are reduced or eliminated, they cannot be raised again, subject to certain exceptions discussed below. Between Canada and the United States, the tariff elimination schedule was governed by CUSFTA, which completed its ten-year schedule in 1998. With the addition of Mexico under NAFTA, a separate schedule was put in place to reduce tariffs in stages between Mexico and the other two members.

For trade with Mexico under NAFTA, products are classified as A, B, C, C+ and D. Category D products were already duty free. Category A tariffs were eliminated on January 1, 1994, when NAFTA came into effect. Category B tariffs were eliminated in equal stages over five years (by January 1, 1998) and Category C over ten years (by January 1, 2003). Category C+ tariffs, on certain sensitive products, are to be eliminated over fifteen years (by January 1, 2008). The NAFTA trade ministers meet periodically to speed up tariff elimination. For example, the first round of accelerated tariff cuts was implemented July 1, 1997. The tariff acceleration process gives business people an opportunity to lobby for faster tariff cuts—for example, on a manufacturing input for which there is no longer a domestic industry seeking tariff protection.

During the transition period, duty rates vary depending on where the goods were produced. For example, a Canadian good entering the United States may have a different rate than the same Mexican good entering the United States. Goods imported into Canada will have three NAFTA rates, depending on whether the goods are of U.S. origin, Mexican origin, or produced jointly with U.S. and Mexican inputs.

Because NAFTA is itself an exception to the GATT MFN rule, NAFTA members charge NAFTA rates of duty on each other's goods, and MFN rates on goods from other WTO members. When goods come from a country that is neither a NAFTA nor a WTO member, an importing country can charge whatever duty rate it wishes to. Because duty rates therefore depend on the country of origin, both NAFTA and WTO contain *rules of origin* that determine the rate that is charged. These rules of origin are discussed below.

The *tariff classification number* of a product determines the applicable rate of duty. The Harmonized Commodity Description and Coding System (HS) provides thousands of different numerical combinations to classify goods. It came into effect January 1, 1998, and is used by nearly all WTO members. HS is amended periodically to add new products. It consists of six digits. The first four indicate the family of product, while the fifth and sixth designate a specific product. For example, 8703 is the number for cars, 8703.10 is for vehicles designed for traveling on snow, and 8703.21 is for vehicles with a cylinder capacity of less than a thousand cubic centimeters. While tariff classification is a highly technical issue, the classification that customs authorities give to a product can have enormous financial consequences, since it determines the rate of duty. The business goal should be to minimize duties, just as one minimizes income taxes; under NAFTA, business people can request *advance rulings* from the customs authorities, which then bind the government to assign the same classification number on every shipment. Advance rulings can be appealed. WTO has no equivalent requirement for members to have an advance ruling-mechanism in place.

Both NAFTA and WTO allow members to use *safeguard measures* where an import surge threatens serious injury to domestic industry due to the implementation of trade concessions. These measures are used when a member agrees to eliminate or lower barriers to trade but, when the time comes to do so, its domestic industry is not ready to face foreign competition. In certain cases, such industries may have the deadline by which it must adjust to foreign competition temporarily extended through such safeguard measures.

NAFTA safeguard provisions apply only until December 31, 2003. If NAFTA tariff reductions cause a good to be imported in such increased quantities and under such conditions that the tariff reductions cause or threaten to cause injury to a domestic producer of like or directly competitive goods, the importing country may suspend scheduled tariff reduction or increase the duty to the MFN rate. The country must provide written notice of the action and hold consultations with the affected parties. The safeguard measure can be maintained for only three years, unless the good falls under the C+ category, in which case it may be extended for another year.

Safeguard action can be taken only once against the same good. When the action ends, the duty rate is set at the rate that otherwise would have been in effect one year after the action began. The NAFTA countries maintain their rights under the WTO Agreement on Safeguards but must exclude each other from WTO safeguard actions, unless imports from a NAFTA member account for a substantial share of total imports or contribute importantly to the serious injury. "Serious injury" is defined as a significant overall impairment of a domestic industry.[10]

The WTO Agreement on Safeguards authorizes extraordinary action on temporary basis. It permits emergency action on imports of particular products being imported in such quantities and under such conditions as to cause or threaten serious injury to domestic producers of like or directly competitive products. The increased imports must be linked to a previously negotiated trade concession. The importing country must hold consultations with the WTO and the affected country beforehand; also, except in critical circumstances, an investigation must be conducted. Factors that are used to determine injury include the amount of increase in imports; the share of domestic market taken by the increased imports; and changes in sales, production, productivity, capacity utilization, profits and losses, and employment. The maximum duration of the safeguard measure is four years, but it may be extended an additional four years. It may take form of a tariff or a quantitative restriction.

The WTO Agreement on Agriculture has a special safeguard measure for agricultural products. In addition to safeguard actions against particular goods, selective safeguard action may be taken in certain circumstances against particular countries. For example, the agreement on China's accession to WTO allows WTO members to use a special safeguard mechanism should imports of Chinese products disrupt their domestic markets during the first twelve years of China's membership. Another safeguard specifically applies to Chinese textile products until 2008.

Rules of Origin

Rules of origin also affect duty rates. WTO has made little progress in this area. The WTO Agreement on Rules of Origin established a harmonization program for rules of origin. Initially, the work was to be completed in three years. However, the deadline was extended to the end of 2001; rules of origin will be negotiated under the Doha Round. The aim is to define "country of origin" as either the country where the good is wholly obtained or, when production takes place in more than one country, the country where last substantial transformation was carried out.

NAFTA chapter 4 contains detailed rules of origin that have harmonized the rules in Canada, Mexico and the United States. These rules are necessary to identify which goods qualify for NAFTA duty rates ("originating" goods), which goods are subject to countervailing or antidumping duties, and which are subject to other trade restrictions.

NAFTA defines "originating" goods in four ways: (1) they may be goods wholly obtained or produced entirely in Canada, Mexico, or the United States that contain no materials or parts from outside the NAFTA territory; (2) they may be goods produced in the NAFTA region wholly from originating materials; (3) they may be goods that contain 60 percent regional-value content using the transaction method, or 50 percent using the net cost method; or (4) they meet the Annex 401 origin rule. The Annex 401 rules of origin are based on a change in tariff classification, a regional value content requirement, or both. "Tariff classification change" refers to the fact that the nonoriginating materials are classified under one tariff provision before processing but under another once processing is complete. Goods also originate if they are produced entirely in Canada,

Mexico, or the United States exclusively from materials that are considered to be originating because they meet the rules of origin in Annex 401.

"Regional value content" means that a certain percentage of the value of the goods must be from NAFTA countries. There are two formulas for calculating the regional value content. The *transaction value method* allows the value of nonoriginating materials to be calculated as a percentage of the invoice price. Because the transaction value method permits the producer to count all of its costs and profit as territorial, the required proportion of regional value content under this method is 60 percent. The *net cost method* calculates the regional value content as a percentage of the net cost only to produce the good. The percentage content required for the net cost method is thus only 50 percent.

NAFTA provides special rules of origin for certain sectors. NAFTA provisions on trade in textiles and apparel are particularly detailed. The aim is to ensure that most of the production relating to textiles and apparel occurs in North America. Indeed, prior to NAFTA, China was the largest exporter of these products to the United States, but after NAFTA Mexico became the largest, due to its NAFTA advantage. The basic origin rule for textile and apparel articles is that the yarn used to form the fabric must originate in a NAFTA country. Exceptions give producers flexibility to import materials not widely produced in North America, such as silk.

To allow flexibility, textile and apparel exports have access to tariff preference levels. This means that specified quantities of certain fibers, yarns and fabrics that do not meet the origin criteria but that are subject to significant processing in one or more NAFTA countries can still be eligible for preferential NAFTA rates. Amounts of these goods exceeding the tariff preference level are subject to MFN rates of duty. Apparel goods made from nonoriginating fabric but that is cut and sewn in North America may be eligible.

The rules of origin for automotive products are designed to encourage investment in manufacturing in North America. NAFTA requires that the regional value content for these products be calculated using only the net cost method. The regional value content requirement for autos and light vehicles was 50 percent on January 1, 1994, but increased to 62.5 percent on January 1, 2002. For other vehicles, the regional value content requirement was 50 percent and increased to 60 percent over the same period.

Because NAFTA is a free trade agreement, not a customs union, each country maintains an independent trade policy with respect to nonmembers. One exception is a requirement that all three countries harmonize their respective MFN tariff rates on computers and computer peripherals. Once the duty rates for these articles are harmonized, duties on goods will be payable only once, on entering the NAFTA territory. Once within the NAFTA territory, these articles can move between Canada, Mexico and the United States without duty payment.

The provisions for agricultural goods were negotiated bilaterally. As a result, the provisions for trade between Mexico and the United States are different from those for trade between Canada and Mexico. For example, for trade between the United States and Canada, NAFTA incorporates the provisions of CUSFTA. This allows the United States or Canada to apply a temporary duty on certain fresh fruits and vegetables.

NAFTA Customs Procedures

Only importers who possess a valid *certificate of origin* can claim preferential tariff treatment. A certificate of origin can cover a single importation of goods or multiple importation of identical goods within any twelve-month period. The certificate of origin must be completed and signed by the exporter of the goods. Importers claiming NAFTA tariff treatment make a declaration, based on a valid certificate of origin in their possession, on the import documentation. When no claim for preferential tariff treatment is made at the time of importation, importers can request preferential tariff treatment up to one year after the date on which the good was imported, as long as a certificate of origin for the goods is obtained.

Importers must provide the certificate to the importing country's customs administration on request. The customs administration of the importing country may deny preferential tariff treatment to the goods if the importer fails to comply with any of the customs procedures set out in chapter 5 of NAFTA. Importers must maintain records pertaining to the importation for five years. Exporters that prepare certificates of origin are to provide copies to their own customs administrations on request. Exporters must also maintain records for five years. To claim preferential tariff treatment under NAFTA, Canadian importers make a written declaration of origin using the Revenue Canada Customs B3 accounting form. Importers must have the certificate of origin in their possession at the time of declaration, but they do not have to present the certificate. On commercial imports valued at less than a thousand U.S. dollars, the formal certificate of origin is not required. Importers can apply for a refund of duties when the imported good would have qualified for preferential treatment at the time of entry but no claim was made because the importer did not have a certificate of origin.

In Mexico, importers must use a customs broker. In the United States, importers must claim NAFTA benefits to receive preferential duty treatment, by inserting "MX" or "CA" as a prefix to the tariff classification number on U.S. Customs Form 7501. The United States does not require a certificate of origin for entries valued at U.S.$1,250 or less. Importers have one year to apply for a refund of any excess duties paid as a result of the goods not having been accorded NAFTA treatment.

NAFTA authorizes the customs administration of an importing country to audit the exporter or producer to verify that goods qualify as originating as certified by the certificate of origin. An exporter or producer who falsely represents on a NAFTA certificate of origin that a good qualifies as originating may be penalized. An importer may also be penalized for making a false claim for preferential NAFTA treatment on the customs import documentation. Importers, exporters and producers who prepare certificate of origins may also be penalized for failing to retain their records as required by NAFTA (as noted, generally five years). These verifications resemble tax audits.

Importers, exporters and producers of goods may obtain advance rulings from the customs administrations of Canada, Mexico or the United States on how NAFTA applies to future imports of goods into each country. Advance rulings are issued on a wide range of issues, such as whether an imported good qualifies for NAFTA tariff treatment. Canada, Mexico and the United States are bound by the rulings they issue. A person who has received an advance ruling has the right to appeal it.

Customs Valuation

The customs value assigned to a good affects the amount of duty payable because duties are assessed as percentages of that value. Under NAFTA, advance rulings are available on customs valuations. However, NAFTA does not impose its own obligations as to how customs valuation is to be conducted; it applies the WTO Customs Valuation Code (CVC) instead of creating a separate set of rules.

The CVC provides clear rules for how goods are to be valued by customs officials.[11] Import duties are levied on a percentage, or *ad valorem*, basis—that is, on the basis of the value assigned to imported products by customs authorities. Several methods of valuation may be used, but only in the order and under conditions set out in the CVC.

The first method used must be the price actually paid or payable when the good is sold for export. To the price actually paid customs officials may add commissions, the cost of containers and packing (as incurred), and certain other costs, such as royalties and license fees payable by the buyer (if not already included in price paid) and proceeds of resale that accrue to the seller.

If the first method is not appropriate, the value of identical goods sold for export to the same importing country must be used. If that does not work, then the transaction value of similar goods sold for export to same importing country is used. If officials cannot determine the transaction value, they must use the price of the good when sold to an unrelated buyer in the country of importation, or a computed value. "Computed value" is the cost or value of materials and fabrication, plus profit, general expenses and other expenses. The importer chooses the order of application of the latter two methods.

If none of the foregoing methods is appropriate, customs officials may use any reasonable means of valuation based on available information. However, they cannot use the price of similar or identical domestic goods, the selling price of the good in its country of origin or other export markets, or fictitious values.

Currency must be given the current value in commercial transactions. Officials must provide confidentiality unless they have permission not to, or unless information must be revealed in judicial proceedings. There must be a right of appeal regarding valuations, and governments must publish the laws, regulations, judicial decisions and administrative rulings relating to customs valuation. Where there is a delay in determining value, officials must release the goods upon guarantee of payment (for example, by posting a bond or making a deposit). There must be a right to request reasons for valuation decisions in writing. Customs officials have the right to determine the accuracy of the information that is provided.

Sometimes business people fabricate a value for products that is less than their true value in order to lower the duties. They accept the risk of being audited, just as they would if they lied about their income in an income tax return. However, there is also another risk. If they understate the price of the goods on the invoice in order to lower tariffs, that same price may be used in an antidumping investigation and result in the application of higher antidumping duties (ADDs) to the product. ADDs are calculated as the difference between the price of the product in its home market and the price in the export market. Misrepresenting the latter price as being lower than it really is therefore increases the risk that a dumping complaint will be filed by a competitor in the export market; it also increases the amount of ADDs.

Agreements on Technical Barriers to Trade (Standards)

NAFTA chapter 9 and the WTO Agreement on Technical Barriers to Trade (known as the Standards Code) impose similar obligations on governments with respect to product standards that may act as barriers to trade. Standards can put foreign producers at a disadvantage by adding unnecessary costs of production. Both NAFTA and WTO provide distinct obligations for sanitary and phytosanitary standards (applied specifically to agricultural trade to protect humans, animals and plants from the risk of pests, diseases and toxins that may be introduced by agricultural imports). Due to the special nature and complexity of agreements on agricultural trade and sanitary and phytosanitary measures, these agriculture-related agreements will not be covered in this book.

The WTO Standards Code applies to all products, including industrial and agricultural products. NAFTA rules similarly apply to trade in goods but, unlike WTO, also apply to standards affecting trade in services (for example, with respect to land transportation). However, neither agreement applies to purchasing specifications in government procurement (which are dealt with separately) or to sanitary and phytosanitary measures.

Both NAFTA and WTO require national treatment in respect to standards. Both require members to ensure that standards do not create unnecessary obstacles to trade. Standards must not be more trade restrictive than necessary to achieve a legitimate objective. The WTO defines legitimate objectives to include national security, the prevention of deceptive practices, or the protection of human animal or plant life or health, or of the environment. Similarly, NAFTA affirms the right to adopt standards for legitimate objectives, which include health and safety, environmental and consumer protection. "Legitimate objective" is defined in NAFTA to exclude the protection of domestic industry.

Both the WTO and NAFTA require members to use international standards as the basis for setting standards, except where this is an ineffective or inappropriate means to fulfill legitimate objective. Acceptable reasons for deviating from international standards in the WTO include fundamental climatic or geographical factors and fundamental technological problems. Similarly, NAFTA allows the consideration of factors such as climate, geography, technology, infrastructure and scientific justification in setting standards. Under both agreements, there is a presumption that standards have legitimate objectives, insofar as they are in accordance with international standards.

Both agreements encourage the harmonization of standards among members without making it mandatory. Under NAFTA, any harmonization must be to the highest common denominator. The WTO encourages only mutual recognition of standards. NAFTA requires members to treat each other's standards as equivalent upon the presentation of proof or to provide reasons in writing for not doing so.

With respect to transparency, WTO members must publish a notice and consider comments for proposed regulations that do not conform to international standards and that have significant effects on trade. They must publish regulations promptly and allow a time lapse before their entry into force. NAFTA provides similar transparency obligations for standards.

Both agreements give members the right to determine the levels of protection set in their standards, but this must be based on a scientific assessment of risks. Under both agreements, relevant factors in conducting risk assessment include available scientific and technical information, related processing technology and the intended end-uses of product.

Government Procurement

Government purchases of goods and services represent a significant portion of total government expenditures. It is estimated that government procurement represents 10–15 percent of gross domestic product (GDP). Opening government purchasing to foreign suppliers can thus have a significant impact on international trade. However, governments often use procurement policies to promote local industries rather than just to seek the best product at the best price.

NAFTA chapter 10 partially opens government purchasing to foreign suppliers. It applies to federal contracts for goods, services and construction, but not to government procurement by provinces or states. Some sectors have exemptions—for example, Canadian shipbuilding and U.S. military supplies. Chapter 10 applies only to contracts over certain threshold amounts, indexed to inflation and converted at prevailing exchange rates —twenty-five thousand U.S. dollars between Canada and the United States, and fifty thousand in Mexico for purchases of goods and services by federal entities. The thresholds are higher for government enterprises and construction services. A percentage of the procurement contracts of Mexico's oil company Pemex and Mexico's electricity utility, CFE, were exempt until 2003.

The rules cover bidding procedures, advertising, breaking up contracts to lower the amount below thresholds, and factors used to evaluate bids. For example, governments cannot require local content as condition for granting a contract. Nor can they use technical specifications to create barriers to foreign bids. Suppliers can challenge bid procedures when there are irregularities.

The WTO Agreement on Government Procurement (GPA) applies to only a small number of WTO members.[12] Among the NAFTA countries, Canada and the United States are covered, but Mexico is not. The GPA works differently from the NAFTA, in that each country that agrees to the GPA submits an individual "schedule of commitments" regarding the extent to which it opens its government procurement market to foreign suppliers. Thus, the schedule of each country must be consulted to determine which contracts are open to bids from foreign suppliers. The schedules list which government entities are open and what the minimum thresholds are for contracts to be open to foreign bids.

GLOBAL BUSINESS STRATEGY AND TRADE IN GOODS

Barriers to trade in goods affect sourcing strategies for importers and for manufacturers. Firms that import goods on a global basis—for example, retailers such as Wal-Mart—generally seek the best products at the lowest price. Import prohibitions entirely prevent the purchase of some imports, while tariffs and other duties may cause the firm to choose one source over another. The same applies to manufacturers who import inputs. For these firms, the main issues are how to reduce the duties that are payable and how to overcome import restrictions.

Differences in product standards affect a firm's choice between a strategy of product standardization and a strategy of adaptation to local market demands. If standards are harmonized, then the choice of strategy can be based on whether the tastes of consumers require that adaptations be made. Without harmonized standards, the cost of production rises, because firms cannot achieve the same economies of scale. Environmental standards may influence the policies of firms where the target market is important enough and where access to the market depends on accepting the cost of changing environmental policies.

The competitiveness of a firm's product in export markets is affected by the price increases implied in the target market's import duties. Import tariffs are designed to protect the domestic industry from foreign competition on the basis of price. If the exporter chooses to absorb the cost of the tariff by charging a lower price in the export market, the exporter runs the risk of antidumping duties. Tariffs can therefore influence whether the firm chooses to compete on price or on other product characteristics, such as the quality or image of the product.

Trade barriers also influence whether a firm chooses to enter a foreign market using an export strategy or a foreign direct investment (FDI) strategy. Where the trade barriers in the target market make exporting impractical, the firm may have to invest in manufacturing facilities inside the country.

CONCLUSION

There is considerable overlap between WTO and NAFTA agreements related to trade in goods. The rules tend to cover the same issues, but NAFTA has made more progress in liberalizing trade in goods than WTO. The general rules and the general exceptions are essentially the same. However, NAFTA generally eliminates tariffs much more quickly than WTO. With respect to rules of origin, NAFTA has an agreement in place, while the WTO agreement remains under negotiation. However, with respect to customs valuation, NAFTA adopts the WTO agreement. With respect to standards, the two agreements provide essentially the same rules. However, in the area of government procurement, NAFTA is more advanced.

Under both agreements, governments enforce these rules for the benefit of their firms. It is important for business people to know what the rules are and how they work, so that they can recognize situations in which they should lobby government to enforce the rules in order to break down barriers to trade. Customs rules and procedures in the NAFTA countries provide business people with mechanisms that they can use to enforce their rights. For example, business people can seek advance rulings on customs decisions to ensure greater predictability in planning.

The main issues facing firms in both regional and global trade are how to minimize duties and how to eliminate import and export bans. Duties and import bans increase the cost of importing inputs in manufacturing. Duties and export bans affect the cost of products in export markets, as well as access to those markets. Duties affect the price competitiveness of a firm's products. This in turn affects decisions regarding the location of manufacturing facilities and the choice of export markets. Firms still use trade barriers to protect home markets against foreign competitors. However, there are fewer barriers to trade in goods under NAFTA than under WTO, which means that trade barriers affect the global competitive position of firms more than it does their competitiveness within the NAFTA region.

CLOSING CASE: CANADA–UNITED STATES LUMBER DISPUTE

A dispute over softwood lumber trade between Canada and the United States has been going on for two decades. In 1982, the softwood lumber dispute began when the Coalition for Fair Canadian Lumber Imports filed a petition to have a countervailing duty (CVD) imposed on Canadian lumber, arguing that provincial stumpage rates constituted a countervailable subsidy.[13] "Stumpage rates" are the fees provincial governments charge lumber companies for the right to cut down timber in lands owned by the provincial governments. In 1983, the U.S. Department of Commerce concluded that stumpage rights were not countervailable, because they were not provided to a "specific enterprise or industry, or group of enterprises or industries," as required by United States subsidies law.[14] This is known as the *specificity test*.

"Lumber II" began in 1986, when the coalition filed another petition based on the same complaint. The key difference from the 1982 case was that the U.S. specificity test had changed in the intervening period. In the Mexican Carbon Black case, the U.S. Court of International Trade had ruled that specificity may be found where a subsidy's availability is not restricted by law but is in fact available only to a specific industry.[15] Thus, in a preliminary determination, the Department of Commerce decided that stumpage was specific, applying this new de facto specificity test. When it became apparent the United States was going to impose a countervailing duty, Canada entered into a memorandum of understanding (MOU) with the United States agreeing to impose an export tax of 15 percent on Canadian lumber exports. In return, the United States terminated the case.

"Lumber III" began in 1991, when Canada terminated the MOU and the U.S. Department of Commerce initiated a third investigation against Canadian lumber imports. In 1992, the department determined that stumpage and Canadian log export controls both constituted countervailable subsidies. After the U.S. International Trade Commission (ITC) determined that the Canadian subsidy was injuring American competitors, the United States imposed a duty of 6.51 percent.[16] Canada appealed the decision to a binational panel under chapter 19 of the Canada–United States Free Trade Agreement, the precursor to chapter 19 of the NAFTA.

In 1993, the panel ruled unanimously that the Department of Commerce had misinterpreted and misapplied its own nation's law and remanded the case to the department for redetermination. The department reaffirmed its original decision. The panel rejected the department's reaffirmation, in a three-to-two decision that split along national lines.[17] The United States then unsuccessfully challenged the second panel decision under the "extraordinary challenge" procedure of chapter 19.[18] Thus, Canada won the third round. The United States had to refund some six hundred million dollars in duties to Canada, plus interest.[19]

After the Lumber III rulings, when it implemented the Uruguay Round agreements, the United States changed its subsidies law. The law was changed in a way that overturned the panel's interpretation. As a result, if the same case were to come before a NAFTA panel, the panel might have to rule in favor of the United States. After the change in the U.S. law, Canada chose to enter into a further bilateral agreement with the United States in order to avoid a fourth countervailing-duty case. In return for five years of trade peace, Canada agreed to impose an export tax on Canadian softwood lumber exports exceeding 14.7 billion board feet per year. The export quota was less than record 1995 exports of 16.2 billion board feet, but more than the average of the previous three years. The United States had threatened to impose a 10 percent countervailing duty on all Canadian softwood lumber exports to the United States. Canada agreed to impose an export quota on softwood lumber from four provinces (British Columbia, Alberta, Ontario and Quebec) for five years beginning on April 1, 1996. If lumber shipments exceeded the quota, the excess shipments would be subject to the export tax. This marked the second time in ten years that Canada had imposed export taxes in order to avoid countervailing duties on softwood lumber.[20]

In the first three lumber cases, the battle was waged between U.S. lumber producers, represented by the Coalition for Fair Lumber Imports, and Canadian lumber exporters. Lumber is a commodity whose price is determined by supply and demand. Demand fluctuates with the ups and downs of the U.S. economy, which affects the quantity of houses and furniture being built. U.S. lumber companies can drive up the price, and their profits, by restricting supply; as roughly 30 percent of the lumber in the

United States comes from Canada, U.S. companies can restrict supply by restricting the flow of lumber from Canada.

As with most trade disputes, the interests of the consumer were not represented in the lumber dispute. An industry that stands to gain or lose from free trade tends to organize itself and lobby for political support the way widely dispersed consumers cannot. However, strategists in the Canadian industry realized that U.S. consumers had to become involved politically and therefore set about organizing them during the five-year truce.

Hewers of Wood Meet Washington Lawyers

On March 31, 2001, the five-year agreement expired. On April 2, 2001, the coalition filed countervailing and antidumping duty petitions with the U.S. government, alleging a subsidy rate of 39.9 percent (based primarily on stumpage fees and log export restraints) and dumping margins of 22.53 percent to 72.91 percent.[21] On April 23, in Washington, D.C., the ITC began hearing allegations by U.S. lumber producers that subsidized and dumped Canadian lumber was harming their industry. At the time, it was estimated that the result could be U.S. tariffs as high as 78 percent.

Meanwhile, a coalition of twenty American home builders and lumber dealers said it would urge the ITC to reject the allegations of subsidies and dumping or of selling at below cost in the U.S. market. "Acceptance of the concepts in these petitions would be the equivalent of a 78 percent hidden tax on consumers wanting to purchase a new home, remodel their home, or even buy a new bed," said Susan Petniunas, a spokeswoman for the group. In its petition, the groups said a 78 percent tariff could cost the United States more than two billion U.S. dollars a year.[22] American Consumers for Affordable Homes, a new Washington lobby group partly funded by the Canadian industry, estimated that the duty demanded by U.S. lumber producers would cut 1.2 million families out of the housing market and raise the average price of a new home by two to four thousand U.S. dollars.[23]

On August 9, 2001, the U.S. Department of Commerce issued a preliminary countervailing duty of 19.3 percent on softwood lumber exports to the United States from all regions of Canada except the Atlantic provinces. The latter were exempted on the grounds that their system of selling timber was closer than the systems of other provinces to that of the United States. Lumber futures rose three dollars per thousand board feet on the Chicago Mercantile Exchange, having already priced-in an expected 15 percent duty. Lumber futures for September delivery had already risen from a six-month low of $237.30 on February 23 to a six-month high of $347.50 on May 21. While analysts expected Canada to win the trade dispute, in the interim the duty could result in mills being closed. In contrast with the earlier lumber disputes, Canada was this time using the WTO dispute settlement process to challenge U.S. laws.

Canada requested a WTO panel to hear Canada's complaint over a U.S. law[24] that prevents the United States from refunding duty deposits collected from foreign companies in situations where the imposition of duties has been found to violate WTO rules. Consultations were held with the United States on March 1, 2001, and a WTO panel was formally established on August 23, 2001.

Consultations were held on June 29, 2001, regarding the Byrd Amendment, which requires U.S. customs authorities to distribute countervailing or antidumping duties to "affected domestic producers" for "qualifying expenses." Canada requested the establishment of a WTO panel to hear this matter as well, arguing that the WTO allows only the imposition of duties and that such additional payments create an incentive for U.S. industry to file complaints.

With respect to the preliminary determination of subsidy, Canada and the United States held consultations on September 17, 2001. When consultations failed to resolve the matter, Canada requested that a WTO panel be established to hear this case as well.[25] In this complaint, Canada challenged the U.S. Department of Commerce's preliminary determination that found a subsidy rate of 19.31 percent. Canada argued that stumpage systems do not meet the WTO definition of "subsidy," because they do not constitute a financial contribution as defined under the WTO agreement.

In the midst of the foregoing proceedings, a WTO panel ruled that export restraints, such as log export controls, do not provide a financial contribution and thus do not confer countervailable subsidies.[26] However, because the U.S. law in question did not "mandate" that the United States treat export restraints as a financial contribution, it was not found to contravene the WTO agreement. This ruling may undermine U.S. claims that log export controls confer subsidies in the current countervailing duty investigation.

On October 31, 2001, the United States assessed preliminary antidumping duties ranging from 6 percent to 20 percent on Canadian lumber.[27]

Once the U.S. government makes final determinations regarding subsidies and dumping, the Canadian government and industry will be able to seek a review of those decisions under NAFTA chapter 19, which could lead to a refund of any duties that are paid. Chapter 19 reviews consider only whether the U.S. agencies properly applied American law. In contrast, the WTO process may be used to challenge the underlying law itself; this is the legal strategy being pursued by the Canadian government in its WTO complaints.

To Litigate or Not to Litigate

Four rounds have been fought in the softwood lumber dispute since 1982. Canada has won two rounds, and the United States has won two rounds. With the expiry of the five-year truce, another round has begun. Twice, Canada has avoided countervailing duties by successfully arguing for a given interpretation and application of the specificity test. Twice, the United States specificity test has changed and thereby changed the outcome for Canadian lumber. Canada and the United States have signed three international trade agreements (CUSFTA, NAFTA, WTO) and two lumber agreements (1986, 1996) since the dispute began. In only one of these five agreements did they reach agreement on a common definition of subsidy and specificity—that of the WTO agreement.

The WTO may be a better forum than NAFTA for settling this issue, for both legal and strategic reasons. A WTO decision would carry more weight than a NAFTA decision, due to the size of the WTO membership. The disproportionate bargaining power of the United States would be offset by that of the other members of the WTO, increasing the likelihood that a decision in favor of Canada's position would be implemented by the United States. Moreover, the WTO has exclusive jurisdiction to interpret the meaning of the WTO Subsidies Agreement.

Canada may choose to negotiate once again a "voluntary export restraint" agreement with the United States to avoid the uncertainty and cost associated with long-term legal disputes. While such agreements violate the WTO rules, the violation would be moot, because neither country would complain to the WTO that their agreement was invalid. The trouble with such agreements is that they run counter to the notion of free trade and give the impression that trade agreements do not work. A recent study calculated that negotiating an export tax and changes to the Canadian system could cost C$2.8 billion more than challenging U.S. measures at the WTO.[28]

This case demonstrates the limits of the dispute-settlement processes under both NAFTA and WTO in the face of protectionist use of trade remedy laws. It also shows that the impact of trade barriers on consumers can be used to organize opposition within the target market. In circumstances such as these, the exporters must choose between negotiating a predictable level of trade barriers and using existing dispute-settlement mechanisms to remove the trade barrier.

NOTES

1. See *US—Import Prohibition of Certain Shrimp and Shrimp Products, Report of the Appellate Body*, AB-1998-4 (1998), available at http://www.wto.org [hereafter Shrimp].

2. *Convention on International Trade in Endangered Species of Wild Fauna and Flora,* done at Washington, March 3,1973, as amended.

3. "General Agreement on Tariffs and Trade, Final Act Embodying the Results of the Uruguay Round of Multilateral Trade Negotiations," April 15, 1994, *Legal Instruments—Results of the Uruguay Round,* Annex 1A, vol. I, 33 ILM 1125 (1994) [hereafter GATT].

4. NAFTA article 102(2).

5. "Understanding on Rules and Procedures Governing the Settlement of Disputes, Apr. 15, 1994, Final Act Embodying the Results of the Uruguay Round of Multilateral Trade Negotiations," *Legal Instruments—Results of the Uruguay Round,* annex 2, vol. 31, 33 ILM 1226 (1994), art. 3(2) [hereafter DSU].

6. *Vienna Convention on the Law of Treaties, done at Vienna, 23 May 1969,* 1155 UNTS 331, 8 ILM 679, article 59 [hereafter Vienna Convention].

7. See *Canada—Patent Protection of Pharmaceutical Products, Report of the Panel* (2000) available at http://www.wto.org.

8. WTO, *Guide to GATT Law and Practice,* 6th ed. (Geneva: Bernan Press, 1995), vol. 1, 600.

9. Australia, Canada, fifteen EU members, Hong Kong, Iceland, Indonesia, Japan, Korea, Liechtenstein, Norway, Chinese Taipei, Singapore, Switzerland, Turkey, the United States, Costa Rica, Czech Republic, Estonia, Israel, India, Macau, Malaysia, New Zealand, Romania, Slovakia, and Thailand.

10. NAFTA chap. 8.

11. *Agreement on Implementation of Article VII of GATT 1994,* arts. 1–17.

12. Austria, Belgium, Canada, Denmark, European Communities, Finland, France, Germany, Greece, Hong Kong China, Iceland, Ireland, Israel, Italy, Japan, Korea, Liechtenstein, Luxembourg, Netherlands, Netherlands with respect to Aruba, Norway, Portugal, Singapore, Spain, Sweden, Switzerland, United Kingdom, the United States.

13. For a more detailed discussion of the lumber case, see, inter alia, A.M. Rugman and S.D. Porteous, "The Softwood Lumber Decision of 1986: Broadening the Nature of US Administered Protection," *Review of International Business Law* 2 (1988), 35; and P.A. Pilouris, "Anatomy of a Trade Dispute: The Question of Softwood Lumber," *Dalhousie Journal of Legal Studies* 1 (1992), 71–86.

14. USC 1677(5)(b)(1988).

15. See *Cabot Corp v. The US,* 620 F. Supp. 722 (1985) (the Mexican Carbon Black case).

16. See *In the Matter of Certain Softwood Lumber Products from Canada, Decision of the Panel,* Q.L. [1993] FTAD No. 5 at 33.

17. See *In the Matter of Certain Softwood Lumber Products from Canada, Decision of the Panel on Remand* (1993), available at http://www.nafta-sec-alena.org/english/index.htm.

18. See *Certain Softwood Lumber Products from Canada,* ECC-94-1904-01USA (3 August 1994), available at http://www.nafta-sec-alena.org/english/index.htm.

19. Jon Fried, "Annual Update on Developments in International Trade Law," paper presented at the Thirteenth Annual International Trade Law Seminar, Ottawa, October 19, 1995, p. 10.

20. Eric Beauchesne, "Canada Winner in Softwood Deal, Minister Says," *Vancouver Sun,* April 10, 1996, C1.

21. See Canadian Department of Foreign Affairs and International Trade, *Softwood Lumber Trade Actions: Chronology and Background,* available at http://www.dfait-maeci.gc.ca~eicb . . . d/SWL_TradeAcitonsBackground-e.htm [*sic*].

22. Barrie McKenna, "Softwood Diplomacy Abandoned: Pettigrew Sees No Negotiated Truce Ahead as Battle Switches to Trade Hearings," *Globe and Mail,* April 23, 2001.

23. Steve Mertl, "Lumber Producers Say US Tariff Will Cost Them $2 Billion Annually," *Vancouver Sun,* August 11, 2001, C1.

24. See *Uruguay Round Agreements Act,* sect. 129(c)(1), PL 103-465 [H.R. 5110] December 8, 1994.

25. Canadian Department of Foreign Affairs and International Trade, *Notice: Request for WTO Panel US Lumber Decisions,* October 27, 2001, available at http://www.dfait-maeci.gc.ca~eicb . . . wood/Req_WTO_Panel_Decisions-e.htm.

26. See *US—Measures Treating Export Restraints as Subsidies, Complaint by Canada, Report of the Panel,* DS194/R (2001), available at http://www.wto.org.

27. Peter Kennedy, "Lumber Duties Could Hit $1.5-Billion," *Globe and Mail,* November 2, 2001.

28. Barrie McKenna and Peter Kennedy, "Legal Action on Softwood Touted," *Globe and Mail,* November 16, 2001, B4.

Chapter 3

International Trade in Services

OPENING CASE: NAFTA TRUCKING AND THE INSURANCE INDUSTRY

By a 285–143 roll call, the U.S. House of Representatives voted on June 26, 2001, that it would block the Transportation Department from issuing permits that would let Mexican trucks operate throughout the United States.[1] This vote was the result of opposition from both the Democrats and the Republicans. The Democrats had been pushed hard by the trucker's lobby and the Republicans by the insurance lobby in Washington.

The U.S. trucking unions had opposed the entry of Mexican truckers into the United States to transport goods on the grounds that the Mexican truckers would not meet U.S. safety standards. Underlying this opposition was the reality that U.S. truckers were likely to lose a lot of business. Each year, about five million crossings are made, hauling about three-fourths of the $250 billion in United States–Mexico trade. Under the new NAFTA panel ruling, instead of transferring their loads to U.S. truckers at the border, the Mexican truckers would be able to carry them to their final destinations in the United States. Moreover, transportation of goods by Mexican truckers would cost less, as the wages earned by the Mexican drivers are a fraction of what the unionized U.S. truckers charge for their services.

In February of 2001, a panel ruled that the U.S. moratorium on free movement of trucks between the United States and Mexico violated NAFTA. The ruling has generated a flurry of lobbying by a number of interest groups in Washington. In what follows, we analyze the history and the current situation, and we take a closer look at the politics and economics behind it. We discuss what might be ahead, given the ruling.

A Bit of History

Prior to 1980, the United States granted operating authority to motor carriers for individual routes, requiring economic justification for each proposed service. It did not distinguish between U.S., Mexican or Canadian applicants. The Interstate Commerce Commission (ICC) severely restricted new entries into the domestic market. However, in 1980 the Motor Carrier Act essentially eliminated regulatory barriers to entry, making it easier for motor carriers from all three countries to obtain operating authority. It did not distinguish between nationals and non-nationals. At the time, Canada already allowed reciprocal access for U.S. truckers in its domestic market, but Mexico did not.[2]

Equal treatment of U.S. and foreign applicants ended in 1982. The Bus Regulatory Reform Act imposed an initial two-year moratorium on the issuance of new motor carrier operating authority to foreign carriers. A presidential memorandum immediately lifted the moratorium with respect to Canada, in response to the Brock-Gotlieb Understanding, which confirmed that U.S. carriers would have continued access to the Canadian market. The same memorandum declined to lift the moratorium with respect to Mexico, citing American truckers' continued lack of access to the Mexican market. The U.S. president repeatedly extended the moratorium against Mexican truckers every two years from 1984 to 1995. The purpose of the moratorium was to encourage Mexico to lift its restrictions on market access for U.S. firms.

However, some exceptions have been allowed, to facilitate cross-border trade. An exemption for commercial zones of border towns has permitted Mexican carriers to operate in the commercial zones associated with municipalities along the border since before 1982, provided they obtain a certificate of registration from the Federal Motor Carrier Safety Administration. Under this procedure, the applicant certifies that he has access to and will comply with Federal Motor Carrier Safety Regulations. Applicants are not required to submit proof of insurance, but inside the commercial zones they must carry proof of insurance on board. In 1999, 8,400 Mexican firms had authority to operate in the commercial zones.

A second exception relates to Mexican operators who transit through the United States to Canada; they are not affected by the moratorium. Congress has not granted the Department of Transportation the authority to require trucks transiting from Mexico to Canada to seek operating authority. These Mexican trucks need only comply with U.S. insurance requirements and safety regulations.

Under a third exception, "grandfathered" Mexican trucking companies that had acquired operating authority prior to 1982, when the moratorium came into effect, are not affected. Five Mexican carriers are entitled to these exemptions.

Under a fourth exception, the ICC Termination Act of 1995 exempts U.S.-owned Mexican-domiciled truck companies, which total approximately 160 companies, from the operation of the moratorium. A fifth exception, which allowed Mexican carriers to lease both trucks and drivers to U.S. carriers, was allowed until January 1, 2000. The Motor Carrier Safety Improvement Act of 1999 ended the leasing exception; the United States had realized that this provision could be used to sell American carriers' operating authority to Mexican carriers for operations beyond the border zone.

On March 1, 1994, the transportation ministers of Canada and Mexico signed three memoranda of understanding to permit truckers to operate between Canada and Mexico.[3] A cargo-exchange agreement permits Canadian truckers to enter Mexico to exchange cargoes at contracted Mexican terminals and facilities along the northern border of Mexico. A commercial drivers license reciprocity agreement lets Canadian and Mexican drivers operate in each other's countries with their own licenses. The third, a transportation training agreement, allows Canada to train Mexican personnel in the areas of maritime and port management and truck-driving simulation.[4]

Under a memorandum of understanding (MOU) between the United States, Mexico and Canada, U.S. truck carriers are able to carry freight from Canada into Mexico as far as twenty kilometers in a nearly barrier-free environment. Despite the MOU, the governments of the United States and Mexico have been at an impasse over permitting each other full access to their respective markets since 1995.

Under NAFTA, the United States agreed to give access to Mexican trucks in 1995, but President Bill Clinton, under heavy pressure from religious, labor, environmental and other interest groups, kept the provision from taking effect, saying Mexico first had to do more to address safety problems. That year, the Mexican government, invoking NAFTA provisions, asked that a five-member panel be set up to determine whether Washington was violating the agreement. In its decision, the panel—two Americans and two Mexicans, with a British chairman—unanimously ruled that the United States would be in violation if it did not begin considering applications from Mexican trucking companies. At the time, more than 160 applications were pending.

Operating authority from the ICC was required to provide interstate or cross-border truck services in the United States. Under NAFTA, a moratorium remained in place on new grants of operating authority for persons from Mexico. However, the United States agreed to phase out the moratorium so that Mexicans would be permitted to obtain operating authority to provide cross-border truck services to or from border states (California, Arizona, New Mexico and Texas) as of December 16, 1995. Cross-border truck services to the remainder of the United States were to start as of January 1, 2000. In addition, Mexicans were to be permitted to establish an enterprise in the United States to provide truck services for the transportation of international cargo between points in the United States as of December 17, 1995. The moratorium remains in place on grants of authority for the provision of truck services by Mexicans between points in the United States for the transportation of goods other than international cargo.[5]

Recent Ruling by NAFTA Panel

The decision of NAFTA panel requires the Department of Transportation to consider applications on individual merit and not to refuse authority to all Mexican companies, across the board. In essence, the United States had argued that it could deny access to all Mexican trucking firms on a blanket basis, regardless of the individual qualifications of particular members of the Mexican industry, unless and until Mexico's domestic regulatory system met U.S. approval. However, under the law of the United States, applications for operating authority from American and Canadian carriers were considered on an individual basis. This differential treatment of Mexicans, on the one hand, and Americans and Canadians, on the other, violated NAFTA articles 1202 (national treatment) and 1203 (most-favored-nation treatment).[6]

Article 1202 requires that each party accord to service providers of another party treatment no *less* favorable than it accords, in like circumstances, to its own service providers. Article 1203 requires that each party accord to service providers of another party treatment no *less* favorable than it accords, in like circumstances, to service providers of any other party or nonparty.

The United States argued that the continuation of the moratorium was nevertheless justified under the general exception of article 2101, which provides that "nothing . . . in Chapter 12 (Cross-border Trade in Services) . . . shall be construed to prevent the adoption or enforcement by any party of measures necessary to secure compliance with laws or regulations . . . relating to health and safety and consumer protection." Citing GATT and WTO jurisprudence, the panel ruled that the United States had to use the least trade-restrictive means available to address its safety concerns. The numerous exceptions the United States was applying to the moratorium proved that there were less restrictive means available to achieve its safety goals with respect to Mexican truckers. Thus, the blanket ban could not be justified under article 2101.

An interesting aspect of the decision involves the nature of reservations taken under a trade agreement. The laws of each country must be congruent with the general rules of trade agreements that it signs, such as the nondiscrimination rules of national and MFN treatment. Trade agreements contain general exceptions to those rules—for example, to permit environmental and safety regulations that may have incidental effects on trade. In addition, at the time of negotiation of the trade agreement, countries may negotiate exemptions for certain industries protected from foreign competition by specific laws. That is, countries may keep certain laws in place notwithstanding their inconsistency with the general rules. However, such laws must be listed as reservations in the annexes of the agreement.

Reservations constitute specific instances where a country maintains laws that go against the main objective of the agreement, which is to liberalize trade. As such, they are often of limited duration and are interpreted strictly. When they expire, such laws must pass muster with the general rules or fit into one of the general exceptions.

In the trucking case, the United States placed a reservation in an annex to permit the moratorium on Mexican trucks to continue, but it also included dates when specific aspects of the moratorium would be phased out. Once the reservation expired, the United States had either to lift the moratorium or justify it under the general rules or exceptions. Not surprisingly, the moratorium did not pass muster; had it been consistent with NAFTA rules, no reservation would have been required in the first place. Thus, by using the reservation procedure the United States virtually admitted a violation of the rules.

The panel made clear that the United States was entitled under NAFTA to set its own safety standards and to ensure that Mexican trucking companies met them. Moreover, the United States is not required to treat applications from Mexican truckers in exactly the same manner as applications from U.S. or Canadian firms, as long as all applications are reviewed on a case-by-case basis, comply with NAFTA, and are decided upon in good faith with respect to legitimate safety concerns.

Following the panel decision, the George W. Bush administration announced that it would reverse the Clinton administration policy and begin allowing Mexican trucks to haul goods throughout the United States.

Economics of Opposition

American trucking is not the only industry opposing the Mexican truckers. The U.S. insurance industry is also up in arms. Why? These firms sell insurance to U.S. truckers, covering not only vehicles and liability but the goods being transported. A reduction in the market share of the U.S. truckers will also reduce the market share of the U.S. companies that insure them; Mexican truckers will buy insurance from Mexican insurance companies. Of course, the American insurance companies may be concerned that Mexican truckers will cause more accidents than U.S. truckers, thereby increasing payouts by insurance companies. But if the Mexican truckers are insured by Mexican insurance companies, those payments will not come out of the pockets of the American insurance companies.

The American Insurance Association (AIA) has said that Mexican trucks should be allowed to operate only in the border states until three programs are implemented. First, the AIA wants safety standards among the three NAFTA countries harmonized. Second, adequate enforcement of those standards must be implemented. Third, an adequate database of Mexican truck safety must be developed. The AIA proposal appears reasonable on the surface but is in fact designed to delay the entry of Mexican truckers beyond the border states for many years. Under NAFTA, there is no requirement to harmonize safety standards, and it may be difficult to get the countries to negotiate such an agreement. Even if such an agreement were reached, corruption in Mexico could delay adequate enforcement there for many years. Finally, the creation of a database on Mexican truck safety would be costly and time consuming; the data collected would likely serve as further ammunition in the effort to keep Mexican trucks out of the U.S. market.

Nevertheless, some progress has been made by the Land Transportation Standards Subcommittee, which is charged with the task of implementing a work program to make standards for bus and truck operations compatible.[7] In 1991, Mexico became a member of the Commercial Vehicles Safety Alliance, together with the United States and Canada. The same year, Mexico and the United States adopted uniform guidelines for roadside inspections and uniform standards for commercial drivers' licenses and for such criteria as knowledge and skills testing, disqualification and physical requirements for drivers.

An In-Depth Look at the DOT Report

In 1998, the Department of Transportation (DOT) in the United States produced a report that sealed the fate of the Mexican truckers in the United States.[8] The report, it is claimed, declares that Mexican trucks do not meet American safety standards; 44 percent of trucks inspected did not pass. Insurance industry trade groups argue that the U.S. government will have to spend four to seven million dollars a year to increase the number of safety inspectors at the border. Mexican trucks have been allowed to cross the border twenty miles into the United States to transfer cargo to U.S. trucks.

A closer inspection of the report reveals a different picture. A much less frequently quoted passage indicates that whereas 44 percent of the Mexican trucks inspected did not pass the safety standards, 27 percent of the U.S. trucks inspected did not either (only 17 percent of Canadian trucks did not). Still, on the face of it, Mexican trucks seem to have a significantly higher failure rate in meeting the safety standards. Such a presumption is false. Why?

When we examine the disaggregated data by state—California (28 percent), Arizona (42 percent), New Mexico (37 percent) and Texas (50 percent)—we find vastly different failure rates for Mexican trucks (in parentheses). The report also quotes more recent figures (that is, from 1998) showing that overall failure rates had become 42 percent rather than the 44 percent quoted for 1997. Thus, the problem is not the same in all border states; there should be no presumption that Mexico only sends "better trucks" to California and "worse trucks" to Texas! The problem lies with the process of inspection. In the report, it is acknowledged that the process is not one of random checking (page 32). If a truck "looks bad," it is inspected more minutely. Therefore, it seems that the inspection process varies substantially across states, making the overall figure of "44 percent bad trucks" completely useless.

Dimension of the Problem

How large is the problem? How many trucks cross the border into the United States? In many press reports the presumed number was in the region of 4.5 million trucks.[9] Thus, it was argued, if the Mexicans were allowed to enter the U.S. roads, they would pose a very large problem. For example, the Public Citizen Organization (a lobby group) declared in a highly charged article called "The Coming NAFTA Crash" that if Mexican trucks were allowed into the United States, the DOT would require at least thirty-two thousand more inspectors to conduct even simple inspections.[10] The volume of work would overwhelm the DOT's border inspection system. It turns out that the actual number of trucks crossing the border (in 1999) is sixty-three thousand. Where did the 4.5 million come from? There seems to be some confusion about the number of crossings and the number of trucks. True, there were 4.5 million crossings made by trucks—but the same trucks crossed the border time and again. Hence the presumed problem turns out to be a storm in a teacup!

Differing Standards

It is true that safety standards in Mexico and the United States differ in many ways: (1) the United States generally limits truck weights to eighty thousand pounds, compared to Mexico's limit of ninety-seven thousand pounds; (2) the United States requires front-wheel brakes, whereas Mexico does not; (3) U.S. laws require drivers to meet licensing standards that include drug testing and limits on the length of their driving shifts, while Mexican laws do not; and (4) Mexico does not require the maintenance of driving logs or other types of data that would be needed for enforcement. However, the lack of mandatory rules of these kinds in Mexico would not prevent Mexican truckers from ensuring they meet U.S. standards. Indeed, trucking companies that seek to operate across the border would be wise to impose the necessary standards in-house. In fact, Mexican truck companies that have applied for operation in the United States have pledged that they will send only trucks that comply with "normal" U.S. standards.

With respect to insurance, U.S. trucking companies must meet minimum financial-responsibility requirements, to protect the right of recovery of third-party claimants. Some interstate trucking companies must also carry cargo insurance. Shippers often obtain similar coverage.

Some State Legislation

NAFTA provisions granting Mexican trucks and buses free access to U.S. border states prompted the Texas legislature to enact several new laws that took effect on December 5, 1995. Mexican carriers doing business beyond the Texas border commercial zones must meet the same safety and insurance requirements as U.S. and Canadian truckers do. Mexican and domestic motor carriers must file proof of liability insurance coverage with the Texas Department of Transportation (TxDOT) in specific amounts ranging from three hundred thousand to five million U.S. dollars, depending on the type of vehicle and cargo.

Coverage must be with a licensed company or through a self-insurance mechanism approved by TxDOT. For-hire motor carriers of household goods must carry cargo insurance in amounts required by federal law (five thousand U.S. dollars per vehicle, up to ten thousand for aggregate loss or damage in one occurrence).

Non-U.S. insurers, through a port of entry law, can obtain a Texas certificate of authority to operate domestically. This law requires alien companies to establish Texas subsidiaries and comply with all Texas capital, asset and surplus requirements. Mexico's third-largest casualty insurer, Aseguradora Mexicana (ASEMEX), was the first Mexican carrier to be granted a Texas certificate of authority under the port of entry law. ASEMEX had sought the certificate in order to sell insurance to Mexican truckers who serve U.S. border zones.[11]

Some Proposals

Cross-border trucking insurance remains a problem to be resolved, as well. Impediments remain to "seamless" insurance coverage for carriers wishing to provide trucking services across the borders to the three NAFTA countries—that is, coverage that is effective throughout the region, without the necessity of more than one policy. In this area, there are concerns regarding the financial ability of Mexican domestic insurers to pay potential claims arising in the other two countries or to issue coverage that complies with the requirements in the other jurisdictions.

Canadian and American insurers use a "managing general agent," or fronting, concept whereby the insurance firm in one country handles the necessary filings of the firm from the other country in the former's jurisdiction and provide the necessary proofs of insurance. However, this service is not available in Mexico. Mexican insurance law requires that the entire risk be retained in Mexico; it does not permit reinsurance through a U.S. or Canadian insurer. Moreover, a Canadian or U.S. insurer that wishes to act as agent for the purpose of issuing a Mexican insurer's paper must first be so authorized by the Mexican National Insurance and Banking Commission. One proposal to solve the problem would be a new Mexican law that would enable Canadian or U.S.-licensed insurers to register in Mexico for the purpose of issuing policies in Mexico to Mexican insureds for motor carrier risks outside Mexico. Another option would be to develop a NAFTA insurance-card system, similar to that used in Europe.

Under international law, countries have jurisdiction to regulate activities within their territory and to regulate the acts of their citizens. Mexico therefore has jurisdiction to regulate insurance contracts between Mexican truckers and insurance companies in Mexico. The U.S. government has no jurisdiction in the matter; however, the United States has jurisdiction to regulate the acts of Mexican truckers operating in American territory. This means that the U.S. government could legally require all trucks operating in the United States to carry insurance, dictating the type of insurance and the nature of the coverage. But can the U.S. government require that insurance be purchased from American companies? One could expect the U.S. insurance industry to lobby for such a law in order to maintain their sales of insurance to truckers, be they Mexican or American.

However, by the WTO Agreement on Trade in Financial Services and NAFTA chapter 14 on Financial Services, the United States made commitments to open up its insurance industry to foreign suppliers. More importantly, it agreed to freeze any existing restrictions on foreign insurance suppliers that had been established by listing them as reservations in schedules submitted to WTO and attached to NAFTA. If the United States were to introduce a new restriction on market access, the law would likely be challenged by Mexico under NAFTA or WTO agreement.

Conclusion

This case illustrates how regional trade agreements, such as NAFTA, can interact with global trade agreements, such as the WTO Agreement on Trade in Financial Services, sometimes in unanticipated ways. Opposition to free trade in trucking services was probably not expected from the American insurance industry, and the reasons for its opposition are not immediately obvious. However, its goal—to ensure that trucks operating in the United States carry insurance issued by American companies—may be complicated by the commitments the U.S. government has made under the global Financial Services Agreement and NAFTA.

Another complexity revealed in this case is the relationship between international agreements and national constitutional law. While the federal government of the United States has signed NAFTA and WTO agreements, the state governments have the power to regulate in many areas, and one of them is insurance. This limits the ability of the federal government to ensure compliance with aspects of international agreements that fall outside its jurisdiction under the Constitution, despite its obligation to seek such compliance.

Finally, this case shows how international agreements affect the range of domestic regulatory options available to national and subnational governments, and to industry interests that lobby those governments for regulations that may offer them protection from foreign competition. On the one hand, NAFTA and WTO agreements allow domestic governments to set their own safety standards. On the other hand, they restrict the manner in which governments may enforce those standards. Such standards must be applied in a nondiscriminatory fashion—that is, they may not be used to create disguised trade barriers to foreign competitors.

International agreements restrict the options available to domestic industry in terms of protecting its national market from foreign competition. The trucking case shows how industry trade groups can influence the trade policy of a government by the selective use of information and by pursuing their economic interests in ways that make them seem to have goals in the public interest. Most often, however, their goal is to protect their domestic markets from foreign competitors.

INTRODUCTION

This chapter focuses on international agreements relating to trade in services. A wide range of business activities fall under this category. NAFTA and WTO agreements take different approaches to the liberalization of trade in services; some services are liberalized under one agreement but not under the other. For example, NAFTA deals with land transportation, such as trucking, because its members share the same land mass; WTO members are distributed around the globe, so land transportation is not a priority. Moreover, the obligations regarding services in NAFTA go farther than do WTO obligations.

THE IMPORTANCE OF SERVICES IN THE GLOBAL ECONOMY

Traditionally, trade agreements have dealt with trade in goods. The reason is simple—the production and sale of goods formed a much larger percentage of economic activity than they do today.

In the 1980s, trade agreements, such as CUSFTA, began adding rules on trade in services. Chapters relating to services trade are also included in NAFTA. This trend stepped onto the global stage with the negotiation of the General Agreement on Trade in Services (GATS) during the Uruguay Round. In many economies of the world, the production and sale of services now account for a higher percentage of activity than goods. A natural outcome was for countries with competitive service industries to seek global access for their providers in the markets of other countries.

Moreover, many services are closely connected to international trade in goods. Transportation services are essential to moving goods. Financial services are required to transfer payment for goods between buyers and sellers and to provide insurance for them and for the conveyances that transport them. Telecommunication services allow transactions to take place by telephone or fax and over the Internet. Documentation of transactions and legal advice in disputes over the sale of goods are also professional services, provided respectively by accountants and lawyers. The globalization of trade in goods has been accompanied by a parallel expansion of international trade in services.

Global manufacturers of goods provide clients for global service providers. Firms with global business strategies, however, need to move more than just goods around the globe. They need to move key people between countries where they operate, people who provide services ranging from engineering to management. They also need to move financial resources across borders, a service that can be most efficiently and effectively provided by global financial services providers. In complex international business transactions, they need sophisticated professional services from global accounting, legal and consulting firms.

Likewise, firms and other customers that operate at the national level seek innovative, high-quality services that globally competitive service companies provide. Less economically advanced countries can gain access to the best services by opening their markets to international competition in services, thereby facilitating their participation in the global economy.

HOW SERVICES ARE DELIVERED INTERNATIONALLY

There are more ways to deliver services than there are to deliver goods. This makes the liberalization of trade in services at least as complicated as free trade in goods. After more than fifty years of pursuing global free trade in goods, the GATT and its related agreements still have some way to go. One can expect that GATS negotiations could take another fifty years to achieve global liberalization of trade in services.

GATS classifies the delivery of services under four modes of supply: (1) cross-border supply; (2) consumption abroad; (3) commercial presence; and (4) the presence of "natural persons." This classification refers as much to kinds of regulatory barriers that impede the international provision of services as to delivery options available to companies.

"Cross-border supply" refers to a company in one country selling a service to a resident of another, without either the provider or the consumer actually crossing the border. An example would be an investor in Canada using the services of a broker in the United States by telephone or over the Internet. The Internet has made it difficult for national governments to erect barriers to this type of trade, as such transactions may be difficult to detect, particularly when the service being provided consists of professional advice.

"Consumption abroad" involves a consumer traveling to the country in which the service provider is located and purchasing the service there. For example, a resident of Mexico might travel to the United States to seek medical care. Residents of one country often purchase services when traveling abroad. Tourists rent hotel rooms and cars, enjoy restaurant services and purchase financial services, such as car rental insurance and currency exchange. As with cross-border supply, it is difficult for governments to erect barriers to this type of service trade.

"Commercial presence" refers to a foreign company setting up operations in another country to provide its services there. For example, a bank may set up a branch overseas or purchase a foreign bank. Commercial presence most often involves some form of foreign direct investment. Government barriers to this mode of service delivery take the form of foreign investment restrictions. However, most countries now actively seek out foreign investment as a means to increase economic growth, create jobs and obtain the technology that often accompanies foreign investment.

"Presence of natural persons" refers to the delivery of a service that requires the importing country to issue entry visas. This situation may range from temporary entry visas that permit a professional to enter the country to advise a client, to longer-term visas that permit a foreign company to station executives in a host country to manage its business activities there. Providing this type of market access is problematic for many countries, since it means relinquishing a degree of control over immigration policy, a politically sensitive area.

The manner in which they deliver their services is a very important issue for companies. The best way depends on the nature of the business. Some modes of delivery are more costly than others. For example, investing in a foreign office is more costly than setting up a Web site. For some services, it is necessary to establish a commercial presence through foreign direct investment, such as retail banking. Restrictions on foreign investment—for example, limiting foreign companies to minority shares in existing domestic firms—may impede control over the investment. Thus, what market-entry strategy a company chooses will depend in part on the mode of service delivery permitted under international trade agreements.

The remainder of this chapter looks at the rules governing international trade in services under NAFTA and GATS. It then looks at the specific rules regarding the delivery of financial services under both agreements. The closing case examines the liberalization of the telecommunications sector in Mexico.

GENERAL RULES ON TRADE IN SERVICES UNDER NAFTA AND GATS

NAFTA and Services

Part V of NAFTA covers investment, services and related matters. Chapter 11 deals with a broad range of foreign investments; it thus covers foreign direct investment as a mode of market entry for service companies. Several other chapters in NAFTA deal with services specifically. Chapter 12 contains general rules that apply to cross-border trade in services. Chapter 16 regulates the provision of temporary entry visas, facilitating the delivery of services through the presence of natural persons.

In addition to the foregoing general rules, NAFTA contains two chapters that govern services that require special rules. Chapter 13 governs telecommunications services, in which foreign companies require access to existing telecommunications networks in order to supply their services. Chapter 14 regulates trade in financial services, an area that requires special rules due to its importance in the economic stability of a country.

In chapter 12, cross-border trade in services is defined as including three of the four modes of delivery mentioned earlier. The fourth, commercial presence, which involves foreign investment, is regulated by chapter 11.[12]

The rules in chapter 12 limit the kinds of restrictions each government may place on a broad range of business activities required to provide a service, including production, distribution, marketing, sale, delivery, purchase and payments. They also apply to the presence of persons from one country who wish to provide services in another. However, none of the three NAFTA countries is obliged to permit the entry of persons seeking access to its employment market or employment on a permanent basis.[13] In other words, NAFTA permits the entry of service providers who are already established in their own countries, not people looking for jobs in another. As a corollary, no country may impose residency requirements or require the establishment of a commercial presence in its territory as a condition for allowing a service to be provided.[14]

Chapter 12 prohibits discrimination against service providers from other NAFTA countries, by applying the principles of national and most-favored-nation treatment.[15] However, the fact that one country recognizes educational qualifications obtained in another member country as meeting professional licensing or certification requirements does not require it automatically to grant the same recognition to qualifications from the other country. Thus, for example, a Canadian law degree may be recognized as equivalent to an American law degree without granting the same recognition to a Mexican degree.

In spite of the foregoing general rules, each country is permitted to keep laws and regulations in place that do not comply with chapter 12, provided they are set out as reservations in the annexes. This applies to both federal and provincial (or state) laws.[16] In addition, restrictions are allowed on the number of service providers granted access to a market, as long as the restrictions are listed in the annexes and notice of any new ones is given to the other parties.[17]

Certain services are excluded from the application of chapter 12—namely, air transportation, services purchased by governments, and financial services. The latter is regulated by chapter 14. Moreover, chapter 12 cannot be construed as preventing governments from providing such services as law enforcement, correction, social security or insurance services, social welfare, public education or health or child care.[18]

With respect to licensing and certification procedures, chapter 12 requires only that each government "endeavor" to ensure that such procedures are based on objective and transparent criteria, use the least trade-restrictive means to ensure quality, and do not create disguised trade restrictions.[19] The nonobligatory nature of this provision reflects the fact that many service industries are self-regulating in this regard, meaning that governments do not determine these procedures directly.

With respect to professional services, annex 1210.5 applies similar obligations to encourage self-regulating professional bodies to develop standards for mutual recognition of qualifications and for temporary licensing, and to process applications for licenses within reasonable times. In addition, it provides specific guidelines for lawyers and engineers. Annex 1212 sets out procedures for the continued negotiation of liberalization of truck and bus transportation services.

Whereas chapter 12 applies to the mode of delivery of services by persons in the territory of another member, chapter 16 sets out the specific obligations regarding the movement of natural persons. Its scope is broader than just services; nevertheless, it may be considered an extension of the obligations contained in chapter 12.

GATS and Services

GATS regulates the kind of measures WTO members may apply to trade in services. It covers the four modes of delivery of services listed above.[20]

Government services that are not supplied on a commercial basis or in competition with the private sector are excluded from the scope of GATS.[21] For example, if a government agency has a monopoly on the provision of automobile insurance, its regulations governing the automobile insurance industry would not have to comply with any GATS obligations. However, if the government allowed private-sector companies to compete with the government agency, GATS would apply.

GATS operates very differently from NAFTA or GATT. While the latter two agreements provide comprehensive sets of rules with which members must comply, GATS is primarily a framework for further negotiation. GATS sets out the general principles that are to apply to trade in services, regarding nondiscrimination (MFN treatment),[22] transparency,[23] and domestic regulation.[24] Unlike other trade agreements, the general obligations of GATS do not include market access or national treatment. Instead, members decide what conditions to set in these areas and specify those conditions in their respective schedules of commitments for each service sector. The design of GATS permits governments to decide which service sectors they will open to foreign competition and to what extent.

Members submit schedules of specific commitments to open particular service sectors to foreign suppliers. Each schedule must specify:

1. Terms, limitations and conditions on market access;
2. Conditions and qualifications on national treatment (i.e., to what extent the nation treats domestic suppliers more favorably than foreign suppliers);
3. Undertakings relating to additional commitments;
4. The time frame for implementing commitments; and
5. The date the commitments enter into force.[25]

These market access commitments must be applied without discrimination to all WTO members, unless exceptions are listed in an annex on MFN exemptions.[26] These exemptions are usually claimed by countries that have granted preferential access to particular sectors. In principle, they are to expire after ten years and are subject to review after five years.[27] The schedules of commitments become part of GATS.[28] A member has three years in which to modify or withdraw any commitment it has made, but any member affected by the modification may seek compensation.[29]

Countries may use their schedules of commitments to place limits on market access and national treatment. However, the limitations apply only to existing measures that would otherwise be inconsistent with these obligations, effectively freezing their restrictions so that future measures they might take will not be more restrictive. For example, a country might permit foreign insurance companies to establish commercial presences but maintain a limit on national treatment by keeping in effect a foreign-investment law that limits the percentage of an insurance firm that foreigners may own.[30]

GATS provides for future negotiations on trade in services.[31] These may take the form of negotiations to liberalize trade across all industries, a "request and offer" approach (through which each WTO member identifies its priorities in other members' markets and presents formal requests and offers for reciprocal concessions), or liberalization by sector. A new round of services negotiations was formally launched on February 25, 2000; they have been incorporated into the Doha Round negotiations. The negotiations are being conducted in two phases. In the "rules-making" phase, WTO members are negotiating new rules for services on subsidies, safeguards and government procurement. In the "request-and-offer" phase, members are negotiating further market access. The Agreement on Trade in Financial Services represents an example of the sectoral approach.

TRADE IN FINANCIAL SERVICES UNDER NAFTA AND WTO

Both NAFTA and WTO contain agreements that serve as vehicles for regulatory change in the financial services industry. NAFTA contains rules regarding the ways Canada, the United States and Mexico may regulate financial services companies. The most important rules are contained in chapter 11, concerning foreign investment, and chapter 14, concerning international trade in financial services. Under the GATS framework, WTO members negotiated the Agreement on Trade in Financial Services (FSA).[32] One hundred four WTO members, including Canada, the United States and Mexico, have made commitments to liberalize financial services regulation under the FSA.[33]

WTO rules on financial services are found in a labyrinth of seven intersecting agreements: the Agreement Establishing the World Trade Organization;[34] the Understanding on Rules and Procedures Governing the Settlement of Disputes;[35] the General Agreement on Trade in Services

(GATS); GATS Annex on Financial Services; the Financial Services Agreement (FSA); the Schedules of Commitments on Financial Services; and the Understanding on Commitments in Financial Services. All WTO members are bound by the first four agreements. Mexico is bound by the first six agreements; Canada and the United States are bound by all seven.

NAFTA versus non-NAFTA Firms

Canada, Mexico and the United States are joined by two sets of international obligations that apply to financial services regulation, one under NAFTA and another under GATS/FSA. In principle, firms from outside NAFTA region are entitled only to FSA treatment. However, they may be able to use the access acquired under FSA to enter the North American market and gain NAFTA treatment.

NAFTA, including chapters 11 (investment) and 14 (financial services), applies to "persons" of a NAFTA country, which means natural persons (citizens or permanent residents of a NAFTA member) or enterprises (corporations, trusts, partnerships, joint ventures and other forms of business organization) constituted or organized under the law of a NAFTA member.[36] Thus, as long as a company from outside the NAFTA region is able to meet the requirements for incorporation (or other forms of business organization) and complies with foreign investment laws, it may become a NAFTA company. For example, it may acquire an existing firm, establish a wholly owned subsidiary, or create a joint venture in one of the NAFTA countries.

Scope and Operation of NAFTA Chapter 14 and GATS/FSA

GATS/FSA and NAFTA chapter 14 both restrict the kinds of measures that governments in one member country can employ to regulate investments and activities of financial services companies from another member country, as well as cross-border trade.[37] Obligations apply primarily to federal governments. However, NAFTA specifically requires federal governments to take all measures "necessary" to ensure that its provisions are observed by state and provincial governments.[38] In addition, chapter 14 requires members to ensure observance of obligations by self-regulatory organizations that play roles in market access for the financial services industry.[39] In contrast, GATS requires each member to take "such reasonable measures as may be available to it" to ensure that obligations are observed by "regional and local governments and authorities and non-governmental bodies within its territory."[40]

Federal governments thus have stricter obligations under NAFTA than under GATS with respect to state and provincial measures. However, under international law, a party to a treaty may not invoke domestic law as justification for failure to perform its duties under the treaty.[41] The normal rule of state responsibility under customary international law makes the party (that is, the federal government) internationally responsible for the acts of its subnational governments.[42]

In NAFTA, financial services are broadly defined as including any "service of a financial matter, including insurance, and a service incidental or auxiliary to a service of a financial nature."[43] The GATS Annex on Financial Services defines financial services as including all insurance and insurance-related services, and all banking and other financial services (excluding insurance). Insurance services are thus treated as a distinct category of financial service.

The annex provides an illustrative list of insurance services; it includes direct insurance (including co-insurance) on life and nonlife; reinsurance and retrocession; insurance intermediation, such as brokerage and agency; and auxiliary services, such as consultancy, actuarial, risk assessment and claim settlement services.[44] It is important to note that this list is not exhaustive. Insurance services that are not listed would still be embraced by the general definition referred to above.

Similarly, the annex provides an illustrative list of banking and other financial services, including acceptance of deposits from the public; lending of all types; financial leasing; all payment and money transmission services, including credit, charge and debit cards, traveler's checks and bankers drafts; guarantees and commitments; trading for one's own account or for accounts of customers, whether on an exchange, in an over-the-counter market, or otherwise; participation in issues of all kinds of securities; money broking; asset management; settlement and clearing services; provision and transfer of financial information, financial data processing and related software by suppliers of other financial services; and advisory, intermediation and other auxiliary financial services.

The Structure of the Agreements

Both agreements set out general principles, general exceptions, and exceptions specific to financial services regarding government social programs, and prudential regulations required for the protection of consumers or the financial system. In addition, each sets out a series of specific exceptions—regarding specific laws or sectors—to the application of the general principles. Such reservations are set out in annexes for each country. All financial services regulations must either comply with the general principles, qualify as exceptions, or be listed as reservations in the annexes.

NAFTA uses a "negative list" of reservations, specific measures that do not comply with the general rules. This approach serves two key functions. First, it prevents governments from creating future restrictions that violate the general rules, except where such restrictions qualify under the exceptions. This limits the circumstances under which governments may create further restrictions on the sale of financial services. Second, the listing of nonconforming measures makes them easier to identify, simplifying future negotiations to eliminate them.

NAFTA thus encourages innovation, by providing financial services firms with an incentive to create new services that are not restricted by the negative list. NAFTA emphasizes the fact by specifically prohibiting governments from discriminating against firms of the other members in the provision of new types of financial services.[45]

The FSA uses the exact opposite of the NAFTA approach to liberalize trade in financial services—it sets out individual "positive lists" of services that are being liberalized. Thus, under the FSA, if a WTO member has not made a specific commitment to liberalize a particular aspect of the financial services industry, it is under no obligation to do so. Even when a general commitment is made to liberalize a particular mode of delivering a specific type of financial service, the country in question may submit lengthy lists of reservations for measures that contradict the commitment.

Relationship between GATS and NAFTA

If there is a conflict between GATS and NAFTA, as a general rule NAFTA prevails.[46] All three NAFTA countries are WTO members and have made commitments under the FSA. Should one of the NAFTA countries make FSA commitments that are more generous than the commitments previously made to the other NAFTA members, NAFTA requires that the better commitment be immediately extended to those partners.[47] It is thus not possible for a NAFTA member to give more favorable access to its financial services market to a nonmember than it does to a NAFTA member.

GATS article V permits WTO members to enter into agreements that liberalize trade in services beyond GATS, just as GATT article XXIV permits members to create free trade areas and customs unions. NAFTA thus constitutes a general exception to MFN requirements under both GATT and GATS, as it covers trade in both goods and services. Therefore, preferential treatment granted to NAFTA members does not have to be extended to WTO members or be listed in the FSA MFN exemptions. Indeed, NAFTA opens up the financial services markets to a greater degree than do WTO financial services agreements.

Nondiscrimination

Under NAFTA, two principles of nondiscrimination, national treatment and most-favored-nation treatment, prohibit discrimination against financial services firms on the basis of nationality. Under national treatment, other members' investments and firms must be treated no less favorably than domestic ones.[48] However, this does not mean they must treat them identically; rather, national treatment for financial services is defined as treatment that affords equal competitive opportunities. This means that differences in treatment are permitted as long as they do not put non-national financial services companies at a disadvantage as compared to national financial services companies. Differences in market share, profitability or size do not in themselves constitute proof that equal competitive opportunities are being denied, but they may be used as evidence of it.[49]

At the state or provincial level, governments must treat member country firms no less favorably than they do firms from other states or provinces. Under MFN, the firms and investments of a member country must be treated no less favorably than those from any other country—that is, MFN prohibits discrimination between different countries.[50]

GATS applies the principle of nondiscrimination only with respect to MFN treatment.[51] Unlike NAFTA, the general obligations of GATS do not include market access or national treatment. Instead, members decide what conditions to set in these areas and specify those conditions in their schedules of commitments for each service sector.

GATS market access commitments must be applied without discrimination to all WTO members, unless exceptions are listed in an annex on MFN exemptions.[52] These exemptions are usually taken when a country has been granted preferential access to a particular sector. In principle, they are to expire after ten years and are subject to review after five years.[53] The schedules of commitments become part of GATS.[54] A member has three years in which it may modify or withdraw any commitment it has made, but any member affected by the modification may seek compensation.[55]

Market access commitments may be restricted by broad or limited MFN exemptions. *Broad MFN exemptions* condition market access on reciprocal access to another member's market. *Limited MFN exemptions* condition market access on another member's compliance with a specific requirement.[56]

Mexico has not submitted a list of MFN exemptions to WTO that affects trade in financial services. This means that Mexico's commitments and limitations in this sector apply equally to all WTO members. Canada and the United States have very limited exemptions. The U.S. commitments in financial services do not apply to any WTO members that restrict the expansion of existing operations, prevent the establishment of a new commercial presence or compel a "person" of the United States, on the basis of its nationality, to reduce its share of ownership in a financial services firm. A Canadian MFN exemption permits Ontario to grant preferential access to nonresident, individual insurance agents from all states in the United States.

Countries may use their schedules of commitments to place limits on market access and national treatment. However, the limitations apply only to existing measures that would otherwise be inconsistent with these obligations, effectively freezing their restrictions so that future measures they might take will not be more restrictive. For example, a country might permit foreign financial services companies to establish commercial presences but maintain a limit on national treatment by keeping in effect a foreign investment law that limits the percentage of a financial services firm foreigners may own.[57]

Transparency and Access to Information

In NAFTA, the principle of transparency requires governments to provide access to regulatory procedures in two ways. First, where a government proposes to enact a new regulation, it must provide an opportunity for interested parties to comment on the proposal. Second, a government must make any existing requirements freely available and process applications in an open and timely fashion.[58] GATS applies similar rules regarding transparency[59] and the administration of domestic regulations.[60]

NAFTA addresses privacy and confidentiality concerns by expressly providing that governments may not be required to furnish or provide access to information regarding the financial affairs of individual customers. This applies as well to the disclosure of confidential information where this would impede law enforcement, be contrary to the public interest or prejudice legitimate commercial interests.[61] However, NAFTA is silent on the matter of access to private-sector, as opposed to public-sector, sources of information.

Mexico's bank-secrecy laws, which prohibit banks from revealing client information, may impede the "discovery" process in both domestic and international private litigation. The secrecy laws would likely qualify under the NAFTA exception, but a client's refusal to provide documents in discovery might still be challenged in litigation. However, it is not clear what the outcome would be if a Mexican court were to decide that the secrecy law protects this information even in litigation.

Privacy laws are also allowed under GATS, so that countries cannot be required to disclose information relating to the affairs and accounts of individual customers or any confidential or proprietary information in the possession of public entities.[62]

General Exceptions

GATS contains a list of exceptions that override any obligations to which a member may have committed itself with respect to trade liberalization in services. However, members may not abuse the exceptions to create disguised restrictions on trade in services or to apply laws that qualify under the various categories of exceptions in such a way as to discriminate arbitrarily between countries. The general exceptions apply to measures:

1. Necessary to protect public morals or to maintain public order;
2. Necessary to protect human, animal or plant life or health;
3. Necessary to secure compliance with laws or regulations, including those relating to:
   a. The prevention of deceptive and fraudulent practices or to deal with the
      effects of a default on services contracts;
   b. The protection of the privacy of individuals in relation to the processing
      and dissemination of personal data and the protection of confidentiality of
      individual records and accounts; and
   c. Safety;
4. Inconsistent with national treatment, provided that the difference in treatment
   is aimed at ensuring the equitable or effective imposition or collection of direct taxes with respect to foreign services or service suppliers;
5. Inconsistent with MFN treatment, provided that the difference in treatment
   is the result of an agreement on the avoidance of double taxation.

With respect to the collection of direct taxes, GATS provides an illustrative list of the types of measures that are included.[63]

NAFTA contains more detailed rules than GATS with respect to the
application to taxation measures to financial services obligations regarding national treatment, MFN treatment, performance requirements; it also
covers claims for expropriation and compensation.[64] However, NAFTA
does not apply the first two GATS exceptions listed above to trade in financial services.[65]

GATS and NAFTA both provide exceptions for national and international security measures. Under these exceptions, no member can be com-
pelled to disclose information if it considers doing so to be contrary to its
essential security interests. Members are also permitted to take any actions
they consider necessary for the protection of essential security interests
relating to military activities, nuclear materials, war or other emergencies
in international relations. This type of exception could be invoked to freeze
the assets of the citizens of another country in order to prevent the international transfer of those assets during an international conflict—for instance, the measures taken in several countries with respect to terrorist
funds following the attacks of September 11, 2001. Finally, nothing in the
agreements can prevent a member from taking actions pursuant to United
Nations obligations on international peace and security.[66]

Exceptions for Government Programs

Nothing in chapter 14 can prevent a member country from acting as the exclusive provider of financial services that form part of a public pension plan or social security.[67] This exception would apply to such government insurance plans as public health insurance and unemployment insurance—those of Canada, for example. Governments may also exclude private-sector financial service companies from activities that involve the use of public finances.[68]

Government services that are not supplied on a commercial basis or in competition with the private sector are excluded from the scope of GATS.[69] For example, if a government agency has a monopoly on the provision of automobile insurance, as in the Canadian province of British Columbia, its regulations would not have to comply with GATS obligations. However, if the government allowed private-sector companies to compete with the government agency, GATS would apply.

Prudential Exceptions

Nothing in part V of NAFTA (chapters 11–16, covering investment and services) can prevent governments from taking measures to protect consumers, maintain the integrity of financial services firms and ensure the stability of their nations' financial systems.[70] Nor does part V apply to nondiscriminatory measures taken with respect to monetary or exchange rate policies.[71] While the governments are generally prohibited from interfering in transfers and international payments,[72] chapter 14 specifically permits nondiscriminatory transfer pricing (the prices related firms charge each other for intra-firm trade in goods and services) rules to maintain the safety, soundness, integrity or financial responsibility of financial services firms.[73] This would likely apply to regulations regarding minimum-deposit and capitalization requirements, for example.

Similarly, GATS provides a blanket exception for prudential measures that allow countries to take measures to protect investors, depositors, policy holders or persons to whom fiduciary duties are owed. Countries are also permitted to take measures to ensure the integrity and stability of the financial system. However, governments may not use the prudential exceptions to avoid their obligations under the financial services agreements.[74]

Canadian Provincial and U.S. State Measures

In NAFTA annex 1409.1, Canada and the United States set out existing provincial and state measures that do not conform to the obligations contained in NAFTA. NAFTA members have a general obligation to ensure that all necessary measures are taken to secure the "observance" of NAFTA provisions by state and provincial governments, except where specific NAFTA clauses provide otherwise.[75] However, constitutional law in Canada and the U.S. limits the ability of the federal governments to enforce compliance by provincial and state governments.[76] Nevertheless, federal governments remain responsible in the international arena for the action of subnational governments.

Not all state and provincial restrictions have to be listed as reservations; many fit the general exceptions. Chapter 14 also contains detailed rules on how national treatment applies to state and provincial measures. Under these rules, if a state discriminates against out-of-state financial services companies of the same country, they must treat financial services companies from NAFTA countries no less favorably.[77] That is, U.S. state restrictions would comply with NAFTA even if they restrict interstate trade, as long as Mexican and Canadian financial services companies are treated no worse than out-of-state companies.

In their WTO schedules of commitments, Canada and the United States both submitted extensive lists of reservations for provincial and state regulations.[78] Mexico submitted no reservations for state regulations, reflecting both the lack of state regulation in this area and the fact that Mexico made commitments only with respect to foreign investment in WTO. Reservations to treaty obligations are construed restrictively to minimize the extent to which they excuse a nation from complying with the treaty, such as the interpretation of the American NAFTA reservation on Mexican trucks.[79]

Modes of Supply

Both NAFTA and the FSA determine market access in terms of the same four modes of supply as listed above: cross-border supply, consumption abroad, presence of natural persons, and commercial presence (where the service is provided by foreign direct investment).[80] Chapter 14 defines the first three modes as constituting "cross-border trade."[81]

The following section compares market access in Canada, Mexico and the United States under NAFTA and the FSA by mode of supply. It looks first at cross-border supply and consumption abroad, followed by presence of natural persons and commercial presence.

Cross-Border Supply and Consumption Abroad

NAFTA. Market access via cross-border sale of financial services, with no established commercial presence in the target market, was not fully liberalized in NAFTA negotiations. Thus, if a firm wishes to sell financial services outside its domestic market—via the Internet, for example—it will find NAFTA rules unclear. NAFTA permits the nationals of each country to purchase financial services outside their country (for example, Canadians would be free to purchase car insurance on rental cars in the United States or Mexico).[82] However, each country remains free to prohibit the other countries' firms from doing business or soliciting in its territory,[83] and to require that cross-border vendors of financial services fulfill registration requirements.[84] Moreover, each NAFTA member is free to adopt its own definition of what "doing business" or "solicitation" means, as long as activities that were permitted on January 1, 1994, are not restricted.[85] Canada's interpretation is that cross-border supply is permitted as long as the consumer initiates the transaction and it does not constitute business in Canada.[86] This reading makes marketing difficult and leaves Canada with plenty of room to restrict business.

WTO. Mexico has made no commitments with respect to consumption abroad or cross-border supply.[87] This means that Mexico has not "frozen" its ability to impose future limitations on these modes of supply.

Canada and the United States have made commitments in these two modes in accordance with the Understanding on Commitments. With respect to cross-border trade, the Understanding on Commitments requires members to permit nonresident suppliers of financial services to provide certain services. Each member must also permit its residents to purchase the same services abroad. The nonresident supplier need not have a commercial presence in the home market of the consumer.

The U.S. and Canadian commitments do not impose any obligation to allow nonresident suppliers to solicit business inside their territories. This seemingly negative approach compares favorably with the equivalent NAFTA provision, which not only permits members to restrict soliciting but permits restrictions on the right to "do business" generally.

However, both Canada and the United States have placed several specific limitations on cross-border supply and consumption abroad, in the form of reservations listing regulations, primarily at the state or provincial level. Most deal with residence or impose requirements to maintain a commercial presence. In other words, they contradict the general requirement to permit nonresidents to supply services without a commercial presence.

Presence of Natural Persons

NAFTA. NAFTA chapter 16 sets out the specific obligations regarding the movement of natural persons. Each country must grant temporary entry to business persons from the other members.[88] "Temporary entry" means entry without the intent to establish permanent residence. "Business person" is defined as a citizen engaged in the trade in goods, the provision of services, or the conduct of investment activities.[89] Chapter 16 does not provide for free movement of labor between NAFTA countries, as does the EU. Rather, it is limited to white-collar workers. In addition, the United States has limited the number of entry visas granted to Mexicans under chapter 16 to 5,500 per year until December 31, 2003.[90]

The principles that apply to temporary entry include reciprocity, transparency, border security, and protection of domestic labor and employment.[91] In addition, people applying for temporary entry must otherwise qualify for entry under measures relating to public health and safety and national security.[92] Thus, for example, a country may refuse entry to individuals carrying communicable diseases, engaged in criminal activity or who have criminal records. NAFTA imposes no obligations regarding immigration measures, other than those set out in chapter 16.[93]

In addition to the general provisions of chapter 16, chapter 14 contains specific rules regarding personnel of financial institutions. No NAFTA country may require the financial institutions of another NAFTA country to engage individuals of any particular nationality for senior managerial positions or other essential posts. Nor may a country require that more than a simple majority of a board of directors be composed of its nationals or persons residing in its territory.[94] Financial services firms thus have greater freedom than other firms to use personnel from non-NAFTA countries.

WTO. Mexico and the United States made no commitment to permit the temporary entry of personnel of a financial services company. This means that they need not list any limitations in this area and that they have not "frozen" their ability to impose future limitations on this mode of supply, for non-NAFTA firms.

The Canadian schedule adopts the rules on temporary entry of personnel contained in the Understanding on Commitments, but the supply of financial services by natural persons is still subject to the limitations placed on the other modes of supply in Canada's schedule. Thus, Canada permits the temporary entry of personnel of a financial services company that is establishing or has established a commercial presence in the country. Senior management and operational specialists are allowed in regardless of the availability of qualified Canadian nationals. However, the admittance of personnel who are specialists in computer services, telecommunications or accounting, as well as of actuarial and legal specialists, is subject to the availability of qualified nationals.

GATS does not apply to persons seeking access to the employment market of a member, or to measures regarding citizenship, residence or employment on a permanent basis. Nor does it prevent a member from regulating the entry of persons into its territory to protect the integrity of its borders.[95] Thus, personnel remain subject to general immigration laws under GATS, as under NAFTA.

Market Access by Commercial Presence

NAFTA. With respect to the establishment of an enterprise, each country recognizes that, in principle, each other's firms should be able to participate widely in the market with respect to the range of services provided, the geographic area covered, and the ownership of firms.[96] However, the degree of market access has been made contingent upon the reform of U.S. laws to permit commercial bank subsidiaries and direct branches to expand into most of the American market.[97]

In Canada and Mexico, banking laws never prevented interstate banking, as the Glass-Steagall Act of 1933 did in the United States. The Riegle-Neal Interstate Banking and Branching Efficiency Act of 1994, which became effective as of June 1997, allows banks to establish branches and acquire banks across the United States. While restrictions remain on the ability of banks to sell insurance in the United States, such restrictions have been largely removed in Canada and Mexico.[98] As the United States moves toward reforms that allow banks to sell insurance, Mexican and Canadian insurers may choose to enter the U.S. insurance market as financial holding companies rather than as insurance companies.

NAFTA prohibits the imposition of performance requirements on foreign investors as a condition of obtaining government approvals, such as export quotas, domestic content rules, or requirements to transfer technology to the operation in the host nation. However, a particular performance requirement that is not prohibited is permitted, as long as it is otherwise consistent with NAFTA.[99]

NAFTA also prohibits restrictions on transfers of profits, proceeds or payments unless the restrictions are due to the application of laws relating to bankruptcy, securities, criminal offenses, currency transfer reporting, or enforcement of judgments.[100] Member countries therefore remain free to restrict transfers under laws such as those relating to money laundering, and those that permit the freezing of assets in litigation and bankruptcy proceedings. However, a specific prudential exception allows governments to regulate transfer pricing.

WTO. In accordance with the Understanding on Commitments, Canada and the United States grant foreign financial services companies the right to establish or expand within their territory, including through the acquisition of existing enterprises. Commercial presence includes wholly or partly owned subsidiaries, joint ventures, partnerships, sole proprietorships, franchising operations, branches, agencies, representative offices and other organizations. Canada and the United States also allow established firms to offer any new financial service that is not yet supplied in the territories. The Understanding on Commitment permits a broad range of financial services to be provided by foreign firms through commercial presence. Mexico's WTO commitments also allow the provision of financial services by foreign companies through a commercial presence in the country, but they are not governed by the Understanding on Commitments and thus are somewhat narrower.

Comparison of North American WTO Commitments

In terms of modes of supply, of the three NAFTA countries, Canada has liberalized financial services trade the most and Mexico the least. Canada has liberalized all four modes of supply. The United States has liberalized three, leaving out presence of natural persons. Mexico has liberalized only one (commercial presence). In terms of restrictions at the state/provincial level, the United States has the most, Canada has fewer, and Mexico has none at all. This reflects the constitutional structures of the three countries.

In terms of the kinds of services that have been liberalized, Canada is the most open, followed by the United States and then Mexico. This reflects Canadian and U.S. commitments to the Understanding on Commitment. However, extensive state restrictions in the United States limit the delivery of a wide range of services to a far greater extent than do Canada's provincial regulations. Nevertheless, Mexico's commitments cover a broad range of services.

Comparison of NAFTA and WTO by Mode of Supply

Because NAFTA permits restrictions on soliciting and "doing business" for firms that seek to supply their services via cross-border supply and consumption abroad, the least restricted method of entering the market is through the establishment of a commercial presence—that is, by way of foreign investment. Restrictions on soliciting require the customer to initiate the transaction, a necessity that limits marketing activities. While WTO also permits restrictions on soliciting, it does not permit, as does NAFTA, restrictions on "doing business." However, this advantage may be negated by the extensive WTO reservations for federal, state and provincial measures submitted by Canada and the United States. Many of these subnational restrictions require commercial presences in the state or the province in order to provide certain services. As a result, a firm may need to establish a commercial presence in each jurisdiction it wishes to serve. In the case of Mexico, non-NAFTA firms may only enter the national market through a commercial presence, but there are no state restrictions.

For a foreign investor, NAFTA provides better treatment than WTO, because the latter has no equivalent to NAFTA chapter 11. Moreover, WTO applies no general national-treatment requirement to trade in services. Under NAFTA, not only are foreign investors entitled to national treatment and MFN treatment, but they may sue national governments directly for expropriation and for measures that are equivalent to expropriation. Finally, there are far fewer reservations made for foreign-investment restrictions in NAFTA than in WTO.

Non-NAFTA firms may acquire rights under NAFTA by investing in one of NAFTA countries. This means that such firms should first establish commercial presences in the NAFTA country that has the fewest foreign-investment restrictions for non-NAFTA firms, then expand into the other NAFTA countries from there.

The restrictions that exist at the state level in the United States are protected by reservations under WTO, and they make entry into the U.S. market more complicated than entry into Mexico, which has no state regulations for financial services. Moreover, the only mode of entry Mexico provides for WTO members is by way of foreign investment. If a non-NAFTA firm establishes a commercial presence in Mexico, it can then expand into the United States through foreign investments that enjoy NAFTA investor protection. As a Mexican enterprise, it may also take advantage of NAFTA provisions permitting the entry of natural persons who are citizens of a NAFTA country (under chapter 16) and of senior managerial and other essential personnel of any nationality (under chapter 14). Moreover, once established in Mexico, it can serve the Mexican market without being impeded by Mexican restrictions on cross-border supply and consumption abroad.

The main drawback of adopting this strategy is that it may not work in Canada, since Canada has reserved the right to require that a company from a NAFTA member be controlled by residents of that member if it is to be entitled to the benefits of chapter 14. However, Canada has liberalized its market under WTO more than has the United States or Mexico, so entry to the Canadian market by a non-NAFTA firm may be achieved directly from its home base. Moreover, the Canadian market is being opened further by the introduction of new financial services legislation at the national level. In any event, the Mexican market is less mature than the Canadian market and is growing faster, making it the better choice.

Canada's "widely held" rule, which limits the number of shares one person may own depending on the size of the firm, complies with national treatment, because it applies to Canadians and foreigners alike. However, it affects international expansion plans by limiting control over the investment. For this reason, firms may prefer to supply services in the cross-border mode. While current restrictions on soliciting and doing business make this difficult, they are likely to be relaxed in future WTO negotiations.

A recent survey commissioned by the federal government in preparation for future negotiations revealed that a majority of Canadians (59 percent) believe freer trade in services helps Canada's economy. A majority also believes that importing services is good for Canadian business (58 percent) and consumers (54 percent). While the majority believes that foreign investment has a positive impact on jobs in Canada (65 percent), most believe that there is a negative impact when foreign investors purchase Canadian companies (52 percent).[101] Thus, the Canadian government may maintain restrictions that prevent foreign firms from acquiring a controlling interest in Canadian firms but welcome other forms of foreign investment.

For European firms, Mexico provides the added advantage of the Mexico-EU Free Trade Agreement (MEUFTA) and bilateral investment treaties (BITs). MEUFTA contains provisions for financial services that mirror those of NAFTA. However, MEUFTA contains no equivalent to NAFTA chapter 11. Nevertheless, thirteen of the fifteen members of the EU (all except the United Kingdom and Ireland) have negotiated BITs with Mexico that provide substantially the same protection for foreign investors as NAFTA chapter 11.

Conclusion

The benefits of increasing growth and diversifying risk through expansion into developed and developing markets with different demographic and economic profiles are obvious to global financial services companies. However, a major challenge lies in integrating the rules of international trade agreements into the strategic planning process. This section has analyzed how two major agreements affect market entry strategies in the world's largest and most economically diverse financial services market. The challenge of regulatory barriers to entry can be mitigated by entering the market through foreign investment in Mexico to take advantage of the market-entry and investment-protection provisions of NAFTA.

Under both NAFTA and WTO, Canada, Mexico and the United States have demonstrated a preference for foreign investment as the market-entry mode for foreign firms. This is due to the perception that foreign investment is more beneficial than allowing imports of financial services. However, they also want their firms to be able to export their services. To open other markets to exports, they have to open their own markets to imports. We can therefore expect to see increasing liberalization of cross-border trade in financial services, which will provoke further consolidation in the industry and widen the selection of market-entry strategies available to firms.

NAFTA has important implications for the international expansion plans of financial services firms. First, it is a trail blazer; it provides clues as to the direction other agreements will take. As a regional agreement involving only three economies, NAFTA can move the liberalization process farther and faster than larger agreements, such as the proposed Free Trade Agreement of the Americas (FTAA). As NAFTA moves forward, its members also push for more rapid global liberalization in WTO that will mirror the achievements of NAFTA. Secondly, NAFTA plays a role in risk reduction. With investment in Mexico as the optimal entry mode, the combined protection foreign investors enjoy under NAFTA chapter 11 and Mexico's bilateral investment treaties reduces the risk of investment loss in all three countries.

NAFTA also reduces political and economic risk in Mexico by locking in the regulatory reforms that have been made, integrating the Mexico economy with those of Canada and the United States, and improving Mexico's long-term growth potential. NAFTA brings a wide range of trade and investment rules under one roof; as a result, Mexico cannot backtrack on one set of commitments without pulling out of the agreement entirely. NAFTA is so important to Mexico's economy that this is highly unlikely to happen. Finally, as NAFTA widens to include the rest of the hemisphere under the FTAA, Mexico will push for a deeper integration of the original three members' economies in order to maintain better access to Canada and the United States than the other developing countries in the Americas enjoy. This will lead to a further reduction in barriers to trade in financial services, blazing yet another trail for other agreements to follow.

Mexico thus enjoys several strategic advantages in its capacity as a gateway for the international expansion of financial services firms. For non-NAFTA firms, it provides a means to enjoy NAFTA benefits in the North American market. For example, the Netherlands-based banking, insurance, and assets-management company ING invested in Mexico and used its Mexican subsidiary rather than its New York subsidiary to enter the California market. Once licensed in California, it was able to expand more easily into Arizona. Even for NAFTA firms, there are benefits. For example, due to the regulatory segmentation of the American market, a firm from one U.S. state may choose to enter another via a Mexican subsidiary, in order to gain foreign-investor protection under NAFTA and thereby challenge barriers to trade in insurance services between states. In addition, with the GDP of the Mexican-American population of the United States approaching that of the population of Mexico itself, entering the U.S. market with a Mexican brand name may overcome cultural marketing barriers. Finally, Mexico's enthusiastic pursuit of foreign investment and trade agreements in all corners of the globe will continue to enhance its potential as a gateway to not only the North American financial services market but the emerging global market as well.

GLOBAL BUSINESS STRATEGY AND TRADE IN SERVICES

In general, trade liberalization affects firms in three areas: buying, selling and competing. In the area of services, where the process of trade liberalization has only recently begun, firms must not only deal with the current state of affairs but prepare for the future by thinking globally in all three areas.

With respect to buying services, firms must seek the best services at the lowest cost on a global level to enhance their competitiveness and reduce operating costs. With respect to selling services, firms must decide how to deliver their services and where. With respect to competing, firms must measure their performance against the best in the world.

The strategies a firm adopts will vary depending on the nature of the service and the barriers to international trade and investment that remain. Market-entry strategies are constrained by the types of limits placed on foreign firms. The cross-border supply of a service—for example, by telephone or the Internet—may be limited in many ways. For instance, in the financial services industry, the United States and Canada liberalized this mode of supply under WTO but maintained restrictions that prevent companies from soliciting business. While a service may be provided in this manner, it may not be possible to market it that way.

With respect to consumption abroad, where the customer travels to the service provider's country and wants to purchase its service there, a country may limit provision of services to nonresidents. For example, nonresidents may not open bank accounts in Mexico, and nonresidents may not use brokerage services in Canada. Nevertheless, Canadian brokerage firms have gained access to nonresident clients through subsidiaries located in countries that do not restrict the service to residents, and access for clients around the world, via telephone, fax and the Internet.

In knowledge-intensive industries, such as consulting, the availability of entry visas for natural persons affects hiring and promotion decisions. This also affects transfer of personnel to facilitate transmission of knowledge and expertise between operations in different countries. Technology can be used to transfer and leverage knowledge without the movement of natural persons. For example, the knowledge databases of McKinsey & Company, a management consulting firm, are accessible to all its consultants over the Internet, and a consultant in one country can contact experts in other countries using telephone and e-mail to access their knowledge.

Foreign-investment restrictions affect the manner in which a firm may exercise control over its operations in other countries. Alliance and merger strategies must vary with the restrictions on the percentage of equity a foreign firm may own (wholly owned subsidiary, joint venture or contractual arrangement). The degree of control that a firm wishes to exercise over its international operations will be restricted where market entry is available only through a minority equity stake in a joint venture with a local firm. Thus, strategic business alliances may be a necessity rather than a choice to be made.

The airline industry provides a good example. Restrictions on foreign investment and landing rights have forced airlines to create alliances with other airlines in order to provide their services globally and to lower their costs through economies of scale in such activities as marketing, reservations and maintenance. Foreign investment restrictions have stood in the way of mergers and acquisitions being pursued to achieve global competitiveness.

Firms need strategies to get around the restrictions and exploit the opportunities created by "loopholes" in the agreements. For example, a European firm may be permitted to incorporate a wholly owned subsidiary in North America in order to gain the greater market access enjoyed by Canadian, American or Mexican firms. Firms must also consider other means of avoiding restrictions. For example, a firm may use contractual relations with other firms to enter a market where other means of entry are not available.

Sometimes contractual arrangements are a superior strategy even where other market entry strategies are available. For example, the Swedish insurance company Skandia has used a global network of contractual relationships to outsource investment management and retail distribution of its mutual fund products, allowing it to expand globally more rapidly than its competitors and at a lower cost. Skandia maintained control only over the product design and administrative coordination functions, areas where it could add the most value.

Modern communications technology has facilitated the globalization of many service industries, allowing firms to adopt global business strategies even where their strategic choices are constrained by government regulations. As international trade agreements gradually eliminate restrictions on trade in services and expand the strategic options available to firms, competition in services will intensify. Firms that have employed strategies to get around the restrictions early on will be better positioned to compete in a more liberalized global services economy.

CONCLUSION

Many businesses are big consumers of services that are increasingly provided on a global scale. Companies that produce goods require transportation services to distribute their goods internationally. They require financial services to process international payments and handle international financing. They require telecommunications services to communicate worldwide. They also require such professional support as accounting and legal services. The growth of international trade in goods has thus spawned the globalization of many service industries, which in turn has led to efforts to liberalize trade in services.

Because the liberalization of trade in services has only begun recently, determining which services may be freely traded and how they may be provided is a complex task. Nevertheless, that determination is an important task for services firms to undertake when formulating business strategies. More importantly, firms must follow the liberalization process closely in order to anticipate the shape of things to come.

This chapter has examined the rules applying to services in NAFTA and GATS. The analysis of rules applying to financial services has illustrated how these agreements apply to a particular industry and how the agreements relate to one another. NAFTA has gone farther than WTO in the liberalization of international trade in services, and in many ways it has blazed a trail for WTO to follow. By watching developments in regional trade agreements, business people may get a clearer picture of the future directions WTO may take.

CLOSING CASE: TELECOMMUNICATIONS SERVICES IN MEXICO

Both NAFTA and WTO apply special rules to telecommunications. This reflects the importance of telecommunications in facilitating international business activities and the manner in which telecommunication services are delivered. The delivery of these services requires access to expensive infrastructure. In many countries, telecommunications infrastructure is controlled by government monopolies or recently privatized firms. Deregulation and privatization in this industry, combined with trade liberalization, has generated intense competition, particularly in the long-distance telephone market. However, due to the importance of the industry, the industry remains highly regulated, particularly with respect to the prices firms charge for their services.

WTO Telecommunications Agreement

During the Uruguay Round of negotiations, many countries made commitments under GATS to open their markets to value-added telecommunications services. The WTO Agreement on Basic Telecommunications (ABT), which entered into force February 5, 1998, is a sectoral agreement negotiated under GATS framework. As such, it consists primarily of schedules of specific commitments that each signatory submits to WTO.

Countries involved in the ABT negotiations agreed to include all public and private telecommunications services that involve end-to-end transmission of customer-supplied information, such as voice or data relay from sender to receiver. They also agreed that basic telecommunications services provided over network infrastructure and resale over private leased circuits would be covered. Market access commitments cover both cross-border supply of telecommunications and commercial presence of foreign firms, including investments in network infrastructure.[102]

Basic services under negotiation included voice telephony, data transmission, telex, telegraph, facsimile, private leased-circuit services, fixed and mobile satellite systems and services, cellular telephony, mobile data services, paging, and personal communications systems. Value-added services, such as online data processing, online database storage, e-mail and voice mail, were not officially part of the negotiations. However, value added services were already included in the GATS commitments of fifty governments as a result of the Uruguay Round; some countries made commitments in this area in the subsequent telecommunications negotiations.

The GATS Annex on Telecommunications requires governments to ensure that foreign suppliers can use public telecommunications networks and services on a reasonable and nondiscriminatory basis. This requirement applies whether or not they have made commitments in the basic telecommunications sector. The annex provides access to these services by users rather than the ability to enter markets to sell such services. Market access to sell telecommunications services is addressed in the schedules of commitments of each member. The use requirement is for the benefit of firms that supply any of the services included in a WTO member's schedule of commitments under other GATS agreements, such as value-added telecommunications suppliers and banking and computer services firms.[103]

Mexico's telecommunications market is worth twelve billion dollars and has more long-term growth potential than the more saturated markets of developed countries like Canada and the United States. Mexico made commitments in value-added services in the Uruguay Round. In the ABT, Mexico made commitments in all types of services delivered over public telecommunications networks except for radio, cable television, satellite transmission, and digital audio services. Mexico's limitations on market access for basic services oblige international traffic to be routed via the installations of a particular Mexican firm that has been granted a concession by the secretary of communications and transport. Foreign investment in such firms is limited to 49 percent. Foreign governments are excluded from making such investments or selling services.[104]

Mexico's WTO obligations essentially mirror its obligations with respect to telecommunications under NAFTA chapter 13. However, under NAFTA annex II, Mexico reserved the right to adopt any measure relating to investment in, or provision of, telecommunications transport networks and services. Like the WTO agreements, NAFTA requires governments to ensure that foreign service suppliers can use public telecommunications networks and services on a reasonable and nondiscriminatory basis.[105]

The U.S.-Mexico Dispute over Market Access

Teléfonos de México (Telmex) is a government-owned monopoly that was privatized by President Carlos Salinas of Mexico in 1990. In 1997,

Mexico opened up its long-distance telephone market to competition. However, Telmex maintained control over Mexico's basic telecommunications structure and continued to dominate the market. Telmex now controls 75 percent of the long-distance market and over 95 percent of local calls.

Due to the foreign-investment limit of 49 percent, AT&T entered the market with a minority interest in a joint venture with the Mexican long-distance company Alestra, while WorldCom did the same with Avantel. Both joint ventures had to use the infrastructure of Telmex, for which they paid an "interconnection" fee. Telmex charged these competitors very high interconnection fees.

The U.S. government, on behalf of AT&T and WorldCom, entered into negotiations with the Mexican government with a view to getting Mexico's Federal Telecommunications Commission (Cofetel) to control anticompetitive practices, and in particular to order Telmex to reduce the interconnection fees. The United States also accused Telmex of withholding critical technical information that would allow competitors to use its network and of failing to provide nondiscriminatory service. In August 2000, after negotiations failed to proceed as hoped, the United States filed a formal complaint against Mexico at the WTO. The complaint was suspended after Cofetel ordered Telmex to reduce the fees by 63 percent, from 3.36 cents a minute to 1.25 cents a minute, beginning January 1, 2001. However, Telmex took advantage of the weak regulatory power of Cofetel and filed numerous injunctions in Mexican courts to delay compliance with its order.[106]

In April 2001, the United States threatened to revive the WTO case unless Mexico resolved the problem with Telmex. However, the United States decided not to pursue the case after Telmex signed private agreements that settled outstanding lawsuits and set lower interconnection fees with AT&T's and WorldCom's affiliates in Mexico. This move by Telmex sufficiently appeased its major competitors that they stopped pressuring the U.S. government over the matter.[107]

In addition, the Mexican telecommunications regulations began the process of being amended in the Mexican Congress in 2001. Possible amendments include granting Cofetel greater autonomy, setting interconnection fees, regulating Telmex and allowing 100 percent foreign ownership of telecommunication companies. While Mexico is not obliged to permit 100 percent ownership under its trade agreements, the issue has been brought to the fore with Citigroup's takeover of Banamex, which owns 55 percent of Avantel. Since WorldCom owns the other 45 percent, either Mexico will have to eliminate the foreign investment restriction or Citigroup will have to sell its interest in Avantel.[108]

Conclusion

Mexico's progressive liberalization of its telecommunications market demonstrates how regional liberalization can lead to global liberalization of trade in services and how both benefit the consumer. Mexico began to open its telecommunications market under NAFTA in 1994 but reserved the right to introduce new restrictions. Mexico then made WTO commitments on a global scale that mirrored its NAFTA obligations, but with less extensive reservations. The liberalization of the Mexican market under these agreements facilitated the international expansion of multinational telecommunications firms.

This case demonstrates the importance of foreign investment as a market-entry strategy in certain services industries and how lack of effective competition regulations can hamper their efforts to achieve market access commensurate with their competitive advantages. It is for this reason that both foreign-investment and competition laws have been put on the negotiating agenda for WTO Doha Round.

This case also demonstrates the value to NAFTA governments of being able to choose between settling disputes under NAFTA or WTO. In this case, the United States chose WTO because it is the better of the two systems (as will be seen in a later chapter of this book) and because Mexico's WTO reservations were less extensive than its NAFTA reservations in telecommunications. The case also shows how firms can benefit from these dispute-resolution systems through their domestic governments. However, the case also demonstrates the limitations of these dispute-settlement mechanisms. Many of the changes that the United State seeks to the regulatory environment in Mexico must pass through the Mexican Congress. Since the election of the first opposition-party president in 2000, the Mexican system has come to resemble more closely that of the United States. With control of Congress in the hands of his opponents, it is more difficult now for the president of Mexico to get legislative initiatives passed.

NOTES

1. This case first appeared as Bradly Condon and Tapen Sinha, "An Analysis of an Alliance: NAFTA Trucking and the US Insurance Industry," *Estey Centre Journal for Law and Economics* 2 (2001), 235–45. Used with permission.

2. *In the Matter of Cross-Border Trucking Services, Final Report of the Panel*, USA-MEX-98-2008-01, February 6, 2001, available at http://www.nafta-sec-alena.org.

3. *MOU on the Use of Terminals and Installations of Transport Companies, MOU on Transportation Technical Cooperation*, and *MOU on Validity of Commercial Drivers Licenses*, signed at Mexico City, March 1, 1994.

4. "Canadian and Mexican Ministers Sign Transportation Agreements," *Canada NewsWire*, March 3, 1994.

5. U.S. annex I, NAFTA.

6. *In the Matter of Cross-Border Trucking Services.*

7. Ibid. Also see *North American Free Trade Agreement between the Government of Canada, the Government of the United Mexican States and the Government of the United States of America,* December 17, 1992, Can.-Mex.-US, 32 ILM 296, and 32 ILM 612 (1993), article 913(5)(a)(i) and annex 913.5.a-1 [hereafter NAFTA].

8. Office of Inspector General Audit Report, *Motor Carrier Safety Program for Commercial Trucks at U.S. Borders,* Office of the Secretary and Federal Highway Administration, report TR-1999-034, December 28, 1998, available at http://www.oig.dot.gov/audits/tr1999034.pdf.

9. Suzanne Gamboa, "Feds: 63,000 Mexican Trucks Crossed," Associated Press, April 17, 2001.

10. "The Coming NAFTA Crash," February 2, 2001, available at http://www.citizen.org/pctrade/nafta/reports/truckstudy.htm.

11. Gloria Leal, "The Truck Stops Here: A Texas Regulator's Perspective," *Business Mexico,* July, 1996.

12. NAFTA article 1213(2).

13. NAFTA article 1201.

14. NAFTA article 1205.

15. NAFTA article 1202 and 1203.

16. NAFTA article 1206.

17. NAFTA article 1207.

18. NAFTA article 1201.

19. NAFTA article 1210.

20. "General Agreement on Trade in Services, Final Act Embodying the Results of the Uruguay Round of Multilateral Trade Negotiations," April 15, 1994, *Legal Instruments—Results of the Uruguay Round,* annex 1B, vol. I, 33 ILM 1125 (1994), article I(2) [hereafter GATS].

21. GATS article I(3).

22. GATS article II.

23. GATS article III.

24. GATS article VI requires regulations to be administered reasonably, objectively and impartially.

25. GATS article XX(1).

26. GATS article II.

27. Christopher Melly, "Renewed Services Trade Negotiations in WTO," *Industry, Trade, and Technology Review* (December 1999), 21–31.

28. GATS article XX(3).

29. GATS article XXI.

30. See Melly.

31. GATS article XIX.

32. Fifth Protocol to GATS, S/L/45, 3 December 1997, available at http://www.wto.org/english/tratop_e/servfi_e/s145.htm [hereafter FSA]. For a comparative analysis of NAFTA and GATS see Joel P. Trachtman, "Trade in Financial Services under GATS, NAFTA and the EC: A Regulatory Jurisdiction Analysis," *Columbia Journal of Transnational Law* 34 (1995), 37.

33. See United States, *Schedule of Specific Commitments, Supplement 3,* GATS/SC/90/Suppl.3, 26 February 1998 (authentic in English only); México, *Lista de compromisos específicos, Suplemento 3,* GATS/SC/56/Suppl.3, 26 de febrero de 1998

(auténtica en español únicamente); Canada, *Schedule of Specific Commitments, Supplement 4*, GATS/SC/16/Suppl.4, 26 February 1998 (authentic in English and French only); and Canada, *Schedule of Specific Commitments, Supplement 4, Revision*, GATS/SC/16/Suppl.4/Rev.1, 6 June 2000 (authentic in English and French only), available at http://www.wto.org.

34. "Marrakesh Agreement Establishing the World Trade Organization, April 15, 1994, Final Act Embodying the Results of the Uruguay Round of Multilateral Trade Negotiations," *Legal Instruments—Results of the Uruguay Round*, vol. I, 33 ILM 1125 (1994) [hereafter WTO agreement].

35. "Understanding on Rules and Procedures Governing the Settlement of Disputes," April 15, 1994, *WTO Agreement*, annex 2, 33 ILM 1226 [hereafter DSU].

36. NAFTA articles 201, 1139, and 1416.

37. NAFTA article 1401, GATS article I.

38. NAFTA article 105.

39. NAFTA article 1402.

40. GATS article I(3).

41. *Vienna Convention on the Law of Treaties, done at Vienna, 23 May 1969*, 1155 UNTS 331, 8 ILM 679, article 27 [hereafter Vienna Convention].

42. See *Metalclad Corporation v. The United Mexican States*, ICSID Case No. ARB(AF)/97/1, 40 ILM 36 (2001); 13 *World Trade and Arbitration Materials* 47 (2001); reversed in part on review, *The United Mexican States v. Metalclad Corporation*, May 2, 2001, BCSC 664 [hereafter Metalclad].

43. NAFTA article 1416.

44. Annex on Financial Services, article 5.

45. NAFTA article 1407(1).

46. NAFTA article 103. Within NAFTA itself, conflicts between chapter 11 and other chapters will be resolved in favor of the latter. See NAFTA article 1112.

47. NAFTA article 1406.

48. NAFTA article 1405. Because it applies to domestic regulatory measures, the national treatment rule may call into question governmental measures that are not necessarily designed for the purpose of restricting trade. The national treatment rule prohibits both explicit and implicit discrimination. It may thus be used to challenge regulations that on their face appear to be nondiscriminatory but have the effect of placing imports at a disadvantage. See John Jackson, "National Treatment Obligations and Non-Tariff Barriers," *Michigan Journal of International Law* 10 (1989), 207.

49. NAFTA article 1405(5), (6), (7).

50. NAFTA article 1406.

51. GATS article II.

52. GATS article II.

53. See Melly.

54. GATS article XX(3).

55. GATS article XXI.

56. See WTO, *Results of the Financial Services Negotiations under the General Agreement on Trade in Services (GATS)*, available at http://www.wto.org/english/tratop_e/servfi_e/financ~1.htm. For a discussion of U.S. policy goals in the FSA negotiations, see Constance Z. Wagner, "The New WTO Agreement on Financial Services and Chapter 14 of NAFTA: Has Free Trade in Banking Finally Arrived?"

NAFTA Law & Business Review Americas 5 (1999), 5. For a developing country perspective, see WTO/World Bank, *The Internationalization of Financial Services: Issues and Lessons for Developing Countries,* ed. Stijn Claessens and Marion Jansen (The Hague: Kluwer Law International, 2001).

57. See Melly.
58. NAFTA article 1411.
59. GATS article III.
60. GATS article VI.
61. NAFTA article 1411(5).
62. Annex on Financial Services, article 2(b).
63. GATS article XIV.
64. NAFTA article 2103.
65. NAFTA article 2101.
66. GATS article XIV bis, NAFTA article 2102.
67. NAFTA article 1401(3)(a).
68. NAFTA article 1401(3)(b).
69. GATS article I(3).
70. NAFTA article 1410(1).
71. NAFTA article 1410(2).
72. NAFTA article 1109.
73. NAFTA article 1410(4).
74. Annex on Financial Services, article 2(a).
75. NAFTA article 105.
76. For a discussion of the Canadian situation, see Stephen A. Scott, "NAFTA, the Canadian Constitution, and the Implementation of International Trade Agreements," in *Beyond NAFTA: An Economic, Political and Sociological Perspective,* ed. A.R. Riggs and T. Velk (Vancouver: Fraser Institute, 1993), 238. For the United States, see Yong K. Kim, "The Beginnings of the Rule of Law in the International Trade System despite US Constitutional Constraints," *Michigan Journal of International Law* 17 (1996), 967; and Charles Tiefer, "Free Trade Agreements and the New Federalism," *Minnesota Journal of Global Trade* 7 (1998), 45.
77. NAFTA article 1405(4).
78. For a detailed discussion of provincial and state reservations relating to insurance, see Bradly Condon, "Smoke and Mirrors: A Comparative Analysis of WTO and NAFTA Provisions Affecting the International Expansion of Insurance Firms in North America," *Connecticut Insurance Law Journal* 8 (2001).
79. See *In the Matter of Cross-Border Trucking Services.*
80. GATS article I(2).
81. NAFTA article 1416.
82. NAFTA article 1404(2).
83. NAFTA article 1404(2).
84. NAFTA article 1404(3).
85. NAFTA article 1404(2).
86. See Organization for Economic Cooperation and Development, *Liberalization of Insurance Operations: Cross-border Trade and Establishment of Foreign Branches* (Paris: Organization for Economic Cooperation and Development, 1999).
87. However, with respect to reinsurance and *reafianzamiento,* foreign firms may participate in the Mexican market via the cross-border supply mode,

provided the Ministry of Finance (Secretaría de Hacienda y Crédito Público) approves their registration. See Mexico, *Lista de compromisos específicos, Suplemento 3*.

88. NAFTA article 1603(1).

89. NAFTA article 1608.

90. NAFTA appendix 1603.D.4.

91. NAFTA article 1601.

92. NAFTA article 1601.

93. NAFTA article 1607.

94. NAFTA article 1408.

95. GATS annex on movement of natural persons supplying services under the agreement.

96. NAFTA article 1403(2).

97. NAFTA article 1403(3).

98. For a comparison of domestic banking regulation in NAFTA countries, see Christopher J. Mailander, *Reshaping North American Banking: The Transforming Effects of Regional Market and Policy Shifts* (Washington, D.C.: Center for Strategic and International Studies, 1999).

99. NAFTA article 1106. While NAFTA chapter 14 does not expressly incorporate the rules regarding performance requirements in article 1106, article 1101 makes it clear that this article applies to "all investments."

100. NAFTA article 1109.

101. EKOS Research Associates Inc., *Canadian Attitudes towards International Trade*, survey conducted March 2001, available at wysiwyg://13/http://www.dfait-maeci.gc.ca/tna-nac/presentations/CATIT/menu-e.htm.

102. See WTO, *Defining Basic Telecommunications*, available at http://www.wto.org/english/tratop_e/servt_e/telor_e.htm.

103. GATS annex on telecommunications.

104. Mexico, *Lista de compromisos específicos, Suplemento 2*, GATS/SC/56/Suppl.2, April 11, 1997, available at http://www.wto.org.

105. NAFTA article 1302.

106. Graham Gori, "Trade Dispute More Likely as Telmex Sues on Connection Fees," *New York Times*, November 1, 2000.

107. Fiona Ortiz, "Reform Seen as Only Hope for Mexico Telecoms Competition," Reuters, November 13, 2001.

108. Josh Tuynman, "A WTO Case Stays in the Background as Telmex Gradually Opens Its Network to US Competitors," *Business Mexico*, October 1, 2001.

Chapter 4

Intellectual Property

OPENING CASE: THE PHARMACEUTICAL INDUSTRY, THE WTO AND THE AIDS CRISIS

On April 27, 2001, African leaders ended the continent's first AIDS summit by declaring a state of emergency and vowing to make the fight against the disease their highest development priority. They agreed to create legislation to ensure that cheap HIV and AIDS drugs were made available and said they would immediately start removing taxes on drugs and would introduce other incentives to reduce drug prices. They supported the call by the secretary-general of the United Nations, Kofi Annan, at the opening of the conference for a seven-to-ten-billion-dollar global AIDS fund. They urged developed countries to support Africa's fight against AIDS by donating 0.7 percent of their respective gross national products to developing countries. They planned to seek changes at the WTO to permit drug patent laws that would make treatment affordable for most Africans.[1] This later became the biggest issue dividing developed and developing countries as they prepared the agenda for the WTO meeting in Doha, Qatar, in November 2001.

The AIDS crisis created a global policy dilemma. The interests of the pharmaceutical industry are served by strong intellectual-property rights and the ability to charge the highest prices the market will bear. Developed countries face conflicting interests—on the one hand, strong patent protection benefits their pharmaceutical industries; on the other hand, high drug prices raise health care costs, even if they can afford high prices. Developing countries are in the most difficult position—they have been hardest hit by AIDS and cannot afford developed-country prices for the drugs. Finally, the global nature of the pandemic requires a global response that involves multilateral organizations serving the interests of the global community.

AIDS in Africa

HIV/AIDS ranks among history's worst epidemics;[2] 21.8 million have died, and 36.1 million more are now infected, including 5.3 million new cases in 2000, six hundred thousand of them children. Sub-Saharan Africa has been hit harder by AIDS than any other part of the world. There an estimated 25.3 million people are living with HIV/AIDS.[3] Infection rates run as high as 35.8 percent of the adult population. The severity of the situation in Africa prompted the UN Security Council to declare the AIDS crisis a global security issue.[4] This is the first time the UN has considered a health issue to be a security matter. There is a strong possibility of major epidemics in Latin America, Eastern Europe, and Asia.[5]

The potential economic and social consequences are profound. In Africa, AIDS is reducing company profits through medical and death expenses, funeral payments, the costs of recruiting and training new employees, and working hours lost because employees are off sick or attending funerals. Through the year 2025, it is estimated that the disease will reduce per capita gross domestic product growth by 0.3 percent in countries that are struggling to grow 1 percent per year.[6] The death rate among teachers is high, resulting in overcrowded classrooms and school closings, and undermining decades of investment in human resources and education.[7]

African health care budgets, most amounting to less than six dollars per citizen annually, have been placed under further strain. Not even the relatively modest eighty-dollar AZT treatment to prevent transmission to children of pregnant and nursing women is affordable.[8] Even if drug prices drop to affordable levels, the countries may not have the necessary health care infrastructure to care for the sick. Without adequate infrastructure, access to combination drug therapies may do more harm than good, by promoting the proliferation of drug-resistant virus mutations.[9]

UNAIDS estimates that prevention programs alone in sub-Saharan Africa will cost two billion dollars per year. Because the first priority is prevention, most of those now infected in Africa are unlikely to receive adequate medical treatment. To provide care to the 40 percent of infected Africans who are dying and the multiple-drug "AIDS cocktail" to another 10 percent would cost about $1.7 billion per year. This estimate assumes a cost of $1,400 per year for the AIDS cocktail—a 90 percent drop in the twelve-thousand-dollars-plus charged in the United States.[10] Another study estimated that a $7.5 billion annual budget is needed to fight AIDS, including $2.5 billion for drugs and palliative care.[11]

According to the World Health Organization (WHO), of the twenty-five million Africans that are infected with HIV, five million are ready for drug therapy, meaning they are sick enough to need the drugs, not too sick to benefit from them, and living in places where they could get them. Only about ten thousand are getting the drugs; if offers of price cuts from patent holders are realized, that number could jump to a hundred thousand.

The Nature of the Pharmaceutical Industry and Patents

Patent systems encourage innovation by granting inventors certain exclusive rights for a limited time in exchange for disclosure of the invention. They provide incentives to invest in research and development by preventing competitors from free-riding on the investment. This time-limited monopoly ensures that inventors have an opportunity to recover their investments and to profit. The system also expands public knowledge through disclosure, which facilitates improvements in the technology and public use of the invention after the patent expires.

The pharmaceutical sector has a number of peculiar characteristics. First, research plays a fundamental role. Because competition revolves around innovation and product substitution, there is a causal relationship between investment in research and market leadership. Second, chemical and pharmaceutical inventions are vulnerable to imitation. Third, distribution channels are unusual, in that in many countries most products are paid for by government social security systems. This has a double impact on price, because governments are involved in setting prices and obtain discounts through volume purchasing. Fourth, the sector is subject to strict control by public authorities, because public health is at stake.

In Canada, for example, both patented and generic products are treated as new drugs requiring regulatory approval, because a generic is only equivalent, not identical, to the patented drug it replicates. It takes eight to twelve years to develop a drug and receive regulatory approval, which takes place during the twenty-year patent term. The time required for a generic manufacturer to complete the approval process ranges from three to six and a half years, including the two to four years necessary to develop a generic drug.[12]

Private patent rights in the pharmaceutical field do not benefit just the owners of patents. They also serve the interest of the public, by promoting the development of new pharmaceuticals; of governments, by advancing public health objectives; and of generic competitors, by providing them with a source of technological information and research data, new products, and new commercial opportunities.

However, rising drug costs are a concern for most countries. Between 1990 and 1997, per capita drug spending in Organization for Economic Cooperation and Development countries increased 35–80 percent.[13] Generic competition lowers prices. In Canada, on average, the first and second generic versions of a previously patented product come on the

market at just under 75 percent of the innovator's price for the same medicine. When a third and a fourth generic enter, the average price drops to
about 54 percent of the innovator's price; and when a fifth enters, the
average falls to just under 46 percent.[14] However, generic manufacturers
in India and Brazil have been able to cut the prices of some generic versions of AIDS medications to 10 to 30 percent of the patent owners' prices
in the United States.

Many countries still lack the facilities and expertise needed to review
the safety, efficacy and quality of drugs destined for their national markets. They depend on foreign authorities to set the necessary standards
and on foreign generic companies to do the necessary testing. For example, a 1993 study of thirty-six African countries conducted by the WHO
found that only three had a "limited drug regulatory capacity." Not one
African nation had what the WHO called a "comprehensive drug regulatory capacity."[15]

Nevertheless, many developing countries have flourishing generic pharmaceutical companies. While a small number of these generic companies
operate on the international level, most operate predominantly in their
domestic markets.[16] Some generic manufacturers in India supply ingre-
dients to drug companies in the United States and must therefore
meet the same standards and pass the same inspections as their U.S.
customers.[17]

The Response of Multilateral Organizations

A major policy goal of the UN has been to lower drug prices. At a special session on AIDS in December 1999, Kofi Annan made a personal appeal to drug companies to lower prices.[18] The UN has also considered
helping African nations to buy generic AIDS drugs from Brazil and India
at lower prices than the discounts the patent owners might offer.[19] At the
UN Millennium Summit in September 2000, world leaders adopted the
following policy goals with respect to the AIDS crisis: to stop the spread
of HIV/AIDS, to give special assistance to children orphaned by AIDS,
and to seek the provision of cheaper pharmaceuticals.[20]

The WTO has not made a specific response to the AIDS crisis, but it
administers and resolves disputes between member countries over the
Agreement on Trade-Related Aspects of Intellectual Property Rights
(TRIPS).[21] TRIPS establishes minimum standards that WTO members
must meet in their intellectual-property laws, including legal protection
of patent rights. The interpretation and application of this agreement restricts the options available to member governments in dealing with the
patent rights of pharmaceutical companies. However, at the ministerial
conference in Doha, WTO members agreed that TRIPS "does not and
should not prevent members from taking measures to protect public

health." This exception applies only to health crises, defined to include AIDS, tuberculosis, malaria and other diseases likely to spread broadly.

The Position of the Patent Holders

The Pharmaceutical Research and Manufacturers of America estimated in 2000 that drug companies would spend $26.4 billion on research that year.[22] The cost of developing a single drug is about five hundred million dollars,[23] and only one out of five thousand compounds investigated ever reaches the market.[24]

In a UN/industry collaboration, five pharmaceutical companies (Boehringer Ingelheim of Germany, Bristol-Myers Squibb and Merck of the United States, Glaxo Wellcome of Britain, and Hoffmann–La Roche of Switzerland) entered negotiations with the WHO, UNAIDS, the World Bank, and the United Nations Children's Fund (UNICEF) to improve access to HIV/AIDS care and treatment in developing countries.[25] The participants endorsed a set of guiding principles on how to tackle the AIDS Epidemic in developing countries:

1. Unequivocal and ongoing political commitment by national governments
2. Strengthened national capacity
3. Engagement of all sectors of national society and the global community
4. Efficient, reliable and secure distribution systems
5. Significant additional funding national and international sources
6. Continued investment in research and development by the pharmaceutical industry.

Merck and the Gates Foundation are donating fifty million dollars each over five years to a new "Botswana Comprehensive HIV/AIDS Partnership," to improve health care infrastructure, expand access to HIV treatment and care, set up distribution systems, and develop public communications and awareness programs in Botswana. Botswana has the highest rate of HIV infection in the world, at 35.8 percent of the adult population.[26]

Uganda has made a deal with pharmaceutical companies to allow AIDS patients to buy retroviral drugs at lower prices. Double-therapy reductions are between 40 and 68 percent, while triple-therapy reductions are between 24 and 70 percent. Merck, Bristol-Myers Squibb, Glaxo Wellcome, and Roche are to provide the drugs. Prior to the reductions, double therapies cost between $214 and $321 a month, while triple therapies ranged between $380 and $602.[27]

Glaxo Wellcome agreed to sell its Combivir, a blend of AZT and 3TC that sells at a global average price of sixteen dollars, for two dollars in poor countries.[28] Boehringer Ingelheim announced it would offer nevirapine, for the prevention of mother-to-child transmission, free of charge for five years in developing countries.[29]

Merck has offered to sell Crixivan to South Africa for six hundred dollars per patient per year, at which price the company says it will make no profit. The same drug sells for $6,016 per year in the United States.[30] Boehringer Ingelheim has also offered preferential pricing of AIDS drugs to developing countries.[31] Bristol-Myers Squibb decided not to block imports of generic versions of its AIDS in South Africa or any other African nation. Bristol-Myers also agreed to reduce the combined price of ddC and ddI in Africa to a dollar a day (in the United States, the cost is eighteen dollars).[32] In Africa, ddC will cost fifty-four dollars a year, compared with $3,589 in the United States.[33] GlaxoSmithKline offered discounts as high as 90 percent to roughly a dozen African nations.

Patent holders have thus begun to address the African crisis. However, the need to protect patents, concerns about inadequate infrastructure, and the risk that cheaper medicines will be resold at higher prices on black markets have slowed negotiations, which are proceeding on a country-by-country basis. Pharmaceutical companies are also concerned that providing cheap drugs overseas may increase pressure to lower prices in the United States and other developed countries. Thirty-nine drug firms launched a court action to stop South Africa from implementing a law to allow imports of generic AIDS drugs and other medicines.[34] (After a public outcry, all thirty-nine companies agreed to withdraw from the case.) At the WTO meeting in Doha, the issue of allowing imports of generic copies from third countries was raised, but the WTO members agreed to postpone debate on this issue for one year.

Generic Drugs in India

India does not recognize intellectual-property rights in chemicals for medicine, a position that dates back to its Patents Act of 1970, which recognized "process patents" rather than "product patents." That is, an inventor patents the multistep recipe for making the drug, not the molecule itself. If a rival can alter the recipe slightly but end up with the same molecule, he may patent and sell that procedure. Under TRIPS, India has until 2005 to recognize twenty-year patents on products that did not enjoy patent protection in India before 1995. Until then, Indian drug companies can reverse-engineer patented drugs and sell copies more cheaply than do the patent holders.

An Indian generic manufacturer is prepared to export AIDS drugs to Africa. Cipla Ltd. of India, a major manufacturer of generic drugs, has offered to supply triple-therapy drug cocktails for $350 a year per patient to Doctors Without Borders. That doctors' group, which won the Nobel Peace Prize in 1999, would distribute the Cipla drugs free in Africa. Cipla also offered to sell the drugs to larger government programs for six hundred dollars a year per patient, about four hundred dollars below the price offered by the companies that hold the patents. The six-hundred-dollar price is near Cipla's break-even point, according to the company's president, but costs could drop with greater production. If that happens, he would cut prices further. In India he sells the same cocktail for about $1,100 a year.

The Cipla drug combination consists of d4T, 3TC and nevirapine. Bristol-Myers Squibb holds the patent on d4T, Glaxo Wellcome holds the patent on 3TC, and Boerhinger Ingelheim holds the patent on nevirapine.

Glaxo Wellcome threatened to sue Cipla when it tried to sell Duovir, its generic version of Glaxo's Combivir in Ghana. Cipla offered the drug for $1.74 a day; Glaxo had cut its price to two dollars, from sixteen. The African regional patent authority ruled that Glaxo's patents were not valid in Ghana, but Cipla stopped selling Duovir.[35]

The U.S. Government Position

Initially, the U.S. trade representative, under pressure from American pharmaceutical companies, threatened trade sanctions against countries that did not respect the American patents. However, this policy changed in 2000. The Clinton administration offered a billion dollars in tax credits to any company that invented a vaccine.[36] It also issued an executive order saying the government would not interfere with African laws and policies that sought greater access to AIDS drugs, as long as they were consistent with TRIPS.[37] The Bush administration agreed to continue the policy of not seeking sanctions against developing countries that break U.S. patent laws to deal with AIDS, as long as they comply with TRIPS.[38]

The U.S. Export-Import Bank offered sub-Saharan African nations a billion dollars in annual loans, most at commercial interest rates, to finance the purchase of American AIDS drugs and medical services.[39] The American loans provide an incentive to buy the drugs from U.S. patent owners. South Africa and Namibia rejected the Export-Import Bank offer, saying they needed affordable drugs, not loans that would further burden their economies.[40]

There is pressure on the U.S. government to allow generic companies to make low-cost versions of essential medicines on which the government holds the patent rights. It holds rights to a variety of drugs, including some AIDS drugs, that were discovered in government labs or by scientists financed by government grants. Some activists have asked the National Institutes of Health to give the World Health Organization the right to use patents owned by the U.S. government to provide cheap medicines for the world's poor. The government's position since 1999 has been that such a move would put the system of developing medicines with government research dollars at risk, arguing that companies would not undertake the development costs of these inventions if they believed the government would allow third parties to use them.[41]

Prior to the WTO Doha meeting, the United States took the position that there was no need to change TRIPS. The United States was backed by Switzerland, Japan and Canada on this issue. However, threats that Canada and the United States had made against Bayer's patent on the anthrax drug Cipro weakened their position. When the debate over patents in the developing countries threatened to derail the negotiations, these developed countries agreed to clarify the exception for health crises to ensure that developing-country actions with respect to AIDS would be covered.

Issues Raised by the AIDS Crisis

The AIDS crisis raises difficult questions with respect to appropriate strategies for patent holders, the response of national governments in rich and poor countries, and the interpretation and application of TRIPS. In the legal profession, there is a saying that hard cases make bad law. On the one hand, strong intellectual-property rights promote investments in innovations; they have led to the development of effective drugs to combat AIDS. However, the research and development behind those drugs cost a lot of money, which is reflected in the price of the drugs. On the other hand, the AIDS crisis in Africa is serious, and the human suffering is real. Moreover, the virus is infectious and is poised to spread rapidly in other poor regions of the world, such as Latin America, Asia and Eastern Europe. Poor countries do not have the resources needed to address the health crisis, and they cannot pay rich-country prices for the drugs. Who should pay?

INTRODUCTION

Obligations to provide legal protection for intellectual-property rights are new to the global trade-law system. Indeed, TRIPS demonstrates how far the scope of the WTO has expanded beyond the GATT's original focus on eliminating barriers to trade in goods. Moreover, the TRIPS obligations are backed up by the same dispute-settlement system as other WTO agreements. If a country does not comply with its obligations, it could face trade sanctions and suffer the economic consequences of losing access to important markets for its products.

Intellectual-property rights are important to a wide range of industries with substantial investments in knowledge. For some, intellectual-property protection is more important than trade liberalization. For example, the pharmaceutical industry is global in that its interests are served by strong patent laws worldwide, which makes TRIPS of utmost importance to this industry. However, international trade in actual finished pharmaceuticals is relatively unimportant, because markets are segmented by national regulatory approval processes. Thus, most trade in this industry consists of intrafirm trade in inputs. Foreign investment liberalization is taking on greater importance for the industry as mergers and acquisitions consolidate the industry internationally.

This chapter begins with a look at the nature of intellectual-property rights. It then analyzes TRIPS in some detail, particularly with respect to patent rights. This is followed by a comparison of the intellectual-property provisions of NAFTA. The chapter then examines how global business strategy is affected by intellectual-property law. The closing case examines how government negotiations to get price discounts from multinational pharmaceutical companies in Brazil and North America created a volatile political climate at the WTO Doha meeting.

THE NATURE OF INTELLECTUAL-PROPERTY RIGHTS

Intellectual property refers to creations of the mind: inventions, literary and artistic works, and symbols, names, images, and designs used in commerce. Intellectual-property rights protect inventions (patents), trademarks, industrial designs, geographic indications (defined below), and copyrights. Copyrights protect literary and artistic works such as novels, poems and plays, films, musical works, artistic works (such as drawings, paintings, photographs and sculptures), and architectural designs. Rights related to copyright include those of artists in performance, those of producers of phonograms (for example, records, tapes and CDs)in their recordings, and those of broadcasters in their radio and television programs.[42]

The strength of intellectual-property rights in a particular market influences the kind of technology that foreign firms will bring to those markets and how that technology will be deployed. The higher the risk that intellectual property will be stolen or expropriated, the less likely a firm is to bring in the latest technology. In today's global business environment, technological innovation is a crucial factor in achieving competitiveness and in staying ahead of the competition. One survey of U.S. firms found that in countries with weak protection for intellectual property, firms were unwilling to invest in joint ventures, transfer their newest technology to subsidiaries, or license their newest technology to unrelated firms.[43]

National competitiveness, economic growth and wealth creation are affected by the creation of and access to technological innovations. Poor countries need modern technology too. It is therefore in the long-term interests of all countries to enforce intellectual-property rights. This is the logic behind TRIPS.

Rich countries with advanced economies increasingly generate wealth through the creation and application of knowledge. In this knowledge economy, rich countries need global protection of intellectual property in order to realize fully the value of their firms' creativity on a global scale. Some of the most important global industries in the developed world depend on intellectual-property rights to maximize their return on investment: the computer hardware and software industries, the entertainment industry (music, books and movies), the telecommunications industry, and the pharmaceutical industry. The growth of such knowledge industries is reshaping the sources of the comparative advantage of the rich countries.

The relationship between intellectual-property rights and international trade is simple. Many products of which the value is derived from intellectual property are easily copied; examples are software, compact discs and videos. Other products, such as pharmaceuticals, can be copied, but only with more effort. To realize the gains from trade associated with the international sale of such products, the countries and firms that produce them need to be paid. Industries that wish to profit from the global sale of such products therefore lobby their national governments to enforce their property rights under TRIPS.

THE AGREEMENT ON TRADE-RELATED ASPECTS OF INTELLECTUAL PROPERTY (TRIPS)

TRIPS is one of several agreements reached at the end of the Uruguay Round of multilateral trade negotiations. All WTO members must ensure that their intellectual-property laws meet the minimum standards set out in TRIPS, though variation is allowed to account for differences in national legal systems. Member governments are free to exceed those standards, but they may not unilaterally try to force other members to exceed those standards.[44] TRIPS obligations are enforced through the WTO dispute-settlement process,[45] as are the other WTO agreements.

The WTO agreements entered into force by January 1, 1995.[46] However, TRIPS allowed developing and least-developed countries to delay the application of TRIPS provisions (except for the general rules of non-discrimination). Developing countries could delay their application for five years, ten years in the case of patent protection for technologies that did not enjoy patent protection before 1995.[47] Least-developed country members could delay application for eleven years, until 2006.[48] At the Doha meeting, WTO members agreed to extend the deadline for least-developed countries with respect to pharmaceuticals until 2016, without prejudice to their rights to seek other extensions.[49]

When a country alleges a violation of TRIPS, it bears the burden of proof. If the defending country wishes to rely on an exception to those obligations, it bears the burden of demonstrating that its legal provisions comply with those exceptions.[50]

Obligations

TRIPS, as noted, sets out minimum standards to be achieved in the domestic intellectual-property law of WTO members. Certain obligations apply generally to all intellectual-property rights, while others apply only to specific types, such as patents, copyrights, trademarks, industrial designs, and trade secrets. In addition, TRIPS incorporates obligations contained in other intellectual-property conventions, including the Paris Convention (1967), the Berne Convention (1971) and the Rome Convention.[51]

General Rules of Nondiscrimination: TRIPS Articles 3 and 4

The principle of national treatment, in article 3, requires members to provide foreign companies intellectual-property protection that is no worse than that provided to domestic companies. The most-favored-nation principle (article 4) prohibits discrimination between foreign companies from different member countries, subject to limited exemptions related to preexisting international agreements.

Exhaustion of Intellectual-Property Rights: TRIPS Article 6

The WTO members were unable to reach agreement on how to deal with the issue of "exhaustion" of intellectual-property rights in the Uruguay Round. (Once a company has sold its product, its patent is exhausted, and it no longer has any rights concerning what happens to it.) Thus, for the purposes of dispute settlement, TRIPS imposes no obligations with respect to the issue of the exhaustion of intellectual-property rights, provided that members do not violate their national treatment and most-favored-nation obligations.

This raises the important issue of "parallel importing" (parallel imports are products sold by the patent owner in one country and imported into another country without the approval of the patent owner). Pharmaceutical companies charge different prices for drugs in different markets, depending on the purchasing power of consumers in a particular market. For example, Glaxo sells Combivir for seventeen dollars a day in the United States and for two dollars a day in Africa. Such a differential pricing strategy would be difficult to maintain if the United States allowed Combivir to be purchased in Africa for two dollars and imported to the United States for sale at five dollars.

One commentator argues that TRIPS gives members discretion to permit parallel importing with respect to AIDS drugs in the context of a domestic health care crisis.[52] At Doha, the issue of allowing countries to import generic copies of patented drugs was deferred for one year.[53] TRIPS lets patent holders prevent third parties from making, using, selling or importing their product without consent. This clearly prohibits imports of nonauthorized generic copies of patented medicines.

Under a system of international exhaustion of patents, the patent owner cannot prevent the importation of his own product from a foreign country once it has been sold there.[54] Exhaustion of patent rights cannot be raised in a WTO dispute, a fact that raises the risk that patented drugs sold cheaply in a developing country could be imported cheaply to a developed-country market. This could threaten differential pricing strategies used by pharmaceutical companies.

At Doha, WTO members agreed that the effect of TRIPS provisions on exhaustion "is to leave each Member free to establish its own regime for such exhaustion without challenge, subject to MFN and national treatment provisions of Articles 3 and 4."[55]

Obligations Specific to Patents: TRIPS Section 5

Members must make patents available in all fields of technology, without discrimination as to the place of invention, field of technology, or whether products are imported or produced locally.[56] It does not prohibit bona fide exceptions to deal with problems that may exist in certain product areas. This provision may be interpreted to require governments to apply exceptions in a nondiscriminatory manner, in order to ensure that governments do not succumb to domestic pressures to limit exceptions to areas where right holders tend to be foreign producers.[57] However, members may exclude certain inventions from patentability to prevent their commercial exploitation within their territory where this is necessary to protect human, animal or plant life or health.[58]

A patent on a product must confer on its owner the following exclusive rights for twenty years, counting from the filing date[59]:

1. The right to prevent third parties not having the owner's consent from making, using, offering for sale, selling, or importing for these purposes that product.[60]
2. The right to assign the patent or transfer it by succession and to conclude licensing contracts.[61]

Applicants for patents must disclose the invention fully enough that it can be reproduced by a person skilled in the art. Countries can also require the applicant to indicate the best method for carrying out the invention.[62] They may also require an applicant to provide information concerning corresponding foreign patent applications and grants.[63]

TRIPS requires enforcement of intellectual-property rights under national law. It requires provisions on evidence, injunctions, damages, and the right of judicial authorities to order disposal or destruction of infringing goods.[64] However, members are free to determine appropriate methods of implementing the provisions of TRIPS within their own legal systems and practices.[65]

The interpretation of TRIPS obligations must take into account the objectives of the agreement. The protection and enforcement of intellectual-property rights should contribute to the promotion of technological innovation and to the transfer and dissemination of technology to the mutual advantage of producers and users, in a manner conducive to social and economic welfare and to a balance of rights and obligations.[66]

TRIPS Exceptions and Their Relation to the AIDS Crisis

Public Health

As a general principle, WTO members may adopt measures necessary to protect public health and nutrition, and to promote the public interest in sectors of vital importance to their socioeconomic and technological development, provided such measures are consistent with the provisions of TRIPS.[67] At first glance, this appears to give African governments carte blanche to take measures that violate patent rights in order to address the AIDS crisis. However, the requirement that the measures be consistent with TRIPS could be interpreted to mean that the rights of patent holders must be respected unless the measures fit other exceptions.

Security

Nothing in TRIPS can be construed as preventing a member from taking any action it considers necessary for the protection of its essential security interests, taken in an emergency in international relations or under its obligations in the UN Charter for the maintenance of international peace and security.[68]

The UN Security Council has declared the AIDS crisis a global security issue. The implication is that the actions African nations may take regarding patent rights to address the AIDS crisis may be permissible as exceptions to their TRIPS obligations. However, it is not clear whether a WTO panel would adopt this view.

Support for the view that AIDS-combating measures may qualify under the security exception may be found in the preparatory work relating to the equivalent GATT article XXI security exception. One of the drafters of the original draft charter stated, "We gave a good deal of thought to the question of the security exception. . . . It is really a question of balance. . . . We cannot make it too tight, because we cannot prohibit measures which are needed purely for security reasons. On the other hand, we cannot make it so broad that, under the guise of security, countries will put on measures which really have a commercial purpose."[69] In the case of African governments taking measures to deal with the AIDS crisis, the purpose is not commercial.

The security exception is also designed to ensure the proper allocation of responsibility between the UN and the WTO, to ensure the WTO does not attempt to take action which would involve passing judgment in any way on essentially political matters. Any measure taken by a member in connection with a political matter brought before the UN in accordance with the provisions of chapters IV or VI of the UN Charter should be deemed to fall within the scope of the UN, not the WTO.[70]

Exceptions That Apply Specifically to Patent Rights: Articles 30 and 31

Article 30 permits Members to provide limited exceptions to patent rights. Article 30 establishes three criteria, each of which must be satisfied in order to qualify for the exception: (1) the exception must be "limited"; (2) the exception must not "unreasonably conflict with the normal exploitation of the patent"; and (3) the exception must not "unreasonably prejudice the legitimate interests of the patent owner, taking into account the legitimate interests of third parties." A WTO panel has ruled that each of the three must be presumed to mean something different from the other two, or there would be redundancy.[71]

The panel ruled that any exception that entirely removes the right to exclude making and using the patented product cannot be considered a "limited exception" under article 30. This exception creates a minimal reduction in the legal rights of the patentee. For example, an exception allowing a generic manufacturer to produce a limited quantity of patented drugs to submit to a national regulatory-review process qualifies as a "limited exception." As long as the exception is confined to conduct needed to comply with the requirements of the regulatory review process, and no commercial use is made of the products resulting from the production runs, the acts permitted will be small and narrowly bounded. The same goes for activities seeking product approvals under foreign regulatory procedures. While the economic impact of this regulatory review exception could be considerable, given the time required for generic producers to develop and obtain regulatory approval, the first condition of article 30 addresses the impact on legal rights, not economic impact.

The regulatory review exception does not conflict with the normal exploitation of patents. It is an unintended consequence of the conjunction of patent laws with product laws, not a normal consequence of enforcing patent rights. Patent owners cannot claim a "legitimate interest" in the economic benefits caused by the length of time required to get regulatory approval for generic drugs. While a number of governments have extended their patent terms to compensate for the delays in obtaining approval, several others have not.

This interpretation of the article 30 exception suggests that seizing patent rights on AIDS drugs in Africa would be too great an intrusion on those rights to qualify as a limited exception.

The article 31 exception allows the use of the subject matter of a patent by the government or third parties without the authorization of the patent holder. This would apply to such measures as authorization of parallel imports of patented products, compulsory licensing of patents, and the revocation or forfeiture of patents. The scope and duration of the use must be limited to the purpose for which it was authorized. The use must be authorized predominantly for the supply of the domestic market of the member. The authorization must be subject to termination if and when the circumstances that led to it cease to exist and are unlikely to recur. The legal validity of any decision relating to the authorization and the remuneration must be subject to judicial review or other independent review.

The use may only be permitted if prior efforts to obtain authorization from the patent holder on reasonable commercial terms and conditions have failed after a reasonable period of time. However, this requirement may be waived by the member in the case of a national emergency or other circumstances of extreme urgency or in cases of noncommercial public use. This exception would appear to fit actions taken by African governments to address the AIDS crisis, and it may have been a motivation for them to declare officially a state of emergency.

However, TRIPS does not define "national emergency" or "extreme urgency." In the case of AIDS, what would the threshold be? An African country with a 30 percent rate of infection that has declared a state of emergency would appear likely to qualify. But what about a country like Brazil, with a much lower infection rate? Would it qualify simply by declaring a state of emergency? That seems unlikely. However, TRIPS is not clear on what factors would determine whether a given situation qualified as a national emergency or a case of extreme urgency.

At Doha, negotiators agreed to a declaration stating that TRIPS "does not and should not prevent Members from taking measure to protect public health."[72] The declaration provides further that WTO members have "the right to grant compulsory licences and the freedom to determine the grounds upon which such licences are granted." It also declares that members have "the right to determine what constitutes a national emergency or other circumstances of extreme urgency, it being understood that public health crises, including those relating to HIV/AIDS, tuberculosis, malaria and other epidemics, can represent a national emergency or other circumstances of extreme urgency." This definition permits "extreme urgency" to be interpreted according to the nature of the disease rather than the number of infections. An epidemic is by definition a rapidly spreading or widely prevalent attack of disease that affects a large number of victims in a community. This means that countries with low infection rates for AIDS, like Brazil (with a rate of 0.47 percent but hundreds of thousands of patients), will clearly be able to avail themselves of the TRIPS declaration to acquire cheaper medicine through compulsory licenses.

However, there is one requirement that may pose a problem. The patent holder must be paid adequate remuneration taking into account the circumstances of each case and the economic value of the authorization. In the circumstances of the AIDS crisis, it is not clear what the economic value of a compulsory license in African markets would be. Offers by patent holders to sell AIDS drugs to Africa at or below cost, together with statements by some companies that these markets would not be sources of profits, provide evidence that the economic value of the authorization may be very little. This is an issue that would have to be confronted by African governments wishing to use this particular exception.

Copyrights and Trademarks

Many developing countries have resisted enforcing copyrights and trademarks because producers of counterfeit-trademark goods and pirated-copyright goods represent an important source of economic activity, and they have seen no economic benefit in restricting them. However, as such countries develop their own knowledge-intensive industries, they have begun to recognize the importance of intellectual-property protection.[73] Still, enforcement remains weak in many large developing-country markets, where counterfeit copies of software and movie videos are readily available from street vendors.

Copyright

Copyright protection extends to expression, not to ideas, procedures, methods of operation or mathematical concepts as such.[74] The products that are protected by copyright represent a significant portion of the fruits of the knowledge economy. Notably, they include books, movies, music and computer software. All of these products are easily copied and thus difficult to protect.

TRIPS incorporates articles 1 through 21 of the Berne Convention (1971) and obliges members to comply with them, but it does not apply to article 6*bis* of that convention.[75] Article 6*bis* grants an author of a copyrighted work the right to object to any modification of the work that would prejudice his or her honor or reputation, independently of the author's economic rights and even after the transfer of those rights to another. The remaining incorporated articles define the works that are included in the term "literary and artistic works"; eligibility for protection; the kind of rights that are protected; enforcement measures (such as border seizures of counterfeit goods); and the term of protection, which is generally for the life of the author plus fifty years.[76]

Under the Berne Convention, the term "literary and artistic works" is defined to include

> every production in the literary, scientific and artistic domain, whatever its form of expression, such as books, pamphlets and other writings; lectures, addresses, sermons and other works of the same nature; dramatic or dramatico-musical works; choreographic works and entertainments; musical compositions with or without words; cinematographic works . . . ; works of drawing, painting, architecture, sculpture, engraving and lithography; photographic works . . . ; works of applied art; illustrations, maps, plans, sketches and three-dimensional works relative to geography, topography, architecture or science.

Translations, adaptations, arrangements of music and other alterations of a literary or artistic work are also protected.[77]

The protection of the Berne Convention applies to authors who are nationals or residents of one of the signatory countries, whether the work is published or not, and to nonnationals whose work is first published in one of the signatory countries. A work is considered as having been published simultaneously in several countries if it has been published in two or more countries within thirty days of its first publication.[78] The convention provides for national treatment, requiring signatories to grant the same protection to nonnationals as they do to nationals. Authors enjoy the rights under the law of the country in question, as well as the rights granted under the convention. The enjoyment and exercise of these rights are not subject to any formality and are independent of the existence of protection in the country of origin.[79]

TRIPS requires members to extend the copyright protection of the Berne Convention to computer programs and databases.[80] The term of copyright protection must be at least fifty years, unless it is calculated based on the life of a natural person, except for photographs or applied art.[81]

Authors of computer programs and movies, and producers of sound recordings must be given the right to authorize or prohibit the commercial rental of their works to the public. WTO members are exempt from this requirement with respect to movies, unless their rental has led to widespread copying that materially impairs the authors' copyrights.[82] Performers must receive protection against the unauthorized recording and broadcast of live performances.[83] Broadcasters enjoy the same protections, but only for twenty years.[84]

The extension of copyright to computer programs and the incorporation of these intellectual-property rights and obligations into the WTO system provides countries with a more effective means to enforce the rights of their companies on a global basis. For example, Microsoft can seek the help of the U.S. government enforcing its rights in China now that China is a member of the WTO. The threat that complaints to the WTO might lead to trade sanctions against countries who fail to comply with their TRIPS obligations gives companies greater bargaining power in seeking the enforcement of their rights.

The economic impact of copyright protection is enormous. In Russia, most computers use Microsoft Windows. Over 90 percent of the computers use pirated copies. In Mexico, pirated copies of movies are readily available for purchase at street stands. It is practically impossible to prevent original movies from being brought into the country for copying. Recently, an elephant was smuggled across the Mexican border; if an elephant can be smuggled, bringing in a video or DVD is a simple matter. Once a video or CD-ROM, etc., is in the country, endless copies can be made. Globally, the loss of royalties and license fees amounts to billions of dollars. At the same time, the sale of counterfeit merchandise creates employment in countries where millions live in poverty.

Trademarks

Under TRIPS, any sign capable of distinguishing the goods or services of one business from another's constitutes a trademark that is eligible for registration. Such signs include words, personal names, letters, numerals, figurative elements and combinations of colors, as well as any combination of such signs. However, a WTO member may deny registration of a trademark on other grounds, provided that they do not derogate from the provisions of the Paris Convention for the Protection of Industrial Property.[85]

Members may make eligibility for registration dependent on use. However, actual use of a trademark cannot be made a condition for filing an application for registration. An application cannot be refused solely on the ground that intended use has not taken place before the expiration of a period of three years from the date of application. The nature of the goods or services to which a trademark is to be applied cannot form an obstacle to registration of the trademark. WTO members must publish each trademark either before it is registered or promptly after it is registered and must provide a reasonable opportunity for petitions to cancel the registration. In addition, WTO members may provide an opportunity for the registration of a trademark to be opposed.[86]

The owner of a registered trademark has the exclusive right to prevent others from using identical or similar signs for goods or services that are identical or similar, where this would likely cause confusion. Article 6bis of the Paris Convention requires countries to refuse or cancel the registration of a trademark that reproduces or imitates a well-known trademark used for identical or similar goods. TRIPS applies this rule to services. If the goods or services are not similar but the use of the trademark would indicate a connection between those goods or services and the owner of the registered trademark, and the interests of the owner of the registered trademark are likely to be damaged, TRIPS applies this rule.[87]

Members may provide limited exceptions to the rights conferred by a trademark, such as fair use of descriptive terms, provided that such exceptions take account of the legitimate interests of the owner of the trademark and of third parties.[88]

Registration of a trademark must be for a minimum term of seven years, renewable indefinitely.[89] If use is required to maintain a registration, the registration may be canceled only after an uninterrupted period of at least three years of nonuse, unless the trademark owner shows valid reasons. Circumstances arising independently of the will of the owner of the trademark that constitute obstacles to the use of the trademark, such as import restrictions or other government requirements, must be recognized as valid reasons for nonuse.[90]

WTO members may determine the conditions that apply to the licensing and assignment of trademarks, but the compulsory licensing of trademarks is not permitted. The owner has the right to assign the trademark with or without the transfer of the business to which the trademark belongs.[91]

The value of a trademark to a company comes from the image and reputation the company has developed through marketing and quality standards. Coca-Cola has one of the best-known trademarks in the world. The company has invested heavily in advertising to develop the value of its trademark. Because it is so widely known, the trademark is often copied onto tee-shirts and spoofed, for example by spelling out the word "cocaine" in the distinctive lettering of "Coca-Cola." The company may seek to maintain its image by enforcing intellectual-property rights in such a case, or it may consider any publicity to be good publicity and expect the public not to confuse it with the illicit drug business. Nevertheless, unauthorized use of the trademark may represent foregone licensing fees.

Designer clothing companies are another frequent target of trademark infringement. A well-known designer can charge more for clothing when the name carries status and represents quality assurance in the mind of the consumer. Poor-quality counterfeit goods can tarnish the reputation of the company and diminish the status value of the brand.

Geographical Indications

TRIPS also provides protection for *geographical indications,* defined as indications that identify a good as originating in a particular country, region or locality, where a given quality, reputation or other characteristic of the good is essentially attributable to its geographical origin.[92] Examples include champagne (from the Champagne region of France) and tequila (from the Tequila region of Mexico). Bubbly wine may not be called champagne, and agave-based liquor may not be called tequila, if they are not produced in these geographic areas, respectively.

Each WTO member must provide the legal means for interested parties to prevent the use of a geographical indication, even where the true origin of the goods is indicated or the geographical indication is used in translation or accompanied by such expressions as "kind," "type," "style," "imitation" or the like.[93] The Doha Round will include further negotiations on geographical indications.

Protection for geographical indications reflects the economic reality that the price of such products is determined by quality, image and supply. For example, poor-quality copies of tequila have damaged the image of the product. In 1999, a shortage of tequila caused the price to rise dramatically. The availability of copies or substitutes in the market place would put downward pressure on prices.

Other Aspects of Intellectual Property Covered by TRIPS

TRIPS also provides rules for the protection of industrial designs (ten years), layout designs of integrated circuits (ten years), and undisclosed information whose commercial value is due to its secrecy.[94]

TRIPS permits members to control anticompetitive practices in contractual licenses, on the basis that such practices may have adverse effects on trade and may impede the transfer and dissemination of technology.[95] A well-known example of such a practice involved Microsoft. The company used the dominant position of its Windows operating system to require licensees that used the Windows system to purchase other Microsoft products. This action led to the antitrust suit against Microsoft to limit its ability to engage in such licensing practices.

Enforcement of Intellectual-Property Rights

TRIPS obliges WTO members to ensure that enforcement procedures are available under their laws to permit effective action against any infringement of intellectual-property rights. However, it does not create any obligation to create a judicial system to enforce intellectual-property rights as distinct from the system for the enforcement of law in general. Most importantly, it creates no obligation with respect to the distribution of resources between the enforcement of intellectual-property rights and the enforcement of law in general.[96] This provides an enormous loophole for developing countries, where the majority of intellectual-property rights violations occur. For example, pirated copies of movies, software and music are sold on a massive scale by street vendors in many countries that do not have the resources to enforce even their general laws effectively. Thus, while the laws on their books may comply with their TRIPS obligations, those laws may not be enforced.

TRIPS requires members to make civil judicial procedures available to rights holders, including minimum standards for procedures, evidence, injunctions, damages and trial costs.[97] This means that the owners of intellectual property may sue producers and vendors of pirated goods for damages. While this is important, in many cases it is not a practical option for companies to pursue. Civil litigation is a costly and lengthy process, and seeking payment of any damages that might be awarded can be problematic. For example, it would not be practical to sue the thousands of individuals who sell pirated copies of music and movies on the streets of Mexico City, simply due to the time and money involved in launching so many court cases. Even if a company chose to do so, the vendors are too poor to pay the damages that would be awarded; their modest profits are all spent on the basic necessities of life.

TRIPS also requires members to provide criminal procedures and penalties in cases of intentional trademark counterfeiting or copyright piracy on a commercial scale. Penalties must include imprisonment or fines sufficient to provide a deterrent, consistent with the level of penalties applied for crimes of a corresponding gravity. Where appropriate, remedies must also include the seizure, forfeiture and destruction of the infringing goods.[98] As tough as this may sound, such criminal laws do not have a great impact on the enforcement of intellectual-property laws in many developing countries. While authorities may occasionally conduct well-publicized raids on highly visible commercial operations, corruption and the lack of adequate human and financial resources allow the vast majority of infractions to go unpunished.

In Mexico, most crimes of all kinds go unreported because of these problems. For example, in Mexico City less than 20 percent of crimes are reported. The procedures involved in filing criminal charges are lengthy and time consuming, involving several half-day visits to the police station over a period of several months. Even when the charges are duly filed, the police will not investigate unless they are paid a bribe. If the suspect pays the investigating police a larger bribe, they will not investigate further. Even where a case makes it to court, the judge may be bribed or threatened by the accused and so rule in his favor. If an accused is jailed, he may bribe or threaten the jailers to allow an "escape" to occur. A survey in 2001 found that 214 million acts of extortion or bribery occur each year in Mexico, which has a population of just under a hundred million people.[99]

The obligations contained in TRIPS apply primarily to the content and application of the intellectual-property laws of each member. As noted above, there is no obligation to dedicate a particular amount of resources to their enforcement. Where those laws do not conform to the requirements of the TRIPS, WTO members may invoke the general dispute settlement mechanisms of the WTO, which may ultimately lead to trade sanctions.

NAFTA RULES REGARDING INTELLECTUAL PROPERTY

NAFTA chapter 17 obliges Canada, Mexico and the United States to provide adequate and effective protection and enforcement for intellectual-property rights[100] and applies the principle of national treatment.[101] The provisions of chapter 17 provide the same kind of protection as TRIPS for copyright (fifty years),[102] trademarks (ten years, renewable),[103] patents (twenty years from the date of filing or seventeen years from the date of grant),[104] trade secrets (unlimited duration),[105] and industrial designs (ten years).[106]

Enforcement of intellectual-property rights must be effective and expeditious,[107] include civil remedies and guarantees of procedural fairness,[108] criminal procedures and penalties,[109] and enforcement at the border.[110]

The obligations imposed by NAFTA are thus similar to those imposed under TRIPS. Like TRIPS, NAFTA incorporates and applies preexisting international intellectual-property treaties (the Geneva Convention, the Berne Convention, the Paris Convention, and the International Convention for the Protection of New Plant Varieties).[111]

An important difference between NAFTA and TRIPS is that NAFTA does not exclude the issue of exhaustion of intellectual-property rights from its application. However, the position of the NAFTA on this issue is not entirely clear. There are specific obligations regarding the exhaustion of rental rights on copyrighted computer programs and sound recordings.[112] However, a party may revoke a patent where the grant of a compulsory license has not remedied the lack of exploitation of the patent.[113] NAFTA makes no specific reference to the issue of parallel imports, but right holders may seek enforcement at the border where there is an infringement of its intellectual-property rights under the laws of the importing country.[114] With respect to copyright, right holders are specifically granted the right to authorize or prohibit the importation of copies made without the right holder's authorization,[115] but this would not prevent parallel imports of authorized copies. Patent owners are provided the right to prevent others from making, using or selling the subject matter of the patent without the patent owner's consent.[116] However, unlike TRIPS, the patent owner's rights do not cover importation.

A major difference between WTO and NAFTA is that NAFTA provides protection for foreign investors, while this issue was put on the WTO negotiating agenda only recently, for the Doha Round. NAFTA chapter 11 gives investors the right to file claims directly for compensation against host governments in cases of expropriation of investments. The definition of investment includes intangible property that is used for economic benefit or other business purpose; it thus covers intellectual-property rights.[117] However, the case of compulsory licenses issued on patents is specifically excluded from the requirement to pay compensation for expropriation.[118] Nevertheless, governments may be liable to pay compensation in cases of revocation, limitation or creation of patent rights where their actions are inconsistent with NAFTA chapter 17 obligations on intellectual-property rights.

There have been no disputes involving NAFTA chapter 17, and for the most part the NAFTA provisions mirror the provisions of TRIPS, which was being negotiated at the same time. Indeed, the WTO appears to be the preferred forum for resolving intellectual-property disputes between the NAFTA members. For instance, the United States chose the WTO as the forum in a complaint against the Canadian term of protection of patents.[119]

BUSINESS STRATEGY AND INTELLECTUAL-PROPERTY LAW

Since most forms of intellectual property are easily copied, it is difficult to protect, even with adequate legal protection. Other means of enhancing protection include technological solutions and political pressure. Sometimes technological solutions are more effective. For example, software can be designed in a way that prevents copying. However, such technological solutions may diminish the value to the consumer and therefore be counterproductive.

Right holders can also lobby their government to put pressure on other governments to enforce intellectual-property laws more vigorously. For example, Microsoft persuaded the U.S. government to put pressure on China. Industry associations can also lobby foreign governments in conjunction with the efforts of their domestic governments. The Motion Picture Association of America pursued this strategy in Mexico.

Legal enforcement of intellectual-property rights can be expensive and may cause other problems. In the case of the pharmaceutical industry, legal enforcement of patent rights in Africa proved damaging to public relations. Moreover, even with modern intellectual-property laws on the books, many countries lack the resources to enforce the laws, and in many the police and judiciary, who play a key role in enforcement, are corrupt.

Sometimes the cost of protecting confidential company information exceeds the benefits. For example, Matsushita has adopted a policy of openly sharing all company information with all its employees. While such a strategy increases the risk that trade secrets may be revealed, the company judged the benefits of knowledge sharing to learning and innovation within the firm to be greater than the benefit of maintaining secrecy.

Despite the potential problems, however, it is in the interest of right holders to enjoy legal protection for intellectual property. Having strong laws in place improves the bargaining position of companies in negotiations over compensation when their rights are lost, and in seeking enforcement of their rights. Most importantly, it keeps the option of formal legal action available.

In the case of the pharmaceutical companies, price discrimination between markets is an important strategy for maximizing sales and profits. The companies charge what each market will bear. As long as they own the patents, the legal protection provided in each market permits them to negotiate the price of the product and seek compensation for their investment. In Africa, for example, the companies can charge low prices and negotiate contractual terms with governments to minimize the risk of resale in developed country markets.

The pharmaceutical industry provides a good example of how proactive efforts can influence the negotiation of international trade agreements. Through lobbying efforts, the industry influenced the Uruguay Round negotiations. Those efforts continue to seek further development of the law so as to enhance the protection of their patent rights. For the Doha meeting, the industry put pressure on the United States and other countries to resist any dilution of TRIPS obligations. While the industry did not entirely succeed, these efforts probably minimized the degree to which those obligations were diminished.

CONCLUSION

Intellectual-property rights are of extreme importance to advanced economies and the increasing number of firms that create wealth through the production of, and international trade in, intellectual property. The inclusion of obligations in this area in the WTO has begun a process of global harmonization of intellectual-property laws. However, this has not solved the problem of extensive violations of intellectual-property rights in the developing world.

Developing countries remain ambivalent about the protection of intellectual-property rights. In many countries, the production and sale of copied products represent important sources of income for many citizens. Moreover, enforcement of intellectual-property laws remains problematic.

While producers of intellectual property may derive benefits from a strong legal regime, they must recognize the limitations of legal enforcement of their rights and continue to seek creative solutions to the infringement of their rights. At the same time, they must consider how legal enforcement strategies may affect other important strategies, such as marketing and public relations.

NAFTA and the WTO have made similar progress in the protection of intellectual-property rights. They contain similar obligations, although there are some important differences. In practical terms, the relatively less effective intellectual-property protection in Mexico, as compared to the other NAFTA members, mirrors the differences in intellectual-property protection found between developed and developing countries at the global level.

CLOSING CASE: AIDS, ANTHRAX, AND PATENTS— THE NORTH-SOUTH DIVIDE NARROWS

The anthrax scare and the preceding terrorist attacks of September 11 have led to an unprecedented convergence of global health, legal, economic and security issues. In their rush to respond to the anthrax threat, the governments of Canada and the United States used negotiation tactics with the German pharmaceutical company, Bayer, that resembled the tactics used in developing countries, such as Brazil, to acquire cheaper AIDS drugs. However, Canada had experienced no anthrax infections, and the United States had experienced less than twenty. In contrast, Brazil had 540,000 people infected with the AIDS virus at the end of 2000, while sub-Saharan Africa had over twenty-five million. To make matters worse, it later turned out that the threats to Bayer's patent on ciprofloxacin were probably unnecessary. Tests of the U.S. anthrax spores conducted by the Center for Disease Control in Atlanta revealed that another antibiotic, the patent on which had already expired, was equally effective, if not more so.

Prior to the North American response to anthrax, the issue of how to deal with patent owners had been framed as a North-South issue. The rich countries of the North were home to the drug-patent owners, and the poor countries of the South sought to circumvent global patent laws to acquire more affordable medicines. At the WTO ministerial meeting in Doha, the issue erupted as a potential deal breaker, threatening to derail the launch of a new round of global trade negotiations.

AIDS and Patents in Brazil

Brazil's AIDS treatment program has made generic medications available free of charge to anyone who is HIV-positive. The program has driven down both drug prices and deaths from AIDS. Brazil began copying AIDS drugs patented abroad before 1997, when its new law went into effect. It has been licensing AIDS drug patents awarded since then to government laboratories, which make generics for the free-drug program.

Before 1997, drugs could not be patented in Brazil, so local manufacturers were free to replicate them. Even now, patent law in Brazil covers only those drugs invented since May 1997. Brazilian law now gives inventors exclusive rights for twenty years and protects drug inventions that are under development, in accordance with TRIPS.

However, Brazilian law says that to maintain a patent, an owner must make use of his technology in Brazil. Importing a product into the country is not enough to satisfy this requirement. American pharmaceutical companies complained that the requirement violates TRIPS. They asked that Brazil be placed on a U.S. government watch list that is usually a first step toward trade sanctions.

In 1999, Brazil's president decreed that his government could grant compulsory licenses on patents in a national emergency. The decree has been exercised to ensure affordable access to AIDS medications. American companies object to the decree, because if an emergency is declared, it requires patent holders to turn over the secrets of their inventions to government officials and local manufacturers, which may then produce the drugs. One clause of the 1999 decree states that a patent owner must transmit the necessary and sufficient information for the effective reproduction of the protected object, as well as other technical and commercial aspects applicable to the case. This requirement is consistent with TRIPS. The Brazilian law says that a national emergency might arise from a threat to the public's health or nutrition, the environment, or the country's state of social, economic or technological development.[120]

Brazil's AIDS program has reduced the nation's death rate from AIDS by half. The health ministry spent $444 million on AIDS drugs in 2000, 4 percent of its health budget. The decline in hospitalizations from opportunistic infections from 1997 to 1999 saved the health ministry $422 million. Since Brazil began making the generic copies of AIDS drugs, it has reduced the price of the patented equivalents. The price of AIDS drugs with no generic competition fell 9 percent between 1996 and 2000. The price of those that faced generic competition fell 79 percent. Brazil now produces certain triple therapies for three thousand dollars per year and expects the price to drop to seven hundred dollars per year in the future. This compares to a cost of ten to fifteen thousand dollars per year in the United States.[121]

The United States challenged Brazil's patent law by lodging a complaint at the WTO under TRIPS. However, the United States dropped the case after world leaders and health organizations said it could hurt Brazil's AIDS program.[122] While this prevented the panel from issuing an interpretation, it may serve as a political precedent should other WTO members consider launching complaints on behalf of their pharmaceutical industries. Given the widespread political objections to the U.S. case, including from the EU, the Swiss government would be unlikely to pursue a case against Brazil at the WTO on behalf of Roche. Even if Roche overcame the political obstacles, a legal victory would be far from certain.

The Roche Negotiations with Brazil

In August 2001, the Brazilian health minister announced that his government would issue a compulsory license on Roche's AIDS drug nelfinavir and begin manufacturing a generic copy in government laboratories in 2002. The announcement came after negotiations between the Swiss drug company and Brazil failed to produce an agreement on price reductions. The health minister said that over a quarter of his AIDS program budget was being spent on nelfinavir alone.[123] Even an agreement to reduce its price by an additional 40 percent, the health minister said, would be insufficient to stop the government from proceeding with its plan.[124]

The company responded that it had already reduced the price in Brazil to 50 percent of the cost in the United States and had donated thousands of doses of the pediatric syrup version to Brazil. It sought further negotiations, a request that the health minister perceived as an attempt to delay preparations to manufacture the drug in the government's laboratory. The company stated its intention to begin manufacturing Viracept (the brand name of nelfinavir) in Brazil in 2002 and to continue to provide the medicine free to Brazilian children with AIDS. Financial analysts said the dispute would affect public relations more than finances; Roche's overall sales of Viracept rose 5 percent, to U.S.$132.6 million in the first half of 2001.[125]

However, on August 31 the Brazilian health minister announced an agreement with Roche to reduce the price by a further 40 percent, making the Brazilian price 30 percent of the U.S. price. In March, a similar threat to break the patent on two AIDS drugs produced by Merck led to an agreement to reduce the price of indinavir and efavirenz by about 60 percent in Brazil.[126]

Anthrax and German Patents: A North-North Spin on a North-South Issue

Following the transmission of anthrax through the mail in the United States, the Canadian government decided to acquire a stockpile of ciprofloxacin (Cipro) in case the same occurred in Canada. At the time, Cipro was considered to be the most potent drug to fight anthrax infections. Health Canada ordered one million pills of Cipro from Canadian generic drug manufacturer Apotex, even though Bayer's patent would not expire until 2004.[127] Under section 19 of the Canadian Patent Act, the government is allowed to apply to the Canadian Commissioner of Patents for the right to use a patented product in a case of national emergency or extreme urgency.[128] This provision reflects Canada's WTO obligations under TRIPS. However, in its haste, the government failed to follow this Patent Act procedure or to seek permission from the patent holder, Bayer.

The Canadian minister of health was heavily criticized by the opposition parties in Parliament for breaking the Patent Act; in addition, Bayer complained. The minister claimed that he had placed the order with the generic manufacturer because Bayer had been unable to fill the order. Bayer denied this.[129] Bayer and Canadian government later reached an agreement in which Bayer agreed not to sue the government and to supply one million Cipro tablets within forty-eight hours of receiving an order. The less expensive generic drugs already purchased by the government would be held by Bayer, to be used in case it was unable to fill an order.[130] When the U.S. government negotiated a price discount with Bayer on its purchase of Cipro, Bayer agreed to give Canada the same discount, which lowered the price to that charged by the generic manufacturer.[131]

In the United States, the secretary of health and human services negotiated a price reduction from the American retail price of four to five dollars per pill (and the $1.75 per pill that Bayer offered to the U.S. government) to just under a dollar per pill. The secretary had said he would consider going to Congress to seek a waiver of the patent and to ask Congress to authorize production of a generic medication if Bayer did not lower its price.[132] Thus, unlike Canada, the United States did not violate the patent. However, a threat was used to lower the price.

Prior to reaching the agreement with Bayer, the secretary publicly stated that the generic alternatives to Cipro, doxycycline and penicillin, had been found to be just as effective as Cipro in treating the strain of anthrax that was the threat in the United States. Doxycycline would cost one-tenth the price of Cipro, according to a generic manufacturer.[133] Ten days later, the Center for Disease Control declared doxycycline to be "the drug of choice" to treat the anthrax strain found in the mail attacks, because it destroys a smaller spectrum of bacteria and has fewer side effects.[134] The Canadian government created a stockpile of forty-seven thousand doses of doxycycline.[135]

Meanwhile, in Geneva...

While negotiations with Bayer were proceeding in North America, trade negotiators in Geneva were preparing for the WTO ministerial meeting that would take place in Doha, Qatar, from November 9 to 13. In the words of a trade negotiator from Brazil, the Canadian and American moves had provoked "a lot of talk in the corridors." One trade delegate said there was considerable anger that a double standard was at work. A group of developing countries began pushing harder for a waiver to allow them to circumvent patents to protect public health.[136]

In a series of prior meetings at the WTO, a group of thirty-eight African nations led by Zimbabwe had pushed for greater leeway under TRIPS. Developed countries, led by the United States and Switzerland, had resisted, arguing that TRIPS already ensured an adequate supply of drugs in case of a health crisis. The United States later offered to extend by ten years the deadline for African nations to comply with TRIPS. In the run-up to the Doha meeting, two competing visions emerged. One approach, backed by the United States, proposed to acknowledge a right "to take measures necessary to address public health crises, in particular to secure affordable access to medicines." Under this proposal TRIPS would take precedence. The concept backed by developing countries reversed the priority, stating that "nothing in TRIPS shall prevent members from taking measures to protect public health."[137] Going into the Doha meeting, the director general of the WTO, Mike Moore, declared that "this could well be the deal-breaker at this conference."[138]

Progress at Doha

At Doha, Brazil and India used their combined leverage in the WTO to champion the cause of creating a public health exception to the patent rules. By the fourth day of the ministerial meeting, the negotiators had reached a tentative agreement stating that TRIPS "shall be interpreted and implemented in a manner supportive of WTO members' rights to protect public health and in particular to ensure access to medicines for all." However, while developing countries were insisting on the word "shall," some developed countries were insisting on the weaker "can and should."[139] They finally agreed to a declaration that TRIPS "does not and should not prevent Members from taking measure to protect public health . . . and, in particular, to promote access to medicines for all."[140]

The Doha Declaration provides further that WTO members have "the right to grant compulsory licences and the freedom to determine the grounds upon which such licences are granted." It also declares that members have "the right to determine what constitutes a national emergency or other circumstances of extreme urgency, it being understood that public health crises, including those relating to HIV/AIDS, tuberculosis, malaria and other epidemics, can represent a national emergency or other circumstances of extreme urgency." This definition permits "extreme urgency" to be interpreted according to the nature of the disease rather than the number of infections. This means that even countries with low infection rates for AIDS—like Brazil, with a rate of 0.47 percent—will clearly be able to avail themselves of the Doha Declaration to acquire cheaper medicine through compulsory licenses. The issue of compulsory licensing in third countries, which would allow countries with no pharmaceutical industry to import generic drugs, was deferred for one year.[141]

Multinational pharmaceutical companies were strongly opposed to the Doha Declaration. A lobbyist for the International Federation of Pharmaceutical Manufacturers Associations described it as "a defeat for drug companies doing research in AIDS, tuberculosis and the like."[142] Pharmaceutical companies argue that the actions allowed by the Doha Declaration increase the risks of investing in research for AIDS, tuberculosis and malaria.

Instead, they should acknowledge the economic reasons why governments must intervene to develop vaccines for such diseases. If a successful vaccine is developed, the disease will disappear, and so will the profits from the patented drug that treats it. If there were fortunes to be made in third-world disease eradication, we should have seen greater advances by now. The industry developed AIDS drugs to serve the developed-country markets. They still serve those markets primarily—hence all the fuss. The industry's argument would have greater force were patent interventions to occur frequently, particularly in developed countries. But they do not; despite the events surrounding anthrax and AIDS, governments have not invoked "national emergency" to issue compulsory licenses for any other drugs that save lives in large numbers (such as the drugs for lowering blood cholesterol level).

Company decisions to develop expensive new drugs should not be affected by the Doha agreement. Expensive drugs are beyond the reach of potential users in developing countries. As long as the generic drugs sold in developing countries do not make their way back to the developed countries, their patents in the developed world are secure.

The Effect of the Doha Agreement on TRIPS

Under existing rules, a member may issue a compulsory license to the government or third parties to produce drugs without the authorization of the patent holder if prior efforts have failed to obtain authorization on reasonable commercial terms. However, this negotiation requirement may be waived in cases of national emergency, extreme urgency, or noncommercial public use. The license to a generic manufacturer to use the patent must be predominantly to supply the domestic market. The patent holder must be paid adequate remuneration, based on the economic value of the license.

TRIPS does not define "national emergency," "extreme urgency," or "commercial use." The Doha Declaration, which permits "extreme urgency" to be interpreted according to the nature of the disease rather than the number of infections, paves the way for compulsory licenses. However, a situation like the anthrax outbreak in the United States is unlikely to be considered an epidemic, due to the paucity of cases. Nevertheless, the anthrax outbreak could qualify under the TRIPS security exception if it proves to be a case of bioterrorism.

At Doha, as noted, the issue of allowing countries to import generic copies of patented drugs was deferred for one year. TRIPS lets patent holders prevent third parties from making, using, selling or importing their product without consent; this clearly prohibits imports of non-authorized generic copies of patented medicines. However, under a system of international exhaustion of patents, the patent owner cannot prevent the importation of his own product from a foreign country once it has been sold there. The Doha Declaration clarifies that each WTO member is free to determine its own regime for exhaustion of patent rights, which raises the risk that patented drugs sold cheaply in a developing country could be imported to a developed country market. This could threaten differential-pricing strategies used by pharmaceutical companies, particularly in developed countries. Allowing unrestricted imports of unauthorized generic copies could pose an even greater risk, which is why the issue was deferred.

NOTES

1. "Africans End 'Uncertainty' in AIDS Fight," Reuters, April 28, 2001.

2. Lawrence K. Altman, M.D., "The AIDS Questions That Linger," *New York Times*, January 30, 2001.

3. "Million New Cases of HIV/AIDS This Year, WHO Says," *Globe and Mail*, November 24, 2000.

4. Barbara Crossette, "Gore Presides over Security Council Debate on AIDS," *New York Times*, January 11, 2000.

5. See Elisabeth Rosenthal, "Scientists Warn of Inaction as AIDS Spreads in China," *New York Times*, August 2, 2000; Jennifer Mena, "AIDS Now a Migrant to Mexico," *Los Angeles Times*, September 15, 2000. The adult infection rate in South Africa climbed from 4 percent in 1993 to 20 percent in 2000. See "Focus on AIDS Epidemic, Mandela Says," *New York Times*, July 15, 2000. As of 2000, Guyana, the Bahamas and Haiti all had infection rates in the same range as South Africa's 1993 rate. See UNAIDS, Table of country-specific HIV/AIDS estimates and data, August 29, 2000.

6. Donald G. McNeil Jr., "AIDS Stalking Africa's Struggling Economies," *New York Times*, November 15, 1998.

7. Norimitsu Onishi, "AIDS Cuts Swath through Africa's Teachers," *New York Times*, August 14, 2000.

8. McNeil, "AIDS Stalking."

9. Lawrence Altman, "Another Approach to AIDS in Africa," *New York Times*, July 16, 2000.

10. Donald G. McNeil Jr., "Writing the Bill for Global AIDS," *New York Times*, July 2, 2000.

11. Paul Knox, "Fight against AIDS Gains Strong New Voices: Africa Needs Easier Access to Medication to Help Cut Deadly Toll, Experts Say," *Globe and Mail*, January 27, 2001.

12. See *Canada—Patent Protection of Pharmaceutical Products, Report of the Panel*, WT/DS114/R (2000), available at http://www.wto.org.

13. Organization for Economic Cooperation and Development, *OECD Health Data, 1998: A Comparative Analysis of 29 Countries* (Paris: Organization for Economic Cooperation and Development [hereafter OECD], 1998) available at http://www.oecd.org.

14. *Savings to Canada's Health Care System* (Ottawa: Canadian Drug Manufacturer's Association, January 1997).

15. World Health Organization, *Status of Drug Regulation and Drug Quality Assurance in WHO African Region and Selected Countries* (Geneva: World Health Organization [hereafter WHO], 1999).

16. National Economic Research Associates (NERA), *Policy Relating to Generic Medicines in the OECD: Final Report for the European Commission* (Brussels: December 20, 1998), 105.

17. Donald G. McNeil Jr., "Selling Cheap 'Generic' Drugs, India's Copycats Irk Industry," *New York Times*, December 1, 2000.

18. Donald G. McNeil Jr., "Companies to Cut Cost of AIDS Drugs for Poor Nations," *New York Times*, May 12, 2000.

19. Joseph Kahn, "US Offers Africa Billions to Fight AIDS," *New York Times*, July 19, 2000.

20. Barbara Crossette, "Millennium Summit Ends with Call for Fundamental Values," *New York Times*, September 8, 2000.

21. Agreement on Trade-Related Aspects of Intellectual Property Rights, April 15, 1994, Final Act Embodying the Results of the Uruguay Round of Multilateral Trade Negotiations, *Legal Instruments—Results of the Uruguay Round*, annex 1C, vol. 31, 33 ILM 1197 (1994) [hereafter TRIPS].

22. See http://www.phrma.org, visited September 28, 2000.

23. Kim Roller, "What Will Drive Pharmacy Sales into the New Millennium?" *Drug Store News*, January 11, 1999, available in Lexis-Nexis.

24. Kevin W. McCabe, "The January 1999 Review of Article 27 of TRIPS: Diverging Views of Developed and Developing Countries toward the Patentability of Biotechnology, *Journal of Intellectual Property* 6 (1998), 49.

25. McNeil, "Companies." See also "The Bill & Melinda Gates Foundation, Merck & Co., Inc. and the Republic of Botswana Launch New HIV Initiative," Merck & Co. press release, July 10, 2000, available at http://www.merck.com.

26. UNAIDS.

27. Paul Busharizi, "Uganda Agrees Deal to Cut Anti-AIDS Drug Prices," Reuters, December 2, 2000.

28. McNeil, "Companies." Only 10 percent of the 1999 sales of Combivir came from outside the United States and Europe. A Merrill Lynch analyst calculated that price cuts to poor countries would not have a significant financial effect. Ibid.

29. Altman, "Another Approach."

30. Sheryl Gay Stolberg, "AIDS Groups Revive a Fight, and Themselves," *New York Times*, March 20, 2001.

31. Rachel Swarns, "AIDS Drug Battle Deepens in Africa," *New York Times*, March 8, 2001.

32. Melody Petersen and Donald McNeil Jr., "Maker Yielding Patent in Africa for AIDS Drug," *New York Times*, March 15, 2001.

33. Stolberg, "AIDS Groups Revive."

34. "South African AIDS Drug Case Postponed," *Globe and Mail*, March 6, 2001.

35. Donald G. McNeil Jr., "Indian Company Offers to Supply AIDS Drugs at Low Cost in Africa," *New York Times*, February 7, 2001.

36. McNeil, "Writing the Bill."

37. McNeil, "Companies." For five years, the USTR has vigorously pursued intellectual property rights under TRIPS, often with favorable results. But Executive Order 13155 (May 8, 2000) stated that the United States will not use section 301 of the Trade Act to seek changes in the intellectual-property laws or policies of sub-Saharan African countries that "promote access" to HIV/AIDS drugs and "provide adequate and effective IP protection consistent with TRIPS." TRIPS allows members to "adopt measures necessary to protect public health." "Trade and Intellectual Property: The 'Essential Medicines' Dilemma," seminar, Tuesday, July 25, 2000, Center for Strategic and International Studies, Washington, D.C..

38. Rachel Swarns, "AIDS Drug Battle Deepens in Africa," *New York Times*, March 8, 2001.

39. Joseph Kahn, "US Offers Africa Billions to Fight AIDS," *New York Times*, July 19, 2000.

40. Rachel L Swarns, "Loans to Buy AIDS Drugs Are Rejected by Africans," *New York Times*, August 22, 2000.

41 Melody Petersen and Donald McNeil Jr., "Maker Yielding Patent in Africa for AIDS Drug," *New York Times*, March 15, 2001.

42. On the World Wide Web at http://www.wipo.org.

43. Edwin Mansfield, *Intellectual Property Protection, Foreign Direct Investment, and Technology Transfer*, International Finance Corporation Discussion Paper 19 (Washington, D.C.: The World Bank, 1994).

44. TRIPS article 1.

45. TRIPS article 64.

46. Marakesh Declaration of 15 April 1994, paragraph 6, Final Act Embodying the Results of the Uruguay Round of Multilateral Trade Negotiations, *Legal Instruments—Results of the Uruguay Round*, vol. I, 33 ILM 1125 (1994).

47. TRIPS article 65.

48. TRIPS article 66. There are no WTO definitions of "developed" and "developing" countries. Members can announce for themselves whether they are developing countries. However, this does not automatically provide rights. Other members can challenge the announcement, and this has sometimes happened in the area of intellectual property. This challenge can then lead to negotiations to clarify the position. The status of countries that negotiated to join the WTO after 1995 depends on the terms agreed in the accessions negotiations. The WTO

recognizes as "least-developed countries" those countries that have been desig-
nated as such by the UN. There are currently forty-eight least-developed countries on the UN list, twenty-nine of which to date have become WTO members.
These are: Angola, Bangladesh, Benin, Burkina Faso, Burundi, the Central Afri-
can Republic, Chad, Congo, the Democratic Republic of the, Djibouti, Gambia,
Guinea, Guinea Bissau, Haiti, Lesotho, Madagascar, Malawi, Maldives, Mali,
Mauritania, Mozambique, Myanmar, Niger, Rwanda, Sierra Leone, Solomon
Islands, Tanzania, Togo, Uganda and Zambia. Seven additional least-developed
countries are in the process of accession to the WTO. They are: Cambodia, Cape
Verde, Laos, Nepal, Samoa, Sudan and Vanuatu. See WTO, "Who Are the
Developing Countries?" available on the World Wide Web at www.wto.org/
english/tratop_e/devel_e/d1who_e.htm.

49. See "Declaration on the TRIPS Agreement and Public Health," available
at http://www.wto.org.

50. *Canada—Patent Protection of Pharmaceutical Products.*

51. TRIPS article 2.

52. Rosemary Sweeney, "Comment: The US Push for Worldwide Patent Protection for Drugs Meets the AIDS Crisis in Thailand: A Devastating Collision,"
Pacific Rim Law and Policy Journal 9 (2000), 445. See also "Blood and Gore: Office
of the US Trade Representative Goes Too Far in Promoting Interests of US Drug
Companies Abroad," *The Nation,* July 19, 1999, 16.

53. See "Declaration on the TRIPS Agreement and Public Health."

54. Claude E. Barfield and Mark A. Groomridge, "Parallel Trade in the Pharmaceutical Industry: Implications for Innovation, Consumer Welfare and Health
Policy," *Fordham Intellectual Property, Media & Entertainment Law Journal* 10 (1999),
185.

55. See "Declaration on the TRIPS Agreement and Public Health."

56. TRIPS article 27(1).

57. *Canada—Patent Protection of Pharmaceutical Products.*

58. TRIPS article 27(2).

59. TRIPS article 33.

60. TRIPS article 28(1)(a).

61. TRIPS article 28(2).

62. TRIPS article 29(1).

63. TRIPS article 29(2).

64. TRIPS articles 41–60.

65. TRIPS article 1.

66. TRIPS article 7.

67. TRIPS article 8(1).

68. TRIPS article 73.

69. WTO, *Guide to GATT Law and Practice,* 6th ed. (Geneva: Bernan Press,
1995), vol. 1, 600.

70. Ibid., 609.

71. *Canada—Patent Protection of Pharmaceutical Products.*

72. See "Declaration on the TRIPS Agreement and Public Health."

73. Ron Hirshhorn, *Foreign Direct Investment and Market Framework Policies:
Reducing Frictions in APEC Policies on Competition and Intellectual Property,* Industry
Canada Discussion Paper 4 (Ottawa: October 1996).

74. TRIPS article 9(2).

75. TRIPS article 9(1).

76. Berne Convention for the Protection of Literary and Artistic Works, available at www.wipo.org [hereafter Berne Convention].

77. Berne Convention, article 2.

78. Berne Convention, article 3.

79. Berne Convention, article 5.

80. TRIPS article 10.

81. TRIPS articles 13, 14(5).

82. TRIPS articles 11, 14(4).

83. TRIPS article 14(1).

84. TRIPS articles 14(3), (5).

85. TRIPS article 15.

86. TRIPS article 15.

87. TRIPS article 16.

88. TRIPS article 17.

89. TRIPS article 18.

90. TRIPS article 19.

91. TRIPS article 21.

92. TRIPS article 22.

93. TRIPS article 23.

94. TRIPS articles 25–26 and 35–39.

95. TRIPS article 40.

96. TRIPS article 41.

97. TRIPS articles 42–49.

98. TRIPS article 61.

99. Transparency Mexico commissioned the poll of 13,790 heads of household. The average bribe cost twelve dollars (110 Mexican pesos). See James F. Smith, "Mexico's Harsh Bribery Reality," *Los Angeles Times*, November 1, 2001.

100. NAFTA article 1701.

101. NAFTA article 1703.

102. NAFTA article 1705.

103. NAFTA article 1708.

104. NAFTA article 1709.

105. NAFTA article 1711.

106. NAFTA article 1713.

107. NAFTA article 1714.

108. NAFTA article 1715.

109. NAFTA article 1717.

110. NAFTA article 1718.

111. NAFTA article 1701.

112. NAFTA articles 1705(2) and 1796(1).

113. NAFTA article 1709(8).

114. NAFTA article 1718.

115. NAFTA article 1705(2).

116. NAFTA article 1709(5).

117. NAFTA article 1139 (g).

118. NAFTA article 1110(7).

119. See *Canada—Term of Patent Protection, Report of the Panel*, WT/DS170/R (2000) available at http://www.wto.org.

120. Sabra Chartrand, "Patents: In Health Emergencies, Brazil Allows the Copying of Drugs," *New York Times*, February 19, 2001.

121. Tina Rosenberg, "Look at Brazil," *New York Times Magazine*, January 28, 2001.

122. Shasta Darlington, "Brazil Latest AIDS Drug Battlefield," *Globe and Mail*, August 24, 2001.

123. Reuters, "Brazil Plans to Ignore Patent on AIDS Drug," *Globe and Mail*, August 23, 2001. In March of 2001, Merck & Co. agreed to cut prices in Brazil on two AIDS drugs by 65 and 59 percent, respectively.

124. Melody Petersen, "Roche Asks for Meeting with Brazil Health Minister," *New York Times*, August 24, 2001.

125. Michael Shields, "Drug Maker, Brazil Near Accord on AIDS Drug Price," Reuters, August 23, 2001.

126. Jennifer L. Rich, "Roche Reaches Accord on Drug with Brazil," *New York Times*, August 31, 2001.

127. Shawn McCarthy and Leonard Zehr, "Ottawa Weighs Paying Bayer after Ignoring Cipro Patent," *Globe and Mail*, October 20, 2001.

128. Richard Gold, "My Body, Your Patent," *Globe and Mail*, October 29, 2001, A13.

129. Jeff Gray, "MPs Grill Rock over Drug Fumbling," *Globe and Mail*, October 25, 2001.

130. Jeff Gray, "Opposition Demands Rock's Resignation," *Globe and Mail*, October 23, 2001.

131. Gray, "MPs Grill Rock."

132. "US Deal Expected on Cipro Prices," Associated Press, October 24, 2001.

133. Robert Pear, "Government Talks with Drug Companies about Buying Anthrax Antibiotics," *New York Times*, October 20, 2001.

134. Shawn McCarthy and André Picard, "Cipro Loses Title of Top Anthrax Drug," *Globe and Mail*, October 30, 2001, at A8.

135. Shawn McCarthy, "Ottawa Adds Doxycycline to Stockpile of Anti-Anthrax Drugs," *Globe and Mail*, October 31, 2001, A4.

136. Elizabeth Olson, "Drug Issue Casts a Shadow on Trade Talks," *New York Times*, November 2, 2001.

137. Ibid.

138. Steven Chase, "Drug Patent Skirmish Threatens WTO Talks," *Globe and Mail*, November 9, 2001, B6.

139. Steve Schifferes, "Poor Countries Want Cheaper Generic Drugs to Save Lives," BBC News Online, November 12, 2001.

140. See *Declaration on the TRIPS Agreement and Public Health,* available at http://www.wto.org, and "WTO Agrees to Change Rules on Generic Drugs Trade: Pact Would Allow Third World Nations to Make or Buy Cheaper Versions of Medications," AP Wire Report, November 13, 2001.

141. Steven Chase, "Drug Access Plan Fuels Optimism at WTO Talks," *Globe and Mail*, November 13, 2001, B1. A recent study found that only 22 percent of the 795 patents theoretically available in Africa's fifty-three countries for the

fifteen recognized AIDS drugs have been awarded. In most cases, this was because the companies that own the patents had not bothered to apply. Donald McNeil Jr., "Patents or Poverty? A New Debate over Poor AIDS Care in Africa," *New York Times*, November 5, 2001.

142. Joseph Khan, "Trade Deal Near for Broad Access to Cut-Rate Drugs," *New York Times*, November 13, 2001.

Chapter 5

Foreign Investment Agreements

OPENING CASE: METALCLAD IN MEXICO

Metalclad, a U.S. company, purchased COTERIN, a Mexican company, on September 10, 1993, together with its hazardous-waste landfill site in Guadalcazar, San Luis Potosi, and associated permits. COTERIN had applied to the municipal government for a construction permit in 1991 but had been refused. Metalclad had made the purchase subject to the condition that either a municipal permit was issued to COTERIN or COTERIN received a definitive judgment from the Mexican courts that a municipal permit was not required. Metalclad completed the purchase without either of these conditions being met, relying instead on assurances from Mexican federal officials that COTERIN had all the authorizations required to undertake the landfill project.

COTERIN's permits included the following:

1. A 1990 federal government authorization to construct and operate a transfer station for hazardous waste;

2. A January 1993 federal permit to construct a hazardous-waste landfill, issued by the National Ecological Institute (INE);

3. A May 1993 state land-use permit to construct the landfill, subject to required specifications of relevant authorities, that specifically did not authorize works, constructions or business activities;

4. An August 1993 federal permit for the operation of the landfill, issued by INE.

Metalclad was told by the president of INE and the director general of the federal environmental secretariat (SEDUE) that these were all the permits that were necessary. In addition to these permits, Metalclad believed it had obtained the state governor's support for the project in a meeting in June 1993. The director general of SEDUE also told Metalclad that the federal government was responsible for obtaining support for the project in the state and the local community.

Shortly after Metalclad purchased COTERIN, the governor began a public campaign to denounce and prevent the operation of the landfill. After negotiations with the governor, in which Metalclad believed it had again secured his support, Metalclad began construction in May 1994. During construction, federal and state officials inspected the site, and Metalclad provided them with written progress reports. However, in October 1994, construction was halted abruptly when the municipality of Guadalcazar ordered building to cease due to the absence of a municipal construction permit. In November 1994, after federal officials declared that Metalclad had all the authority necessary to build and operate the landfill, it resumed construction, though applied for the municipal permit in order to facilitate relations with the municipality.

In January 1995, INE granted an additional permit to build the hazardous-waste cell and structures, including the administrative building and a laboratory. In the spring of 1995, an independent university study and a federal audit of the site both confirmed that the site was geographically suitable for a hazardous-waste landfill.

Metalclad Is Prevented from Operating the Landfill

In March 1995, Metalclad completed construction of the landfill and held an inauguration ceremony, which was attended by dignitaries from the United States and from Mexico's federal, state and local governments. However, the inauguration was disrupted by demonstrators who blocked the entry and exit of buses carrying guests and workers. Metalclad would charge that the state and local governments helped to organize the demonstration and that state troopers helped to block traffic. Thereafter, Metalclad was prevented from operating the landfill, despite efforts to negotiate a solution.

In November of 1995, Metalclad signed an agreement with federal environmental agencies under which the company agreed to follow an action plan, including the setting aside of thirty-four hectares of its property to conserve local species. The agreement allowed Metalclad to operate the landfill for a renewable five-year term. However, the state governor immediately denounced the agreement. In December 1995 the municipality denied Metalclad's application for a construction permit.

The municipality did not notify Metalclad of the Town Council meeting at which the permit application was discussed and rejected, nor did it allow Metalclad to participate in the process. Moreover, there was no evidence that the municipality had ever required or issued a municipal construction permit before or even had an administrative process in place to do so. In January 1996, the municipality launched legal challenges to Metalclad's agreement with the federal agencies, litigation that ended unsuccessfully in May 1999.

From May to December of 1996, Metalclad negotiated with the state government, without success. On January 2, 1997, Metalclad began legal proceedings against the government of Mexico under chapter 11 of NAFTA. On September 23, 1997, three days before the end of his term, the governor issued an ecological decree declaring a natural area for the protection of rare cactus, which included Metalclad's landfill, permanently preventing the operation of the landfill. Metalclad added the ecological decree to its NAFTA claim.

The Decision of the Chapter 11 Tribunal

The three-person tribunal held that the federal government was responsible for the actions of the state and local governments and that those actions violated NAFTA article 1105(1), which required that investors be given treatment that was fair and equitable and in accordance with international law. Mexico had failed to ensure the transparency required by NAFTA, in that there had been no clear rule as to whether or not a municipal construction permit was required. The municipality had improperly required and denied a construction permit after construction was virtually complete and the federal permit had been granted. Its reasons for denying the construction permit had had nothing to do with any defects in construction and it had given Metalclad no opportunity to participate in the decision. Finally, NAFTA article 1114, which allows members to ensure that investment activity is undertaken in an environmentally sensitive matter, could not affect the outcome, because the federal permits and agreements had demonstrated that Mexico was satisfied that the project was consistent with its environmental concerns.

The tribunal held further that under NAFTA article 1110, Mexico had taken a measure tantamount to expropriation by acquiescing in the denial of the municipal permit when the federal government had exclusive authority for siting and permitting a hazardous-waste landfill. The tribunal defined expropriation under article 1110 to include "not only open, deliberate and acknowledged takings of property . . . but also covert or incidental interference with the use of property which has the effect of depriving the owner, in whole or in significant part, of the use or reasonably-to-be-expected economic benefit of property even if not necessarily to the obvious benefit of the host State."[1] The tribunal identified the governor's ecological decree as a further ground for a finding of expropriation, because it had had the effect of barring forever the operation of the landfill.

Having found that Mexico had indirectly expropriated Metalclad's investment without providing compensation, the tribunal held that Metalclad had lost 100 percent of its investment. In its calculation of the compensation payable under NAFTA article 1110(2), the tribunal decided that fair market value should be determined by reference to Metalclad's actual investment, less the cost of site remediation that the Mexican government would incur. In addition, the tribunal awarded Metalclad interest at 6 percent per year, compounded annually, from the date on which the municipality had wrongly denied Metalclad's application for a construction permit. Mexico was ordered to pay U.S.$16,685,000, plus 6 percent interest compounded monthly until the compensation was paid.

The Decision of the Supreme Court of British Columbia

Because the arbitration had taken place in Vancouver, British Columbia, Mexico appealed the tribunal's decision in the Supreme Court of British Columbia (BCSC). The Court's authority to interfere in the decision of an arbitration tribunal was limited by legislation that provided that an award could be set aside only if:

1. The dispute does not fall within the terms of the submission to arbitration; or
2. The composition of the tribunal or the arbitration procedure does not accord with the agreement of the parties; or
3. The award is in conflict with public policy.

Unless the tribunal's award contained decisions beyond the scope of the submission to arbitration, the Court had no jurisdiction to set it aside, even if it could be shown that the tribunal had erred in interpreting the agreement. The issue that Metalclad had posed in its submission to arbitration was whether Mexico had breached its obligations under NAFTA chapter 11 "guaranteeing national treatment; most-favored-nation treatment; minimum treatment in accordance with international law, fair and equitable treatment, and full protection and security, prohibiting performance requirements; and depriving [Metalclad] of its investment through [Mexico's] actions that directly and indirectly resulted in, and were tantamount to, expropriation of that investment without due process and full compensation."[2]

The Court observed that the right of a foreign investor to submit a claim under chapter 11 was limited to violations of chapter 11, section A (articles 1101 to 1114), and two articles contained in NAFTA chapter 15. Article 105 requires that investors be treated in accordance with international law, which the court interpreted to mean customary international law (developed by the common practices of countries) as opposed to conventional international law (which comprises treaties). The Court held that the tribunal had based its decision regarding the actions of the municipality on a matter beyond the scope of the submission to arbitration—that is, there are no transparency obligations contained in chapter 11, and the concept of "transparency" is not part of customary international law. The Court ruled that in relying on the concept of transparency to conclude that there had been an indirect expropriation within the meaning of article 1110, the tribunal had yet again decided a matter beyond the scope of the submission to arbitration.

However, the Court found that Metalclad's claim based on the ecological decree did fall within the scope of the agreement to arbitrate. While in the tribunal's definition of expropriation under article 1110 was extremely broad, the Court was not entitled to interfere with a question of law that fell within the scope of Metalclad's submission, and the tribunal's conclusion that this constituted an act tantamount to expropriation was not patently unreasonable. The Court therefore declined to set aside the award as it related to the ecological decree. However, because the ecological decree occurred later than the refusal to issue the municipal permit, the Court reduced the award of interest by calculating the interest from the date of the ecological decree (September 20, 1997) rather than the date the municipality refused to issue a permit (December 5, 1995). Because Mexico had succeeded in its legal arguments regarding transparency and in reducing the interest payable, the court required Mexico to pay only 75 percent of the legal costs Metalclad had incurred in the appeal.

Mexico had also argued that the award was in conflict with public policy, because it included the reimbursement of a bribe. However, the Court was not persuaded that Mexico had proved any corruption in which Metalclad had participated.

Following the Court's decision, Metalclad president Grant Keseler declared that the ruling on the transparency issue violated the spirit of NAFTA and would discourage foreign investors fearful of secretive and arbitrary government actions. He said that his company had liquidated all of its Mexican holdings and would not invest in Mexico again until the legal protections for foreign investors improved. The company had once had the largest waste-collection operation in Mexico, with sites in eleven states. The Mexican government, for its part, was pleased that the judge had set limitations on the rights of private investors under NAFTA and hoped the case would set a precedent for future chapter 11 cases.[3] Both sides later agreed not to appeal the Court's decision; Metalclad accepted a Mexican offer to pay U.S.$15, 626,260 plus daily interest of $2,559 after June 1, until the settlement was paid in full.[4] However, at the beginning of October 2001 Metalclad began legal action against the Mexican government, because the payment had not been made. The Mexican government paid the company by check on October 26, 2001, and received the deed to the property from Metalclad. Mexico issued a statement saying the government "honors its international obligations, even when it does not agree with the findings of the international tribunal nor with the way the tribunal works."[5]

This case demonstrates the operation of NAFTA provisions on expropriation and dispute settlement. It also confirms the responsibility of federal governments for the actions of states. The case also clarifies the relationship between environmental law and foreign investors' rights. Finally, it provides a good example of the potential impact of legal protection for foreign investors on investment decisions.

INTRODUCTION

The globalization of production and markets is closely linked to the liberalization of international trade and investment laws. Foreign direct investment (FDI) and international trade, in the form of exports of goods or services, represent different strategies by which firms might enter foreign markets. The choice between the entry strategies of FDI and exports is influenced by such factors as market size, geographic location, the degree to which a firm has penetrated the market and the legal restrictions that are in place. In the case of services, FDI may be the only viable strategy if the firm needs a commercial presence in order to sell the service. However, FDI and international trade can also be complementary strategies, in that FDI often implies importing inputs and exporting final products in manufacturing industries. In recent years, as the majority of the world's economies have adopted free market reforms, international trade liberalization agreements have been accompanied by foreign-investment agreements. Some agreements, notably NAFTA, have been negotiated that contain both trade and FDI obligations.

This chapter considers the relationship between foreign-investment agreements and global business strategy. The chapter first examines the growth of FDI flows in the global economy in recent years. Second, it examines the relationship between international trade, FDI and business strategy. Third, the chapter reviews the economic goals that underlie the foreign-investment policies reflected in bilateral foreign-investment agreements and NAFTA. Fourth, the chapter provides a detailed review of the investment provisions of NAFTA, together with recent interpretations by arbitration panels and the Free Trade Commission. Fifth, it compares the progress made multilaterally under the Organization for Economic Cooperation and Development (OECD) and WTO. Finally, the chapter considers the strategic goals served by FDI decisions. While portfolio investment serves important business goals, by providing a source of capital, this chapter will focus on FDI, because legal issues and strategic business goals with respect to FDI and portfolio investment differ greatly.

The closing case examines the process of foreign-investment liberalization that has occurred in Mexico over the past three decades.

THE GROWTH OF FDI FLOWS IN THE GLOBAL ECONOMY

FDI flows have increased dramatically since the 1980s, reflecting the globalization of business and increasing integration of the global economy. FDI may be defined as "capital invested for the purpose of acquiring a lasting interest in an enterprise and of exerting a degree of influence on that enterprise's operation."[6] The degree of control exerted by the investor is what distinguishes FDI from portfolio investment; ownership of 10 percent of the shares of a corporation is used as the benchmark for classifying an investment as FDI. The degree of influence a given percentage of shares provides will depend on the size of the company. A controlling interest may require a majority of shares in a small company or a substantial minority in a large company. "Portfolio investment" refers to investments that do not result in a controlling interest, such as stocks (less than 10 percent of the outstanding shares of the company), bonds and other financial instruments. More than three-quarters of global FDI flows occur between the OECD countries; they have grown from less than fifty billion U.S. dollars in the early 1980s to over $250 billion in the late 1990s. Most of these flows occur between developed countries, which excludes Mexico and Turkey, even though they are OECD members.

There are three major reasons for this growth in FDI. First, many governments have removed barriers to foreign investment, both unilaterally and through such regional initiatives as the European Union and NAFTA. Second, many governments have decreased government involvement in their economies, through deregulation, privatization and demonopolization. Finally, FDI has played a major role in the global business strategies of large corporations who wish to reduce costs by globalizing production and expanding into new or growing markets. The growth of international cooperation between firms, such as licensing agreements, joint ventures, strategic alliances, mergers and acquisitions, has further increased FDI flows.

For thirty years, international trade has grown faster than GDP. FDI flows have grown twice as fast as trade since 1983. The foregoing factors have also led to increases in the collective developing-countries share of world trade and FDI. From 1983 to 1993, the total share of developing countries of world trade increased from 13.1 percent to 23.8 percent, while their share of FDI grew from 24.2 percent to 39.4 percent.[7] However, inflows of FDI are unevenly distributed among developing countries, most of it going to China, Southeast Asia (Malaysia, Indonesia and Thailand) and Latin America (Mexico, Brazil and Argentina).[8]

TRADE, FOREIGN INVESTMENT AND BUSINESS STRATEGY

A prior strategy of exports establishing a foothold in a foreign market later facilitates FDI by familiarizing the firm with the business environment and achieving sales volumes large enough to justify the long-term commitment that FDI implies. An export strategy involves less financial commitment to the market and lets the firm test the waters to see whether its product will succeed in that particular market. However, FDI can achieve strategic goals that a simple export strategy does not, such as adapting the product to the needs of the local market, incorporating local inputs and gathering more sophisticated market intelligence.

An increase in FDI does not necessarily mean a reduction in international trade flows. FDI can stimulate imports of capital goods and inputs that are not produced locally and that a firm needs for its production process in its foreign subsidiary. FDI can also stimulate exports from the subsidiary and from local firms, initially through local inputs to the subsidiary. Open trade policies encourage FDI by facilitating these imports of inputs and exports of finished products. In this sense, FDI and international trade are complementary strategies.

In the middle of the twentieth century, many countries, such as Mexico and Brazil, adopted "import substitution" policies that promoted industrialization by imposing trade barriers. Thus, if a foreign company wished to sell its product in Mexico, it had to invest in the establishment of a plant in Mexico to serve the market. However, nationalist foreign-investment policies placed limits on the percentage of companies foreigners could own and imposed performance requirements on foreign companies, such as the use of local inputs and the export of a certain percentage of production. With the reduction of trade barriers in the 1980s and 1990s, such countries changed to an export-oriented policy. However, they still needed to attract foreign investment to provide the capital and technology needed to produce goods for export. Mexico, for example, encouraged foreign investment by opening up its economy to foreign ownership (in a new Foreign Investment Law)[9] and agreeing to rules to protect foreign investors, both in NAFTA chapter 11 and in a series of bilateral investment treaties (BITs).

An important link between international trade and investment relates to intrafirm trade. In industries with "globalized" production, components are imported from all over the world and assembled in various locations; the finished product is then exported to various markets. For example, Volkswagen's plant in Mexico imports many components and services from Germany, produces the "new" Volkswagen Beetle in Mexico, then exports the car to dealers around the world. Indeed, this car is only produced in Mexico. The trade that takes place between the international operations of such firms—intrafirm trade—substantially increases the volume of international trade in goods. It is estimated that about half of all trade takes place between firms that are related through equity holdings.[10] These equity relationships can take many forms. For example, the relationship may be a parent company that owns 100 percent of the shares of a foreign subsidiary; two parent companies that each own 50 percent of a joint venture company; or international strategic alliance members that own minority stakes in each other.

When a country simultaneously reduces or eliminates barriers to trade and investment, it becomes a more attractive location for the FDI than if it only lowers barriers to investment. Liberalizing both trade and investment laws allows the firm to choose its entry strategy on the basis of business rather than legal considerations. Trade and investment strategies are not always alternatives. Not all firms have sufficient capital to engage in FDI, and not all goods lend themselves to an export strategy (for example, where transportation costs are high). With respect to trade in services, as noted, FDI may be the only viable strategy where a local presence is required to sell the service. From the perspective of the firm, the ability to choose is thus very important.

An FDI strategy represents a greater commitment to the market than does exporting, both in terms of firm resources and the time frame involved. For this reason, investors seek more legal protections than do exporters. Fair treatment, national treatment, and the right to transfer funds in a convertible currency are important considerations for both foreign investors and exporters, but they become even more important when the stakes are raised by FDI. Foreign investors also require protection against expropriation.

NAFTA contains a more comprehensive set of provisions regulating the treatment of foreign investors than WTO, which has virtually none.[11] However, most WTO members have signed BITs that contain provisions similar to NAFTA, including with respect to expropriation.[12] Nevertheless, the minimum standard of treatment required by NAFTA is not always identical to that contained in the BITs—for example with respect to transparency.[13] Some BITs are based on the OECD Model Investment Treaty of 1987, while others are based on NAFTA chapter 11 model.[14] Both models provide protection against expropriation, but the type of property that is covered varies.

Governments enter into such agreements in order to attract FDI and its potential benefits to their national economies. FDI provides a means to transfer technology, management expertise and other firms' assets to the host country. It can also provide skilled jobs, export diversification, and stronger links with foreign markets. Through their relationships with local suppliers and competitors, foreign firms contribute to the development of local firms. Capital exporting countries benefit from the outflow of FDI, in that FDI provides a means for their firms to grow and expand into new markets, enhancing their international competitiveness.

THE NATURE OF FOREIGN-INVESTMENT TREATIES

International obligations regarding the treatment of foreign investors operate like those relating to international trade in that they impose limits on the governments that sign them. Investment treaties, whether independent bilateral agreements or parts of larger trade agreements, impose obligations on governments, not on investors.[15] However, as with trade agreements, as investment agreements progressively eliminate formal barriers to foreign investment, informal barriers become relatively more important.[16] As with nontariff barriers to trade, informal investment barriers are more difficult to overcome, and negotiations over their elimination are more complex.

Informal investment barriers include rules governing mergers and take-overs, research and development subsidies, international taxation laws, and the manner in which antitrust laws are applied.[17] Treaties to avoid double taxation, such as those in place between NAFTA countries, facilitate investment by clarifying the rules that apply and reducing withholding taxes. However, they also make it more difficult for firms to manipulate intrafirm transfer prices to reduce taxes, because the signatory governments share information as well.

Another potential barrier to investment concerns the laws to which firms are subject under international law. For example, the Helms-Burton Act of the United States sought to discourage foreign investment in Cuba by all firms, regardless of national origin. If a Canadian law sought to counter this by requiring Canadian firms to ignore the U.S. directive, which law would a Canadian firm with investments in Canada, Cuba and the United States follow? Such conflicts are generally not dealt with in investment treaties.[18]

As with trade negotiations, gaining sufficient political support for investment treaties requires gaining the support of influential sectors. For this reason, agreements like NAFTA contain reservations and exceptions that were necessary to secure the passage of the agreement.[19] Multinational firms generally are ahead of governments in expanding and integrating their operations internationally, and it is these firms that push governments to negotiate the removal of barriers to trade and investment. At the same time, however, these firms may seek rules of origin that give preferential treatment to goods produced regionally, as the North American automobile industry did in NAFTA to maintain an advantage over imported vehicles.[20] Thus, while they seek the removal of intraregional barriers to trade and investment, these firms may lobby for rules that increase interregional barriers. However, in highly competitive global industries, with high research and development costs and short product cycles, firms may need to obtain strategic market knowledge and technologies through "greenfield" investments, international acquisitions, joint ventures, and strategic and technological alliances.[21] It is therefore not surprising that the liberalization of foreign-investment regimes in a country is often followed by an increase in FDI, often in the form of mergers, joint ventures and acquisitions. These investments serve strategic purposes and help make firms more competitive.

In FDI policy as in trade policy, there exists a tension between firms seeking protection in their home markets, firms seeking the elimination of entry barriers in foreign markets, and firms seeking to eliminate barriers to equity investments in foreign firms that hold strategic technology. While it is the governments that negotiate and implement the rules, the rules are ultimately for the benefit of these firms, with their sometimes conflicting demands.

NAFTA, BILATERAL INVESTMENT TREATIES AND INVESTMENT POLICY

Bilateral investment treaties provide foreign investors with protections similar to that contained in NAFTA chapter 11. Perhaps due to the lack of any multilateral investment agreement under WTO or the OECD, the number of BITs has grown rapidly in recent years; today, a web of more than 1,300 BITs involves approximately 160 countries.[22]

Kenneth Vandevelde has analyzed BITs in terms of the degree to which they advance *economic nationalism* versus *economic liberalism*. The former theory espouses the regulation of foreign investment to ensure that it promotes national political objectives. The latter advocates the free movement of capital across borders, with governments allowing the market to determine the flow of international investment. Vandevelde argues that a truly liberal investment regime would conform to three principles: "investment neutrality, the principle that the state should not interfere with transfrontier investment flows; investment security, the principle that the state should protect private investment; and market facilitation, the principle that the state should facilitate the operation of the market by correcting market failures."[23] He concludes that the typical BIT, while it affirms liberal economic objectives and liberalizes foreign investment to a degree, is in fact principally driven by economic nationalism.

Investment neutrality requires free access and freedom from discrimination based on nationality. However, BITs subject access to local laws that may prevent the entry of personnel needed to operate the investment; regulate the outward flow of investment; and impose performance requirements on the investor. With respect to nondiscrimination, BITs allow exceptions to national treatment and MFN treatment; also, they protect only foreign investments, not domestic investors, further undermining the principle of neutrality.

BITs normally provide broad guarantees of investment security and require that direct or indirect expropriation be for a public purpose, non-discriminatory, in accordance with due process, and accompanied by prompt payment of adequate and effective compensation. They also guarantee the right of free transfer of investments in a convertible currency. Most importantly, these protections are enforced through binding arbitration between the investor and the host government, usually through the World Bank's International Center for the Settlement of Investment Disputes (ICSID). These investment-protection provisions reduce political risks of expropriation, currency controls and lack of effective legal recourse. All of these provisions are found in NAFTA chapter 11. However, it is important to point out that this protection is from government interference with investments, not from private interference. Commercial disputes between private parties are not covered; they must be settled in the domestic courts.

Market facilitation is not normally advanced in BITs. While some have transparency provisions that address the market failure represented by lack of information, most do not. Other market failures are not addressed. Rather, such matters are left to the discretion of the host government. It is important to note that lack of transparency can have a significant impact on foreign investors and that it is not covered in NAFTA chapter 11.[24] In this context, lack of transparency means that government officials make decisions that do not respect due process and that are based on factors other than published laws and evidence—for example, on the basis of corrupt practices.

The reasons why countries sign these agreements vary. Countries like Canada and the United States, which both import and export capital, want to attract FDI and seek protection for their investors in other countries. Capital-importing countries such as Mexico seek to attract foreign investors by lowering the perceived political risk. However, they maintain considerable discretion, which may be exercised poorly where there is political pressure, corruption or administrative incompetence.

Claims for compensation against governments under NAFTA chapter 11 have garnered considerable press coverage. Critics argue that the agreement gives foreign companies too much power to challenge government regulations. In 1997, such political opposition succeeded in derailing OECD negotiations to create a multilateral agreement on investment that could have superceded the plethora of existing BITs between countries that signed it. Plans to negotiate a similar agreement in WTO are also on hold. However, foreign investors already enjoy protection under BITs, and multilateral negotiations could simplify the existing regime by folding hundreds of separate agreements into a more accessible, single agreement.

With BITs, foreign investors enjoy protection, but sorting through the hundreds of agreements makes the identification of specific rules for specific situations more complex.

NAFTA CHAPTER 11

Chapter 11 of NAFTA serves a dual function. On the one hand, it is an agreement between countries defining the parameters of their treatment of foreign investors. On the other hand, it serves as an agreement between each country and its respective foreign investors regarding their treatment and modes of dispute settlement. However, in the latter respect it is not like a normal contract, because the terms of the agreement are determined without the participation of the investors, and the terms of the agreement can be renegotiated by NAFTA countries without investors' consent. However, as long as the countries do not change its provisions, chapter 11 sets out rules that each country must obey and arbitration procedures that can lead to the payment of damages to investors when the rules are broken.

Chapter 11 is not the only chapter that is relevant to foreign investors. However, other chapters—which apply specifically to government enterprises, monopolies, services, intellectual property and the temporary entry of business people—are covered in other chapters of this book.

NAFTA versus Non-NAFTA Firms

NAFTA, including chapter 11, applies to "persons" of NAFTA countries, which means natural persons (citizens or permanent residents of a NAFTA member) or enterprises (corporations, trusts, partnerships, joint ventures and other forms of business organization) constituted or organized under the law of a NAFTA member.[25] Thus, as long as a company from outside NAFTA region is able to meet the requirements for incorporation (or other forms of business organization) and complies with foreign-investment laws, it may become a NAFTA company. For example, it may acquire an existing firm, establish a wholly owned subsidiary, or create a joint venture in one of NAFTA countries. However, companies that are controlled by investors from outside NAFTA countries may be denied the benefits of NAFTA where the enterprise has no substantial business activities in the territory of the country under whose laws it is constituted.[26] Benefits may also be denied if a NAFTA country does not maintain diplomatic relations with the investor's home country or prohibits business transactions with enterprises from that country[27]—as is case between the United States and Cuba.

While chapter 11 prohibits requirements that senior managers be of any particular nationality, NAFTA members may require that a majority of the board of directors be residents or nationals of a particular country, as long as this does not materially impair control by the owner.[28] Given the importance of senior management in implementing strategy and the nature of the global market for senior executives, this freedom to appoint management of any nationality is necessary for the operations of companies. It also benefits the host country by facilitating the transfer of management practices that enhance the competitiveness of the firm. However, due to the supervisory function of the board of directors and their liability for the actions of companies under domestic laws, the host country may need to ensure that directors have assets in the country to satisfy judgments against them. While this may restrict the freedom of international firms, directors are often drawn from companies with whom the firm does business. Directors who are nationals or residents of the host country may facilitate the development of business relationships that enhance the success of the firm.

The Standard of Treatment Required by NAFTA Chapter 11

NAFTA provides two types of standards for the treatment of foreign investors. National treatment and MFN rules set out standards of non-discrimination. In addition, foreign investors are entitled to a minimum standard of treatment that applies regardless of whether a government's actions are discriminatory.

National treatment for investors requires a government to treat foreign investors no worse than its own investors with respect to the establishment, acquisition, expansion, management, conduct, operation, and sale or other disposition of investments. With respect to a state or province, this means treatment no worse than the most favorable treatment accorded to investors of the country of which it forms a part. No NAFTA party may require that a minimum level of equity in an enterprise in its territory be held by its nationals, other than nominal qualifying shares for directors or incorporators of corporations. Nor may it require an investor, by reason of its nationality, to sell an investment.[29] MFN treatment requires each party to treat foreign investors from a NAFTA country no worse than any other foreign investors.[30] Foreign investors from NAFTA members must receive the better of these two standards.[31] Both standards are based on a comparison of how the party treats other investors, its own and foreign.

NAFTA also imposes a minimum standard of treatment that applies independently of how other investors are treated. Each party must treat investors in accordance with international law, including fair and equitable treatment and full protection and security.[32] While a government's treatment of its own nationals may fall below this standard, its treatment of foreign investors may not. After different chapter 11 tribunals reached inconsistent interpretations of this provision,[33] NAFTA parties agreed to an interpretive note that adopted the approach taken by the Supreme Court of British Columbia in the Metalclad case.

The NAFTA Free Trade Commission adopted the following interpretation of article 1105(1):

1. Article 1105(1) prescribes the customary international law minimum standard of treatment of aliens as the minimum standard of treatment to be afforded to investments of investors of another party.

2. The concepts of "fair and equitable treatment" and "full protection and security" do not require treatment in addition to or beyond that which is required by the customary international-law minimum standard of treatment of aliens.

3. A determination that there has been a breach of another provision of NAFTA or of a separate international agreement does not establish that there has been a breach of article 1105(1).[34]

This interpretation is consistent with the decision of the BCSC. Arguably, this interpretation precludes future claims involving issues of transparency. Interpretations of the commission are binding on chapter 11 tribunals.[35]

Performance Requirements and Transfers

NAFTA prohibits the imposition of performance requirements on foreign investors as a precondition for obtaining government approvals, such as export quotas, domestic content rules, or mandatory technology transfer. However, if a particular performance requirement is not prohibited, then it is permitted, as long as it is otherwise consistent with NAFTA.[36] The rules on performance requirements apply to all investments, whether from NAFTA or non-NAFTA countries.[37]

NAFTA also prohibits restrictions on transfers of profits, proceeds or payments unless the restrictions are due to the application of laws relating to bankruptcy, securities, criminal offenses, currency transfer reporting, or enforcement of judgments.[38] NAFTA members therefore remain free to restrict transfers under laws such as those relating to money laundering, and those that permit the freezing of assets in litigation and bankruptcy proceedings. All payments into and out of a host country related to an investment may be transferred freely and without delay. Such transfers shall be made in a freely convertible currency. However, there is a specific prudential exception that allows governments to regulate transfer pricing. This allows governments to enact laws to prevent the use of intrafirm transfers to avoid taxes by transferring income from high-tax to low-tax jurisdictions.

Following the terrorist attacks of September 11, NAFTA governments used money-laundering laws to deal with terrorist funds. While such measures would likely fit the specific exception discussed above, the NAFTA national security exception applies to all of its provisions, including the treatment of foreign investors.[39] Because it is so broad and discretionary, this exception could be used to restrict capital movements whenever one of the governments considers such restrictions necessary for the protection of its essential security interests in a time of war or other emergency in international relations. While there have been no cases interpreting this provision under NAFTA or the equivalent provision under GATT, capital restrictions placed on terrorist funds in the context of the September 11 attacks would very likely qualify under this exception.

Exceptions and Reservations

NAFTA annexes list specific measures and sectors that are exempt from all or some of the provisions of chapter 11. These "negative lists" serve the purpose of making investment restrictions more accessible to foreign investors, and they provide a foundation for negotiating the further liberalization of each country's foreign-investment regime. The lists are quite detailed; they cover sectors each country wishes to continue to protect from foreign competition. For example, Canada has maintained restrictions on foreign investment in cultural industries,[40] Mexico continues to prohibit private investment in oil and electricity,[41] and the United States prohibits foreign involvement in the atomic energy sector.[42]

In addition to the reservations, there are several exceptions that apply either specifically to chapter 11 or to NAFTA in general. For example, the national security exception applies to all of NAFTA, as discussed above.[43] Because it is so broad and discretionary, it may be used to restrict foreign investment in many sectors of the economy. Another general exception relates to taxation measures. Some types of taxation are exempt from the provisions of chapter 11, while others are not. In order to balance the right of governments to impose taxes against the risk that taxes will be applied to achieve a "creeping" expropriation of investments, special provisions apply to claims for compensation for expropriation involving taxation. Such claims must be submitted to the taxation authorities for consideration before the issue can go before a chapter 11 tribunal.[44] The remaining general exceptions deal with measures relating to balance of payment difficulties[45] and investments in cultural industries.[46]

Chapter 11 contains a specific exception for environmental measures that affect foreign investment. This exception provides that nothing in chapter 11 can be interpreted to prevent a government from adopting, maintaining or enforcing any measure that it considers appropriate to ensure that investment activity is undertaken in a manner sensitive to environmental concerns.[47] However, the measure in question must be otherwise consistent with the provisions of chapter 11. Thus, governments may not disguise investment restrictions as environmental measures. This exception applies to all investments, not just those from NAFTA countries.[48]

The Metalclad case provides a good example of how this exception works in practice. In that case, the federal government of Mexico did apply measures to ensure that the company's investment in the hazardous-waste facility was undertaken in an environmentally safe manner. The company having met the requirements of the environmental measures, its investment was effectively expropriated by ecological decree. Because the ecological decree was inconsistent with the obligation to compensate investors in cases of expropriation, and because the environmental concerns of the government had previously been met, the ecological decree could not be exempted from the expropriation provisions.

A second environmental provision in chapter 11 recommends that NAFTA governments not seek to attract foreign investment by relaxing environmental, health or safety standards. However, this "pollution haven" provision imposes no binding legal obligation, merely requiring the countries to engage in consultations should one of them contravene this principle.[49]

NAFTA Dispute Settlement between Private Investors and Governments

NAFTA chapter 11 allows foreign investors from one NAFTA country to sue the host government of another NAFTA country for compensation or restitution in the event of expropriation or measures equivalent to expropriation. While the tribunal cannot order the government to repeal the legislation that led to the expropriation, in practice restitution of the expropriated investment may require the government to do just that.[50] This procedure is available to NAFTA companies that invest in other NAFTA countries.[51]

Article 1110(1) states that "no Party may directly or indirectly nationalize or expropriate an investment of an investor of another Party . . . or take a measure tantamount to nationalization or expropriation . . . except: (a) for a public purpose; (b) on a nondiscriminatory basis; (c) in accordance with due process of law and [international law]; and (d) in payment of compensation [at fair market value, plus interest]."

Article 1139 provides a very broad definition of the kinds of investments that are protected to include, among other things, "property, tangible or intangible, acquired in the expectation or used for the purpose of economic benefit or other business purpose." The definition thus has the potential to cover investments in intellectual property, such as trademarks and patents. However, article 1110 does not apply to the issuance of compulsory licenses granted in relation to intellectual property rights or other measures that are consistent with NAFTA chapter 17 (on intellectual property).[52] This provision is especially significant for the pharmaceutical industry, both in NAFTA region and in the rest of the world, where NAFTA chapter 11 may serve as a precedent for future agreements. In emergencies, governments may issue compulsory licenses to allow generic drug manufacturers to produce patented medicines without the patent holder's consent. For example, as discussed in the previous chapter, in the aftermath of the anthrax attacks the Canadian government was ready to do so with respect to Bayer's drug ciprofloxacin, to ensure an adequate supply in the event of widespread anthrax infections.[53] Similarly, in negotiations between the government and the pharmaceutical companies Merck and Company of the United States and Roche of Switzerland, Brazil has threatened to issue compulsory licenses for AIDS drugs in order to force patent holders to lower their prices.[54]

The definition in article 1139 may also cover intangible property, such as the goodwill and reputation of a company. Indeed, Ethyl Corporation sought compensation from the Canadian government for expropriation of goodwill based on statements of government officials in the media alleging that the company's product was harmful to the environment and health.[55] However, since the case was settled before a tribunal could rule on that aspect of the claim, it remains unclear whether such a claim could succeed.

Chapter 11 provides NAFTA investors with the power to demand compensation whenever government measures interfere with business activities to such an extent as to amount to expropriation. The responsibility of federal governments includes measures of state and local governments, as well as courts. In the case of courts, a decision must be clearly incompatible with a rule of international law, constitute a denial of justice, or in exceptional circumstances, be contrary to the law of the country in question. This does not mean that court decisions can be appealed to international investment tribunals. Rather, it means that a claimant must show either a denial of justice or a pretense of form to achieve an internationally unlawful end.[56]

The crucial question is how to define the term "tantamount to expropriation." A measure that prevents the use, enjoyment or disposal of the property may qualify, but a mere reduction in profits does not constitute a sufficient degree of interference to constitute expropriation.[57] However, government regulations can be applied in a way that would constitute "creeping" expropriation, where they have the effect of "taking" the property in whole or in large part, outright or in stages.[58]

In the Metalclad case, the tribunal gave an interpretation of expropriation under article 1110 that was sufficiently broad to include a legitimate rezoning of property by a municipality or other zoning authority—and therefore too broad, in the opinion of the British Columbia Supreme Court. The tribunal concluded that

expropriation under NAFTA includes not only open, deliberate and acknowl-edged takings of property, such as outright seizure or formal or obligatory trans-fer of title in favour of the host State, but also covert or incidental interference with the use of property which has the effect of depriving the owner, in whole or significant part, of the use or reasonably-to-be-expected economic benefit of property even if not necessarily to the obvious benefit of the host State [paragraph 103].

Given the ruling of the BCSC on the transparency issue and the official interpretation of the Free Trade Commission regarding the minimum stan-dard of treatment, this interpretation is too broad to be sustained under chapter 11.

An important issue is whether "tantamount to expropriation" makes NAFTA governments liable for the economic impact of regulatory action. The answer appears to be that it does not. The Myers tribunal, after not-ing that the primary meaning of the word "tantamount" is "equivalent," concluded that something that is equivalent cannot logically encompass more. The Myers tribunal agreed with the Pope & Talbot (a lumber com-pany) tribunal that the drafters of NAFTA had intended the word "tanta-mount" to embrace the concept of "creeping expropriation," not to expand the internationally accepted scope of "expropriation."

The general body of international legal precedent does not normally treat regulatory action as amounting to expropriation. The Myers tribu-nal therefore concluded that regulatory conduct is unlikely to provide a legitimate basis for complaints under article 1110. In this regard, the tri-bunal stated,

Expropriations tend to involve the deprivation of ownership rights; regulations a lesser interference. The distinction between expropriation and regulation screens out most potential cases of complaints concerning economic intervention by a state and reduces the risk that governments will be subject to claims as they go about their business of managing public affairs [paragraph 282].

The claims that have been successful, through negotiation or favorable arbitral awards, provide examples of the kinds of measures that may be covered. Canada settled a claim by Ethyl Corporation of the United States by paying thirteen million U.S. dollars in compensation and repealing legislation banning trade in the gasoline additive MMT, which Ethyl processed and sold in Canada. Ethyl Canada's MMT business constituted 50 percent of the company's activity. Mexico was ordered to pay U.S.$15,626,260 to Metalclad Corporation of the United States after the state government of San Luis Potosí established an ecological zone to prevent the operation of the company's hazardous-waste disposal facility in the state.[59] However, Pope & Talbot, Inc., was unsuccessful when it sought compensation from Canada after Canada restricted lumber exports to the United States under a bilateral trade agreement.[60]

Claims for compensation under chapter 11 represent a powerful tool for companies to use to dissuade NAFTA governments from implementing legislation that will cause significant harm to their cross-border investments. Even if a claim is ultimately unsuccessful, the mere threat of a claim can be used as a bargaining tool, particularly at this early stage, before enough cases have been settled to clarify what claims might succeed. Indeed, the Canadian government has publicly expressed its desire to renegotiate chapter 11 in order to limit the kinds of claims that may be brought.[61] The threshold requirements for seeking arbitration are sufficiently low that firms may abuse the process in order to harass a government.[62] However, launching claims for compensation for ordinary regulatory actions that diminish the value of investments to a relatively small degree are likely not only to fail but to result in the claimant's paying the legal costs of the government, as well as its own.

Procedural Issues

An investor cannot make a claim if more than three years have elapsed from the date on which the investor first acquired, or should have first acquired, knowledge of the measure in question and the loss incurred therefrom.[63] Six months must have passed since the events giving rise to the claim before any claim can be submitted.[64] However, the investor must deliver written notice of its intent to submit a claim ninety days before the claim is submitted.[65] Investors must also waive their right to initiate or continue any other legal proceedings involving the same measure.[66] Failure to do all this properly may prove fatal to the claim.[67]

The arbitration rules that normally apply are those of the ICSID Convention or the Additional Facility Rules of ICSID, but the investor may choose either one of these or the UNCITRAL Arbitration Rules. Where either of the ICSID rules are chosen, the tribunal is made up of three arbitrators. Each party chooses one arbitrator, and all agree on the third, who acts as president of the tribunal.[68] The other NAFTA countries must be notified of the claim and may make submissions regarding the interpretation of NAFTA at the hearing.[69] The tribunal must make its decision based on the provisions of NAFTA and the applicable rules of international law (which in practice means the Vienna Convention on the Law of Treaties).[70]

The decisions of the tribunals do not become precedent[71] but may have persuasive value in future cases. If a NAFTA country does not comply with the decision of the tribunal, the NAFTA Commission must establish a dispute panel under NAFTA chapter 20 to resolve the matter. The investor may also seek enforcement of the award in domestic courts.[72]

Certain decisions are not subject to investor-state dispute settlement. A decision to prohibit or restrict the acquisition of an investment under the article 2102 national security exception is not subject to review. Thus, for example, decisions of the president of the United States to prohibit an acquisition under the Exon-Florio Amendment could not be the subject of a claim. In addition, decisions of Canada under the Investment Canada Act and decisions of Mexico's National Commission on Foreign Investment regarding whether to permit an acquisition cannot be the subject of a claim.

WTO AGREEMENT ON TRADE-RELATED INVESTMENT MEASURES

WTO has no equivalent to NAFTA chapter 11, and it provides no rights under which foreign investors can claim compensation from governments for expropriation. The WTO Agreement on Trade-Related Investment Measures (TRIMS) applies to investment measures related to trade in goods only.[73] However, TRIMS does not add any new obligations; it merely interprets and clarifies the application of GATT articles III and XI to trade-related investment measures.[74] The term "investment measure" is not defined but has been interpreted to mean measures that have "a significant impact on investment."[75] The agreement prohibits TRIMS that are inconsistent with national treatment or that impose quantitative restrictions on trade in goods. For example, governments may not impose requirements on foreign investors to use domestic products or limit the use of imports to an amount related to the volume or value of local products that it exports.[76] Members were required to notify the WTO of existing nonconforming measures and eliminate them within two years, though the deadline could be extended on request for developing country members.[77] TRIMS obligations are subject to all general GATT exceptions.

TRIMS also imposes transparency obligations that require governments to notify the WTO Secretariat of the publications in which TRIMS may be found, including those applied by regional and local governments, and to provide information on request to other WTO members unless such disclosure would impede law enforcement, be contrary to the public interest, or prejudice the legitimate commercial interests of firms.[78]

Other than TRIMS, WTO does not impose any obligations specific to investment, other than those relating to trade in services and intellectual property. The investment provisions in the area of services are far more significant than those found in TRIMS. At Doha, the members of WTO agreed to place foreign investment on the negotiating agenda of the Doha Round. It is too early to tell whether those negotiations will succeed or, if they do, whether liberalization will follow the NAFTA model or the GATS model. However, it is likely that the draft text produced under the failed negotiations for an OECD multilateral agreement on investment will serve as a precedent for the WTO negotiation.

OECD MULTILATERAL AGREEMENT ON INVESTMENT (MAI)

The OECD led a round of negotiations from 1995 to 1998 to create a Multilateral Agreement on Investment (the MAI), after the GATT Uruguay Round failed to produce a comprehensive agreement on investment. However, the negotiations collapsed under political pressure from domestic opponents of the agreement in France and elsewhere, who were concerned that the agreement would give transnational corporations undue influence over the decisions of national governments. The agreement would have contained provisions similar to those contained in NAFTA chapter 11 and the OECD Model Bilateral Investment Treaty. Although the negotiations were ultimately unsuccessful, it is useful to review the main provisions of the MAI draft agreement, as it will likely form (as noted above) the basis of future negotiations in the WTO Doha Round.

Investments were defined to include direct investments (the creation, expansion or participation in an enterprise), portfolio investments (whether debt or equity), real estate, intellectual property rights, rights under contract and rights conferred by authorizations or permits. Only government measures were covered, including laws, regulations and administrative practices. Key principles imposed nondiscrimination obligations (the better of MFN or national treatment) and transparency (obliging signatories to publish terms and conditions that might affect investors and investments).

An expropriation, or other measure having equivalent effect, would only be permitted if it were in the public interest and nondiscriminatory; was imposed against payment of prompt, adequate and effective compensation; and was in accordance with due process of law. Exceptions included national security, public order, prudential measures (stability of the domestic financial system, protection for investors and depositors) and tax policy. A safeguards provision permitted temporary restrictions on investment transactions and cross-border payments and transfers in the event of serious difficulties in the balance of payments. Dispute settlement provisions provided for state-to-state arbitration and investor-to-state arbitration.

GLOBAL BUSINESS STRATEGY AND FOREIGN-INVESTMENT LAW

The strategic goals served by FDI vary considerably depending on the sector, the target client, and the strategic purpose of the investment. FDI in the manufacturing sector may serve different strategic objectives than FDI in the services sector. Firms that provide support services to multinationals or firms from their home countries may use FDI abroad to enhance services for those clients, while other firms may seek customers in the host country. The strategic purpose of the investment may be to secure resources or to serve the host market. Similarly, an investment in a joint venture may provide a vehicle to gain market access or may be designed to gain access to new technology that the partner has. This section will consider these distinctions and consider how foreign-investment law may affect strategic decisions relating to FDI.

It is important for several reasons to distinguish between FDI that sets up manufacturing facilities and FDI that establishes a commercial presence for service firms. First, trade in services and trade in goods are governed separately, and differently, in international trade agreements. Secondly, manufacturing is more likely to be resource seeking, and services are more likely to be market seeking.

Where there are low barriers to trade in goods, manufacturers do not have to set up a factory in each market, as they can export from the location that is most cost effective. Thus, FDI in manufacturing chooses locations based on the attractiveness of factor costs and other variables, such as proximity to markets, labor cost and quality, natural resources and the competitive structure of the market. Depending on the type of resource the manufacturer seeks, the FDI may be long term or short term. If the resource is specific to the location (for example, oil in Saudi Arabia) or the location enjoys a long-term advantage over other locations, manufacturing FDI may be long-term. However, where the resource is generally available, as with cheap labor, and the location can quickly lose its cost or quality advantage to other locations, the FDI in manufacturing may be shorter term, as firms seek the same resource elsewhere at a better price.

FDI in manufacturing may be a market-entry strategy rather than a resource-seeking strategy in three sets of circumstances. First, where transport costs are high and the product has to be customized to suit local preferences, it may be better to manufacture the product in the target market. However, the market would have to be sufficiently attractive to justify the cost of the investment—for example, due to its size, purchasing power, the sophistication of its consumers, its demographic profile or its future growth potential. Second, trade barriers may make FDI the only strategy available for market entry, and minority stake in a joint venture with a local firm may be the only way to penetrate the market, due to investment restrictions. Third, a firm may choose to enter a market through an equity-based joint venture to achieve technological innovation that provides the firm a strategic advantage over competitors. Sometimes, a combination of strategic goals and trade/investment restrictions may be the motivating force, as in the case of Xerox's joint venture in Japan with Fuji Film, Fuji-Xerox. In that case, the initial motivation was market access, on the basis of existing government restrictions, but the joint venture also led to the development of new technologies and products that gave Fuji-Xerox a competitive advantage.

FDI in Manufacturing: The Case of Mexico's Assembly Plants

The presence or absence of trade barriers and trade-related investment barriers has become an important consideration in the FDI decisions of firms that base location of manufacturing on worldwide or regionwide sourcing of inputs and exporting of finished products. For example, Mexico has attracted considerable FDI in automobile production, for several reasons. Initially, Mexico attracted automobile producers by making access to its market conditional upon FDI and the use of local inputs. As investment and trade regimes were liberalized, car manufacturers chose to locate or expand operations in Mexico for other reasons as well.

First, Mexico's geographic location is attractive for a product that is expensive to transport. With its proximity to the wealthy markets of North America and the growing markets of Latin America (including Mexico itself), Mexico's location is strategic. Moreover, with ports on both the Atlantic and Pacific Oceans, Mexico is relatively close to both Asia and Europe, in terms of transporting both inputs and finished products.

Second, Mexico has pursued a "hub-and-spoke" strategy of aggressively seeking free trade agreements with North America, Latin America, Europe and Asia. This strategy makes Mexico a most attractive location for FDI in car manufacturing, because it is the only country that provides preferential access to all these markets.

Third, Mexico enjoys a labor-cost advantage over other members of NAFTA and the Mexico-European Union Free Trade Agreement.

Fourth, the rules of origin that apply to automobiles in NAFTA require an increasingly higher percentage of NAFTA content to qualify for duty-free treatment. This was designed to give North American–based manufacturers an advantage over those based in Europe and Asia. To level the playing field in the North American market, European and Asian car manufacturers had to produce cars in North America. While many already did, those who did not or chose to expand North American production had a strong incentive to choose Mexico over the United States or Canada. For example, VW expanded its FDI in Mexico not only to serve the North

American market in certain makes but also to serve the global market with the popular new Beetle.

Finally, Mexico has improved its treatment of foreign investors through amendments to its Foreign Investment Law, the signing of NAFTA, and the negotiation of BITs, all of which provide better property rights for investors. Other changes in Mexico have reduced political risk (through democratic reforms prior to the 2000 election) and economic risk (through the introduction of a floating exchange rate in 1994).

Manufacturing FDI may serve the firm's home market, the host market, other markets or all of the above. Where the FDI is purely resource seeking, the production of goods for export rather than for the host market is the main strategic goal. The Mexican *maquiladora* zone provides a good example. Initially, Mexican law allowed the duty-free import of inputs as long as most of the production was then exported, after Mexico had added labor to the value chain. U.S. firms invested in assembly plants, seeking Mexico's cheap labor to produce products for sale in the American market. However, Asian firms also used Mexico as an assembly location, to exploit the cheap labor and Mexico's proximity to the United States, with the final products destined for the U.S. market. Finally, with the removal of Mexico's domestic sales restrictions under NAFTA, these firms also were able to serve the growing Mexican market from the same plants. However, the initial raison d'être of these plants was to exploit cheap labor and proximity to the U.S. market, not to serve the Mexican market.

FDI in Services

Today, FDI in the services sector is more likely to be a market-entry strategy than a resource-seeking one.[79] There are two principal reasons for this. First, many services require a commercial presence in the target market, which means FDI is a prerequisite for entry. For example, retail banking services cannot be provided without establishing branches in the target market, through mergers, acquisitions, joint ventures or equity investments. Secondly, most countries still limit the ability of firms to engage in cross-border trade in services. For example, cross-border trade in financial services (without the establishment of a commercial presence) is subject to many restrictions in Canada, Mexico and the United States.

A distinction may be made between services firms that enter the market to serve local firms versus those that enter to serve other multinationals operating in the market.[80] When manufacturers integrate their operations on a regional or global basis, service firms may set up regional or global operations the better to serve their multinational clients. For example, the Bank of Montreal invested in banks in the United States and Mexico in order to provide North American banking services for the rapidly growing cross-border trade and investment in the region. Similarly, Canadian National Railway acquired assets in the United States and Mexico in light of increasingly north-to-south movement of goods in the region. On a global scale, Citibank is pursuing a strategy of building a global brand in banking; AT&T does the same in telecommunications.

In sum, the location of manufacturing operations will be affected not only by the attractiveness of the country as a location but by the trade and investment restrictions maintained by that country. The nature of the country's foreign-investment laws will likely determine whether FDI in manufacturing constitutes a market-entry strategy or is destined to produce goods for export. The viability of mergers, acquisitions, joint ventures and alliances in the international expansion plans of firms, in both manufacturing and services, will also be determined by formal and informal investment barriers that a country maintains, in addition to measures relating to repatriation of profits and to management of political and economic risk.

CONCLUSION

The integration of the global economy is reflected in the rapid growth of international trade and FDI flows. Generally speaking, participation in international agreements that lock in reductions of trade and investment barriers makes a country a more attractive destination for the FDI of multinational firms. The reduction of legal barriers enhances the ability of these firms to choose international business strategies based on business considerations rather than legal limitations. FDI may serve a wide variety of strategic goals that enhance competitiveness. Thus, the ability to choose strategies rather than have strategies dictated by national laws will affect the competitiveness of firms and influence investment decisions.

However, existing international investment agreements do not fully liberalize the regulation of FDI. The principles of investment neutrality, investment security and market facilitation are not fully met. Moreover, international investment agreements contain numerous exceptions and reservations. Some, like national security, are necessary to allow governments the flexibility to deal with issues like international terrorism. Others, however, serve only to gain political support for the agreements. Finally, there are many informal barriers to foreign-investment flows that are simply not addressed in foreign-investment agreements. Despite these shortcomings, liberalization of foreign-investment laws through domestic legislation and international agreements enhances the competitiveness of firms by allowing them greater flexibility in their choice of global business strategies.

NAFTA has liberalized foreign investment far more than WTO has. However, an extensive network of bilateral investment treaties exists between many WTO members, and some agreements under GATS liberalize FDI on a selective basis. Progress in this area has been politically difficult to achieve, as evidenced by the failure of the OECD negotiations. It remains to be seen how much progress will be achieved in the Doha Round on foreign investment and how that progress will in turn affect the global investment strategies of firms.

CLOSING CASE: FOREIGN-INVESTMENT LIBERALIZATION IN MEXICO

The ever-increasing pace of global economic integration, driven by advances in technology, transportation and communications, has produced dramatic growth in world merchandise trade and FDI. Ongoing reforms to international and domestic legal regimes that govern trade and investment are integral parts of the process of globalization. Active participation of governments in the "legalization" of international commerce is necessary to provide their national firms competitive advantages and make their nations attractive locations for FDI on the part of multinational enterprises. Recognizing the need to be proactive in the face of change, Mexico has undergone a rapid transition from a closed economy that restricted trade and investment to a relatively open economy that now promotes both.

The 1993 Mexican Foreign-Investment Law

In anticipation of the passage of NAFTA, Mexico introduced the 1993 Foreign Investment Law (1993 FIL), which opened over 90 percent of the Mexican economy to 100 percent foreign ownership.[81] The 1993 FIL applies to all countries, with the exception of certain provisions that give more favorable treatment to NAFTA members. For example, the 1993 FIL requires a foreign commercial enterprise to establish a local presence in Mexico, provided this requirement does not contravene any of Mexico's international agreements.[82] NAFTA forbids the imposition of such a requirement for service providers from NAFTA countries, thereby exempting them from this requirement of the 1993 FIL.[83]

Prior to the introduction of the 1993 FIL, foreign investment in Mexico had been governed by a nationalistic 1973 investment law (1973 FIL), which required the permission of the National Commission on Foreign investment to exceed a 49 percent interest in any Mexican enterprise.[84] The seventeen criteria employed by the commission included the following: that the foreign enterprise would not displace Mexican enterprises; that the business would have a positive impact on the balance of payments and increase exports; and that the country of origin of the investment would diversify Mexico's sources of investment.[85] Moreover, the amount of discretion exercised by the commission and the lack of any time limits in which their decision had to be made introduced uncertainty into the process and provided an ideal environment for corruption.[86]

Such restrictions would not sit well with the global business strategies of most multinational enterprises. For example, Wal-Mart's entry into the Mexican market through its joint venture with Mexican retail giant Grupo Cifra would not have met any of these three criteria, nor would it have met many of the remaining fourteen. The highly competitive Wal-Mart would be likely to displace Mexican competitors; Wal-Mart's offerings of imported consumer goods would have a negative impact on the balance of payments; and as a U.S. company, Wal-Mart would increase already dominant U.S. investment in Mexico rather than diversify Mexican sources of investment.

In 1989, Mexico issued new regulations to the 1973 law that had the effect of amending it substantially.[87] In unrestricted business activities (which included retailing), 100 percent foreign ownership was expressly permitted without the authorization of the commission. In restricted activities that required approval, if the commission did not issue a negative decision within forty-five working days, approval was deemed to have been granted. The 1989 regulations paved the way for the unrestricted entry of foreign retailers into the Mexican market. Wal-Mart could have chosen to enter the market on its own after the introduction of the regulations. With the introduction of the new foreign-investment regime, Wal-Mart was able to acquire its initial 50 percent share of the joint venture.

The 1993 FIL formalized the liberalization that had occurred under the 1989 regulations and further liberalized the investment regime. The objective of the 1993 FIL is to attract to Mexico foreign investment that will contribute to the economic development of the country,[88] whereas the purpose of the 1973 law had been to promote *Mexican* investment and to *regulate* foreign investment.[89] Among developing countries, in 1990–96 Mexico received the second-highest amount of FDI in the world, after China. In terms of inflows of FDI, Mexico ranked ninth during this period, receiving roughly the same amount as Canada.[90]

As a general rule, foreign investors may acquire any percentage of Mexican corporations, enter into new fields of economic activity, manufacture new products, open and operate business establishments and expand or relocate existing operations, unless the 1993 FIL specifies otherwise.[91] Certain activities are reserved exclusively for the Mexican government[92] and Mexicans or Mexican companies by an exclusion-of-foreigners clause.[93] An exclusion clause in articles of incorporation prohibits the participation of foreign investors in a company.[94] In certain other activities, foreign investment is limited to maximum percentages of 10 percent, 25 percent or 49 percent,[95] or requires the permission of the National Commission of Foreign Investment to exceed 49 percent.[96] Again, if the commission fails to make a decision within forty-five working days, permission is granted automatically.[97] This latter provision prevents delays and makes the process less prone to abuse of discretion or corruption than under the 1973 FIL.

The acquisition of land by foreigners is regulated according to the zone in which it is located. In the restricted zone (within a hundred kilometers of the international borders or within fifty kilometers of the coastline), article 27 of the Mexican constitution prohibits the purchase of land by foreigners for residential purposes, and such acquisitions must be made in the form a renewable thirty-year trust. If the land is used for nonresidential purposes, the purchase must be recorded with the secretary of foreign relations.[98] Land in Mexico can be purchased by foreigners only if the foreign investors agree to consider themselves Mexican nationals, to subject themselves to Mexican law and jurisdiction and to forego any legal remedies they may have with their home government (the "Calvo clause"—article 27 of the constitution; 1993 FIL, articles 10 and 10A). Under the 1973 law, the Calvo clause had been applied to all foreign investments; the 1993 FIL reduced the scope of its application to land only.

The FIL and NAFTA Chapter 11

The 1993 FIL further enhanced investment opportunities for foreign companies in Mexico but did not provide protection for those investments beyond that already available under the Mexican legal system. NAFTA chapter 11 provides an additional layer of legal protection that can be enforced at the international level, providing greater security and predictability for foreign investors from the United States and Canada. Chapter 11 also applies to enterprises that are owned by non-NAFTA citizens, provided an enterprise is incorporated under the law of a NAFTA member.[99] Thus, for example, a European or Asian company may incorporate a subsidiary under U.S. law, and the investments of the subsidiary in Canada and Mexico would enjoy the same rights under NAFTA as a U.S. corporation that was owned by citizens of the United States.

Chapter 11 imposes the rule of law on the treatment of international investments, through rules requiring national treatment and through disciplines concerning expropriation and compensation. The principle of national treatment requires Mexican law to treat U.S. investors no less favorably than Mexican nationals.[100] However, NAFTA contains reservations that exempt certain laws, such as article 27 of the Mexican constitution, from the application of the principle of national treatment. One of Mexico's reservations provides that foreign nationals, foreign enterprises or Mexican enterprises without a foreigner-exclusion clause may not acquire property rights in the restricted zone.[101] However, the 1993 FIL permits Mexican corporations without a foreigner-exclusion clause to purchase land in the restricted zone, provided that the land is dedicated to nonresidential purposes and the company agrees to consider itself a Mexican national and to forego any remedies it might have with its own government, where the Mexican corporation is controlled by foreigners.

The protection afforded to investors under chapter 11 only covers foreign investments coming from a NAFTA member. The national treatment principle does not prevent a government from providing *more* favorable treatment to foreign investors than to its own nationals. This process is not available to domestic investors, whose only remedy against expropriation by their own government is to pursue the matter under the laws of their own country in the domestic courts. Thus, if the Mexican government were to expropriate the assets of a Mexican company, no claim could be made under chapter 11. On the other hand, a U.S. company would have the option of pursuing the matter through the Mexican courts or filing a claim under chapter 11. The widely reported corruption and delays in the Mexican legal system makes the domestic courts a less attractive option than international arbitration, which can be enforced under NAFTA.[102]

The Relation between Mexican Law and NAFTA

Under Mexican law, international treaties are given the same weight as federal laws, provided the provisions of the treaties do not conflict with the Constitution.[103] With respect to investments in land, there appears to be a conflict between the Calvo clause of the Mexican constitution and the investor-state arbitration procedure of chapter 11. The Calvo clause requires foreign purchasers of Mexican land to treat themselves as Mexican nationals when determining who has jurisdiction over any claims related to the property. Mexican nationals do not have access to chapter 11 arbitration regarding investments in Mexico, since the arbitration option is only available to foreign investors. The Calvo clause would therefore prevent foreign investors from seeking this remedy with respect to investments in Mexican land, thereby limiting the coverage of chapter 11 to investments other than land. Should foreign investors make a claim under chapter 11 for land, thereby violating the agreement to treat themselves as nationals, they would become subject to the penalty of forfeiting the land to the Mexican government.[104]

However, some authors argue that Mexico's having agreed to the investor-state arbitration provisions of NAFTA suggests a retreat from the Calvo doctrine.[105] The fact that Mexico has listed article 27 as a reservation against the national-treatment obligation of article 1102, in annex I, suggests that Mexico's intention is to maintain the application of the Calvo clause with respect to investments in land. Nevertheless, Mexico's agreement to compensate Metalclad for the expropriation of its investment, which included land, demonstrates that NAFTA chapter 11 is likely to prevail in practice.

NOTES

1. See *Metalclad Corporation v. The United Mexican States,* 40 ILM 36 (2001), 13 *World Trade & Arbitration Materials* 47 (2001), paragraph 103 [hereafter Metalclad, Tribunal].

2. See *The United Mexican States v. Metalclad Corporation* (BCSC), 2001 BCSC 664, paragraph 56 [hereafter Metalclad BCSC].

3. Evelyn Iritani, "Ruling in Canada Strikes at Companies' NAFTA Trade Suits Courts: Decision Could Blunt Legal Challenges to Governments' Power to Enforce Health and Safety Regulations," *Los Angeles Times,* June 5, 2001, C1.

4. "Metalclad Reaches Preliminary Agreement with Mexico; $15,626,260 to Be Paid in Settlement of NAFTA Case," *PR Newswire,* June 13, 2001.

5. "Eye on Investors, Mexico Pays US Company," *New York Times,* October 29, 2001.

6. Organization for Economic Co-operation and Development, Survey of OECD Work on International Investment 6 (Paris: OECD) (1998) [hereafter OECD Survey].

7. Erich Gundlach and Peter Nunnekamp, "Some Consequences of Globalization for Developing Countries," in *Globalization, Trade and Foreign Direct Investment,* ed. John Dunning (Oxford: Elsevier, 1998), 153–74.

8. OECD Survey.

9. The "Ley de Inversión Extranjera," *Diario Oficial,* 27 de diciembre de 1993, replaced the "Ley Para Promover la Inversión Mexicana y Regular la Inversión Extranjera," *Diario Oficial,* 9 de marzo de 1973.

10. OECD Survey, 18.

11. "The Agreement on Trade-related Investment Measures, Final Act Embodying the Results of the Uruguay Round of Multilateral Trade Negotiations, April 15, 1994, Legal Instruments—Results of the Uruguay Round," annex 1A, vol. I, 33 ILM 1125 (1994) [hereafter TRIMS], only applies to trade in goods, not services. See TRIMS, article I. TRIMS does not create new obligations, but rather clarifies the application of GATT articles III and XI to trade-related investment measures. See *Indonesia—Certain Measures Affecting the Automobile Industry, Report of the Panel,* WT/DS55 (1998) and *European Communities—Regime for the Importation, Sale and Distribution of Bananas, Report of the Panel,* WT/DS27 (1997), both available at http://www.wto.org.

12. For a list of WTO members, see www.wto.org. For a list of countries that have signed BITs, see http://www.worldbank.org/icsid/.

13. See Metalclad BCSC.

14. See, for example, the "Listing of Canada's Foreign Investment Protection and Promotion Agreements," available on the Web at http://www.dfait-maeci.gc.ca/tna-nac/fipa-e.asp.

15. An exception would be the procedural rules investors must follow in order to enforce their rights—for example, under NAFTA.

16. See Someshwar Rao and Ash Ahmad, "Formal and Informal Investment

Barriers in the G-7 Countries," in *Investment Rules for the Global Economy*, ed. Sauvé and Schwanen (Toronto: CD Howe Institute, 1996), 176–218.

17. See Daniel Schwanen, "Investment and the Global Economy: Key Issues in Rulemaking," in *Investment Rules for the Global Economy*, ed. Sauvé and Schwanen (Toronto: CD Howe Institute, 1996), 13.

18. See Edward Graham and Pierre Sauvé, "Towards a Rules-Based Regime for Investment: Issues and Challenges," in *Investment Rules for the Global Economy*, ed. Sauvé and Schwanen (Toronto: CD Howe Institute, 1996), 100–46.

19. See Alan Rugman and Michael Gestrin, "A Conceptual Framework for a Multilateral Agreement on Investment: Learning from NAFTA," in *Investment Rules for the Global Economy*, ed. Sauvé and Schwanen (Toronto: CD Howe Institute, 1996), 147–75.

20. See NAFTA articles 402(5)(d) and 403, esp. 403(5). These rules of origin increase the percentage of the net cost of automobiles that must be North American content from 50 percent in 1994 to 62.5 percent in 2002.

21. Rao and Ahmad, 176–77.

22. Kenneth J. Vandevelde, "The Political Economy of a Bilateral Investment Treaty," *American Journal of International Law* 92 (1998), 621.

23. Ibid., 631.

24. See Metalclad BCSC.

25. NAFTA articles 201, 1139, and 1416.

26. NAFTA article 1113(2).

27. NAFTA article 1113(1).

28. NAFTA article 1107.

29. NAFTA article 1102.

30. NAFTA article 1103.

31. NAFTA article 1104.

32. NAFTA article 1105.

33. See *S.D. Myers Inc. v. Government of Canada* (November 13, 2000) and *Pope & Talbot Inc. v. Government of Canada* (April 10, 2001), both available on the Web at http://www.dfait-maeci.gc.ca/tna-nac/dispute-e.asp#chapter11. See also the discussion of these conflicting interpretations in Metalclad BCSC.

34. *NAFTA—Chapter 11—Investment, Notes of Interpretation of Certain Chapter 11 Provisions* (NAFTA Free Trade Commission, July 31, 2001), done at Washington, D.C., July 31, 2001, available on the Web at http://www.dfait-maeci.gc.ca/tna-nac/NAFTA-Interpr-e.asp.

35. NAFTA article 1131.

36. NAFTA article 1106. While NAFTA chapter 14 does not expressly incorporate the rules regarding performance requirements in article 1106, article 1101 makes it clear that this article applies to "all investments."

37. NAFTA article 1101(1)(c).

38. NAFTA article 1109.

39. NAFTA article 2102.

40. NAFTA annex 2106.

41. NAFTA annex III.

42. NAFTA annex I.

43. NAFTA article 2102.

44. NAFTA article 2103(6).

45. NAFTA article 2104.

46. NAFTA article 2106.

47. NAFTA article 1114(1).

48. NAFTA article 1101(1)(c).

49. NAFTA article 1114(2).

50. See, for example, *Ethyl Corporation v. Government of Canada*, documents available on the Web at http://www.dfait-maeci.gc.ca/tna-nac/dispute-e.asp#chapter11.

51. NAFTA article 1401(2).

52. NAFTA article 1110(7).

53. Jeff Gray, "MPs Grill Rock over Drug Fumbling," *Globe and Mail*, October 25, 2001.

54. Jennifer L. Rich, "Roche Reaches Accord on Drug with Brazil," *New York Times*, August 31, 2001.

55. See *Ethyl Corporation*.

56. See *Robert Azinian, Kenneth Davitian, & Ellen Baca v. The United Mexican States*, 14 ICSID Rev.-FILJ 538 (1999); 39 ILM 537 (2000).

57. See *Pope & Talbot Inc.*

58. *Third Restatement of the Foreign Relations Law of the US*, s. 712, comment (g), cited with approval in ibid.

59. Metalclad BCSC.

60. See *Pope & Talbot Inc.*

61. *Canada Calls for Rewriting of NAFTA Chapter 21* [sic], El Universal, Mexico City, September 6, 2000.

62. See Graham and Sauvé.

63. NAFTA articles 1116(2), 1117(2).

64. NAFTA article 1120.

65. NAFTA article 1119.

66. NAFTA article 1121. There is an exception for proceedings before domestic courts or tribunals seeking injunctive, declaratory or other extraordinary relief, not involving the payment of damages.

67. See *Waste Management Inc. v. United Mexican States*, 15 ICSID Rev.—FILJ 214 (2000); 40 ILM 56 (2001).

68. NAFTA article 1123.

69. NAFTA articles 1127 and 1128.

70. NAFTA article 1131.

71. NAFTA article 1136(1).

72. NAFTA article 1136(5) and (6).

73. TRIMS article 1.

74. See *Indonesia—Certain Measures Affecting the Automobile Industry* and *European Communities—Regime for the Importation, Sale and Distribution of Bananas*.

75. See *Indonesia—Certain Measures Affecting the Automobile Industry*.

76. TRIMS article 2.

77. TRIMS article 5.

78. TRIMS article 6.

79. See Julian Birkinshaw and Neil Hood, "Multinational Subsidiary Evolution: Capability and Charter Change in Foreign-Owned Subsidiary Companies," *Academy of Management Review* 23 (1998), 773–95.

80. See, for example, the case of foreign banks in Hungary, discussed in Yusaf Akbar and Brad McBride, "Multinational Enterprise Strategy, Foreign Direct Investment and Economic Development: The Case of Hungary," Academy of International Business, SE Regional Conference, New Orleans, November 2001.

81. "Ley de Inversión Extranjera," *Diario Oficial*, 27 de diciembre de 1993 [hereafter 1993 FIL].

82. 1993 FIL article 17A.

83. NAFTA article 1205.

84. "Ley Para Promover la Inversión Mexicana y Regular la Inversión Extranjera," *Diario Oficial*, 9 de marzo de 1973 [hereafter 1973 FIL] article 5.

85. 1973 FIL article 13.

86. Michael Johnston, "What Can Be Done about Entrenched Corruption," in *World Bank Annual Bank Conference on Development Economics* (Washington, D.C.: World Bank, 1997).

87. "Reglamento de la Ley Para Promover la Inversión Mexicana y Regular la Inversión Extranjera," *Diario Oficial*, 16 de mayo de 1989.

88. 1993 FIL article 1.

89. Ibid.

90. OECD Survey 10. Canada received $44,921 billion, and Mexico received $44,806 billion, in 1990–1996. The United States was the largest recipient of FDI, with $327,753 billion. China ranked second, with $156,342 billion.

91. 1993 FIL article 4.

92. 1993 FIL article 5.

93. 1993 FIL article 6.

94. 1993 FIL article 2.

95. 1993 FIL article 7.

96. 1993 FIL article 8.

97. 1993 FIL article 28.

98. 1993 FIL article 10.

99. NAFTA article 1139.

100. NAFTA article 1102.

101. NAFTA annex I—Schedule of Mexico.

102. Sam Dillon and Craig Pyes, "Failed Drug Pursuit of a Mexican Bares a System Rife with Graft," *New York Times*, April 15,1998.

103. *Constitución Política de los Estados Unidos Mexicanos* (Mexico: Ediciones Delma, 1998), article 133.

104. Ibid., article 27.

105. Alan Rugman, "The Rules of Foreign Investment in NAFTA," *Latin American Business Review* 1 (1998), 77–94.

Chapter 6

Firm Strategy in Negotiations and Enforcement of Trade Agreements

INTRODUCTION

Corporations can influence trade policies to enhance their own competitive strategies and to hobble competitors. The goals of the corporate strategist can be divided into two broad categories. On the one hand, the firm may seek to challenge existing or proposed laws that disadvantage the firm in some way. On the other hand, the firm may seek the creation of new laws, such as trade or investment barriers that will put competitors at a disadvantage, or free trade agreements that may enhance competitiveness by lowering the cost of imported inputs. The first may be viewed as a reaction to adverse environmental conditions and the latter a proactive effort to shape the environment in which the firm competes.

Free trade increases wealth. However, the distribution of that wealth is addressed not in trade rules but in the domestic laws and policies of each country. It is tempting for firms to influence domestic policies so that they receive bigger pieces of the bigger pie. For example, by restricting the supply of Canadian lumber, U.S. lumber companies are able to increase their profits at the expense of Canadian lumber companies and American consumers. Firms should bear in mind, however, the ethical and business implications of pursuing a strategy that enriches shareholders at the expense of customers.[1]

This chapter begins with an examination of proactive strategies to shape the competitive environment through the creation or elimination of trade barriers, or the implementation of other laws. Having considered the realm of possibilities from the proactive perspective, the chapter will examine strategies to respond to such laws.

THE STRATEGY OF INFLUENCING TRADE RULES

Firms will have different goals with respect to what they seek in trade negotiations and the enforcement of trade agreements. Their goals are affected by the competitiveness of the firm. Generally speaking, competitive firms want to eliminate barriers to trade and investment to expand into new markets. This enhances their competitiveness by lowering the cost of expansion, which in turn creates the potential for greater economies of scale. Uncompetitive firms want to maintain or create barriers to foreign competition. This does not lower their costs but increases those of their competitors.

Competitive firms with international expansion plans seek access to foreign markets through exports or FDI and thus seek the elimination of trade or investment barriers in the target market. The market-entry strategy varies with the firm and the nature of its business. For example, goods may be more susceptible than services to an export strategy. However, some goods may require an FDI strategy, due to transportation costs or the need to adapt the product to the target market.

Manufacturers may set as their goal the reduction of trade and investment barriers for a slightly different purpose—to lower the cost of inputs. To that end they would seek a reduction in trade barriers for imports to the country in which their plant is located. This will not only lower the cost of imported inputs but may also expand the selection of suppliers the firm has to choose from and thus the quality of the inputs. They would also seek the elimination of investment barriers in countries where they extract natural resources. Finally, they would seek to eliminate trade barriers that impede the export of finished products.

For knowledge-intensive industries with easy-to-copy intellectual property, intellectual property rights and their enforcement form an important part of their competitive advantage and have a significant impact on profits. Pharmaceutical, entertainment and software firms would fall into this category. Indeed, the degree to which intellectual property rights are enforceable in a particular market may be the determining factor in choosing an entry strategy, and in deciding whether the market is to be entered at all.

Thus, some firms seek trade policies that enhance their competitiveness in some way. On the other side of the coin are the firms that seek to hobble their competitors through protectionist measures that do nothing to enhance their own competitiveness but impose costs on competitors. Alternatively, these firms may seek government subsidies to lower their costs vis-à-vis competitors.

In sum, firms may seek to influence trade policy for competitive or anticompetitive reasons. Rugman and Verbeke classify these two approaches as *efficiency-based* strategies and *nonefficiency-based* strategies. They define the former as "decisions and actions that aim at achieving survival, profit and growth through the provision of products and services to the firm's customers that are cheaper than or differentiated from those of potential competitors."[2] The latter strategies seek their objectives by other means, such as trade barriers, cartels and government monopolies.

A protectionist strategy is generally viewed as unhealthy for both firms and countries. While it may allow firms to achieve success in the short term, protection may cause or perpetuate inefficiencies that decrease competitiveness in the long run.[3] In some cases, such as infant industries, protection may be necessary in the short term. However, a protectionist strategy only makes uncompetitive firms more vulnerable over time.[4]

Regardless of the motive, firms, be they foreign or domestic firms, need to incorporate strategies to influence trade policy into their overall business strategies. The impact of trade policy on the firm's competitive position with respect to foreign competitors makes understanding trade agreements essential for corporate strategists.

STRATEGIES FOR CHALLENGING LAWS THAT HAMPER BUSINESS

The central point of this chapter is that regulatory barriers to international business are an environmental factor that firms do not necessarily have to accept. If a national government decides to pass a law that will have a negative impact on a firm's business interests, there are several strategies available to change the law, both before and after it is passed. There are essentially four approaches: extralegal, illegal, domestic and international. "Extralegal" refers to such strategies as lobbying. "Illegal" refers to such strategies as corrupt practice. Domestic legal strategies make use of the domestic laws and court systems. International legal strategies make use of the rules and dispute settlement procedures found in international agreements like NAFTA and WTO.

Before the Law Passes

Lobbying politicians or bureaucrats is a time-honored method of influencing trade policy. Whether a firm lobbies politicians or bureaucrats will depend on the structure of the decision-making process in government. Politicians may insulate themselves from such pressures by legally delegating decisions to administrative bodies. A good example is the delegation of decisions on countervailing-duties (CVD) and antidumping-duties (ADD) cases. The channels through which lobbying takes place will also depend on both the rules governing lobbyists and the formal structures that have been set up to channel industry concerns. In many countries (Canada, for example), former politicians may be obliged to let a minimum period of time elapse between leaving elected office and becoming a professional lobbyist. In the United States, advisory bodies provide input to the House Ways and Means Committee and the Senate Trade and Finance Committee, providing a formalized structure for influencing trade policy in the United States. Lobbying efforts need not be limited to formal channels, however.

In many countries, government policies can be influenced by financial contributions from firms. These take the form of either campaign contributions or bribes. Campaign contributions have come under closer scrutiny in recent years, precisely due to the perception that they have a corrupting effect on government decision making. Nevertheless, large campaign contributions can buy access to key politicians and permit a firm to raise trade policy issues that are relevant to its industry.

Bribery can be distinguished from campaign contributions in that it is generally illegal and transactions are not recorded. It remains common, particularly in the developing world. In some countries, it is difficult to do business without resorting to bribery. However, some countries have attempted to discourage bribery through laws that make it illegal for their citizens to engage in this practice in foreign countries. The best-known example is the U.S. Foreign Corrupt Practices Act. However, where they consider it necessary, companies are able to circumvent such laws by hiring "consultants" to make the bribes on their behalf.

NAFTA chapter 18 contains a formal mechanism for influencing trade-related laws that are in the development stage. Each country must publish, in advance, measures that it proposes to adopt and provide interested persons and the other governments a reasonable opportunity to comment on them.[5] This covers laws, regulations, procedures and administrative decisions that are of a general nature, but not decisions that apply to a particular person or a specific case. The latter type of decision is subject to judicial review, which means that a firm can have the decision reviewed by a judge.

After the Law Passes

After a law passed, it may be challenged under either domestic laws or international agreements. The advantage of using domestic laws is that an order of a domestic court legally compels the government to comply, whereas decisions under international agreements generally do not have the same weight. In a domestic legal system, there are essentially two courses of action—civil action and constitutional challenge.

Challenges to the constitutional validity of a law can in turn be divided into two categories. The first is an argument that the law has been enacted by the wrong branch of government, in terms of the constitutional division of powers. This argument is available in countries where legislative authority is divided between a federal government and state or provincial governments. This is the case in all three NAFTA countries. For example, in all of NAFTA countries the federal governments have constitutional jurisdiction to pass laws that deal with international and interstate or interprovincial trade. Thus, if a state or a province passes a law that restricts that trade, the law would be constitutionally invalid.

The second category of constitutional challenge relates to civil rights, such as freedom of expression. For example, advertising restrictions on products such as cigarettes might be challenged as violations of free speech. A civil rights argument can be used to challenge a law passed at either the federal or state level, as long as the civil right in question is protected under the constitution.

However, courts in different countries may interpret the same constitutional right differently, and different constitutions may express such guarantees in different language. For example, the right to free speech has been interpreted more liberally in the United States than it has in Canada. In addition, the Canadian constitution expressly permits some rights to be limited, including freedom of speech. As a result, Canada has stronger laws than the United States against forms of communication that promote the hatred of specific groups—for example, on the basis of race or religion.

As for civil action, companies may sue governments for damages in domestic courts. For example, a company might sue for breach of contract in cases of government procurement (that is, when the government has agreed to purchase goods or services from a company). A company can also sue a government under domestic law for compensation for expropriation. If a government official abuses a position of power in a way that causes economic damage to an individual or company, he might be sued for damages caused in excess of his jurisdiction. For example, a Montreal restauranteur successfully sued the premier of Quebec for wrongfully canceling his liquor license, in the well-known Canadian case of *Roncarelli v. Duplessis*.

International agreements provide another forum in which companies may seek to have laws challenged. Under NAFTA chapter 11, foreign investors may file claims for compensation where a law constitutes expropriation. Other dispute settlement forums may be available only to governments. For example, a company would have to persuade its government to challenge the law before a NAFTA chapter 20 panel or a WTO panel, since those forums are reserved for governments. With respect to trade-remedy laws, companies and governments may both have access to international dispute-settlement panels.

TRADE-REMEDY LAWS

Trade laws that address dumping and subsidies are collectively referred to as *trade-remedy laws*. "Dumping" occurs when a firm sells exports for less than their normal value, in effect subsidizing its exports to one market with the profits from its home market or other export markets. Differential pricing strategies may be considered dumping that is subject to anti-dumping duties where the exports cause injury to domestic producers in the export market. Similarly, government subsidies to exporters may trigger countervailing duties where the subsidized export causes injury to domestic producers in the export market. The rationale behind both ADDs and CVDs is to counteract anticompetitive practices in international trade. However, critics argue that trade-remedy laws are used in practice to protect inefficient industries from foreign competition—itself an anti-competitive practice.

Where there is no domestic competitor in the target market, companies can use differential pricing strategies without running the risk of ADDs. However, where domestic competition exists, industries that use differential pricing strategies must exercise caution to ensure that those pricing strategies do not backfire. Similarly, companies that receive subsidies from government need to ensure that the subsidies are structured in a way that will not attract CVDs in foreign markets. Trade-remedy laws can have a serious impact on a firm's position in a foreign market. For this reason, firm strategists need to understand this rather technical area of international trade law.

The WTO regulates the circumstances in which its members may impose ADDs and CVDs. WTO rules define the parameters of each country's trade-remedy laws by governing the content of such laws. In contrast, NAFTA imposes no obligations regarding the content of each country's trade-remedy laws. Instead, it provides a procedure for resolving disputes over the manner in which the trade authorities of each country apply domestic laws. NAFTA chapter 19 replaces appeals to the domestic courts of each country with appeals to binational panels of experts on trade-remedy law. The result is that disputes over the content of a country's trade-remedy laws go before WTO panels, while disputes over the application of those laws go before NAFTA chapter 19 panels.

Subsidies

The WTO Subsidies Agreement contains an internationally agreed-upon definition of "subsidy." This agreement was intended to limit the ability of countries to take unilateral action in defining subsidies and taking countervailing action. There are three categories of subsidy—strictly *prohibited* subsidies, *nonactionable* (permissible) subsidies and *actionable* subsidies—referred to as "red light" subsidies, "green light" subsidies and "yellow light" subsidies (as in traffic lights).

Prohibited subsidies are those that are made contingent upon export performance or the use of domestic inputs.[6] For example, this prohibits subsidies that a government provides to companies that export a certain percentage of their production or that purchase a given value of manufacturing inputs from local producers. Least-developed countries were exempted, and developing countries were given eight years (from January 1, 1995) to eliminate export subsidies.[7] However, where a developing country has reached export competitiveness in any given product, it must phase out those export subsidies over two years.[8] With respect to domestic input subsidies, developing country members are exempt for five years and least-developed countries for eight years.

The idea behind this prohibition is that companies should choose where to sell their products and where to buy their inputs based on market conditions rather than government enticements. Moreover, there are those who argue that such subsidies are bad for the competitive position of firms and nations in the long run, in that they make their competitive positions subject to the whims of politicians rather than the discipline of the marketplace.[9] Others argue that subsidies are necessary where countries are nurturing the establishment of infant industries.

If a WTO member uses prohibited subsidies, another may invoke WTO dispute-settlement procedures. The first step is consultations. Should that fail to resolve the matter within thirty days, the matter may be referred to a dispute-settlement panel. If the panel finds that the measure in question is a prohibited subsidy, it recommends the removal of the subsidy. Barring appeals, should the member not remove the subsidy, the WTO may authorize the complaining member to take countermeasures (that is, trade sanctions) against the member that is using a prohibited subsidy.[10]

All WTO members may use four categories of nonactionable subsidies.[11] First, they may subsidize up to 75 percent of the research costs of a firm and up to 50 percent of its development costs. Second, they may use subsidies to assist disadvantaged regions inside a country. (A region is considered "disadvantaged" if its per capita GDP is less than 85 percent of the nation as a whole or its unemployment rate is more than 110 percent of the national rate.) Third, governments may subsidize up to 20 percent of the cost of a firm complying with new environmental regulations. Finally, there are exceptions for certain agricultural support programs.

Actionable subsidies are the most difficult to identify. They must fit into the WTO definition,[12] which has three elements. First, the subsidy must be a financial or other commercial benefit from government, such as a direct transfer of funds, forgiveness of amounts owing to the government, or a government sale or purchase of goods or services at less or more than fair market value. (For example, in the Canada–United States lumber dispute, the U.S. lumber producers argued that the Canadian government sold trees to the Canadian lumber industry at less than fair market value.) Second, the subsidy may be direct or indirect; for example, a subsidy given to one firm that supplies a major input for the production of a second firm may constitute an indirect subsidy to the second firm. Third, the government benefit must be specific to one industry or sector—that is, not generally available. The purpose of the specificity test is to ensure that generally available government services (such as roads and public education) are not counted as actionable subsidies. Where actionable subsidies cause adverse effects to the interests of another WTO member (injury to domestic industry, nullification of GATT benefits or serious prejudice to the interests of another member), the same dispute-settlement process may be invoked as for prohibited subsidies.[13]

Where a domestic industry is being injured by subsidized imports, the industry may request its own government to initiate an investigation that could lead to the imposition of CVDs.[14] At least 25 percent of the domestic producers of the product in question must expressly support the application. Of the producers expressing support for or opposition to the application, at least 50 percent must be in favor.

Once it is determined that there is an actionable subsidy, two more elements are required before a country may impose a CVD. First, there must be proof of material injury, or the threat of it, to the domestic industry or proof that the subsidized imports materially retard the establishment of a domestic industry. Indicators of material injury include negative effects on the output, employment, market share, profits, or growth of the domestic industry, or high inventories, price erosion or underutilized capacity.

Second, there must be a causal relation between the subsidy and the material injury. That subsidized imports exist in a market does not necessarily mean that they are the cause of all economic problems faced by the domestic industry. Take the case of a lumber mill in the United States that is forced to close because its supply of lumber from federal forests is cut off in order to protect the forest habitat of an endangered bird under federal environmental laws. This closure would not be caused by imports of subsidized lumber from Canada. In this case, notwithstanding material injury to domestic industry and actionable subsidies, no duties could be imposed.

If all three elements are in place (subsidy, injury and causal connection), the maximum CVD that may be imposed is the estimated subsidy. However, under the *de minimus* rule, no duties may be imposed where the subsidy is less than 1 percent of the value of the product in question or where the volume of the imports in question constitutes less than 3 percent of total imports of that product. For developing countries, these percentages are 2 percent and 4 percent, respectively. The duties terminate after five years (unless a new complaint is filed) or when the subsidy ends, whichever comes first.

The process of investigating subsidized imports and imposing CVDs must conform to the rules set out by WTO. However, decisions to impose

CVDs are made independently of WTO dispute-resolution processes. Once the decision to impose duties has been made by a government, there must be an opportunity to seek judicial review of the decision.[15] WTO dispute-settlement procedures do not apply to the review of CVD decisions. Rather, the review is conducted by the domestic courts or arbitration tribunals of the country imposing the duty. In NAFTA countries, judicial review by domestic courts has been replaced by judicial review by binational panels of arbitrators for cases involving NAFTA companies.

Dumping

Dumping is price discrimination between markets where the export price is less than the normal value. "Normal value" may be calculated in three ways. Usually, normal value is based on the home market or domestic sales price. However, where this is inappropriate—for example, due to lack of sales or low sales volume in the home market—the *constructed-cost* method or the *third-country* method may be used. The constructed-cost method calculates the costs of production then adds a reasonable amount for administrative, selling and general costs and a profit margin. Alternatively, the third country method may be used. For example, in the case of Chinese exports to Mexico, the sales price of the same Chinese product in the United States might be used.[16]

As with subsidies, three elements are required to impose an ADD. First, there must be dumping. Second, there must be material injury or the threat of material injury to domestic producers, or the dumping must materially retard the establishment of a domestic industry. Third, there must be a causal relation between the dumping and the material injury. If all three elements are present, the maximum ADD that may be imposed is the "margin of dumping"—that is, the difference between the normal value and the export price. Under the *de minimus* rule, no duties are imposed where the margin of dumping is less than 2 percent of the export price or the volume of the imports in question is less than 3 percent of total imports. Unlike the case with subsidies, the *de minimus* rule is the same for developed and developing countries in dumping cases. As with subsidies, the duties terminate after five years (unless a new complaint is filed) or when the dumping ends, whichever comes first. As with subsidies, dumping decisions are subject to domestic judicial review. In NAFTA countries, judicial review by domestic courts has been replaced by judicial review by binational panels of arbitrators for cases involving NAFTA companies.

In addition, dumping decisions may be reviewed using the WTO dispute-resolution system. Only governments have access to the latter system, and the parameters of the review of the panel is limited. If the establishment of the facts was proper and the evaluation was unbiased and objective, even though the panel might have reached a different conclusion, the dumping decision cannot be overturned by the panel. Moreover, where a provision of the Agreement on Dumping is open to more than one interpretation, as long as the dumping decision was consistent with one of those interpretations, the dumping law of the country shall be found consistent with the agreement.[17]

In the case of both dumping and subsidies, complaints may be filed by the domestic industry, or investigations may be initiated by the government agency charged with the investigation. In Canada and the United States, separate government agencies investigate material injury on the one hand and the existence of subsidies or dumping on the other. In Mexico, the same government ministry investigates both kinds of issues.[18]

For example, the U.S. countervailing-duty process begins with a petition to the Department of Commerce (or initiation by the department itself). The first stage of the investigation is conducted by the International Trade Commission (ITC), which makes a preliminary determination whether the import in question is causing, or threatening to cause, material injury to a domestic industry. If the ITC makes a positive finding of injury, the International Trade Administration branch of the Department of Commerce makes a preliminary determination as to whether the import is subsidized and if so, to what extent. The Department of Commerce and the ITC must then make a final determination of subsidy and injury, respectively, before a CVD is imposed. An importer may challenge either of these final determinations under chapter 19 of the NAFTA, if the import is from Canada or Mexico. Appeals regarding imports from non-NAFTA countries go to the Court of International Trade.

Competition Law (Antitrust Law)

Competition law, which is known as "antitrust law" in the United States, provides governments with tools to police the anticompetitive practices of companies in their markets. The aim of such laws is to maintain healthy levels of competition by legislating against monopolistic and predatory practices by companies or groups of companies.[19] Critics of antidumping laws argue that competition laws should be used instead of antidumping laws in free trade areas. In some free trade agreements, this has happened. The Canada-Chile Free Trade Agreement, for example, eliminates the application of antidumping laws to the goods of the two countries.[20] However, NAFTA does not.

NAFTA chapter 15 requires each NAFTA country to have competition laws in place. It also requires the parties to cooperate with each other with respect to competition policy. However, NAFTA imposes no obligations regarding the content of those competition laws and prohibits recourse to dispute settlement with respect to these very limited obligations.[21] No harmonization of competition laws is required.

WTO does not impose obligations in the area of competition policy. However, in 1996 WTO members decided to set up a working group to analyze the relationship between trade and competition policy. At Doha, WTO members agreed to make competition policy the subject of Doha Round negotiations.

It is difficult to assess the prospects for replacing trade-remedy laws with a regional competition law in NAFTA. As noted, some argue that antidumping laws should be eliminated and existing competition laws used in their place. Some have proposed harmonization of competition laws, while others have gone further and proposed the creation of a North American Competition Commission. They argue that the degree of economic integration in the region and the cross-border mergers and acquisitions that take place require an integrated competition policy.[22]

The trouble with antidumping laws and subsidy laws is that they can be abused by a domestic industry that seeks protection from legitimate foreign competition. Domestic industries that use trade-remedy laws to seek administered protection oppose their elimination. In the United States, such political opposition to the elimination of trade-remedy laws within the free trade area has caused the U.S. government to reject both Canadian and Mexican proposals to eliminate them. However, competition laws could be harmonized without necessarily eliminating trade-remedy laws. Indeed, that could be the first step toward eliminating the use of trade-remedy laws between NAFTA members.

Business Strategy and Trade-Remedy Laws

Trade-remedy laws affect business strategy in three ways. First, companies need to assess the effect of dumping laws on differential pricing strategies. As long as the export market has no domestic competitor that can file a dumping complaint, antidumping duties do not become an issue. However, where the export market has antidumping laws and a domestic industry that might file a complaint, the risk of duties may influence the pricing strategy. For example, U.S. pharmaceutical companies that charge far lower prices for AIDS drugs in developing countries need not worry about antidumping duties against patented medicines, because they are the exclusive supplier of the patented product.

Second, companies must consider the potential effect of subsidies laws on government assistance strategies. Where firms receive financial support from government, the subsidies should be structured so as to fit one of the green-light categories, such as research and development. For example, Canada has sought to structure subsidies to aircraft maker Bombardier in a way that avoids violating WTO rules.

Third, firms in the importing market may use trade-remedy laws to seek protection against competitors' imports. For example, the U.S. lumber industry has used trade-remedy laws very effectively to limit competition in the lumber market and to increase profits by restricting the supply of lumber in their domestic market.

NAFTA DISPUTE SETTLEMENT

There are three principal types of dispute settlement under NAFTA. Foreign investors may make claims against governments under chapter 11. Second, under NAFTA chapter 20, member governments may challenge the laws of other members as not conforming to the obligations of the agreement. This mechanism focuses on the interpretation and application of NAFTA to the substance of domestic laws. Private parties have no direct access to the chapter 20 dispute-settlement mechanism.[23] Therefore, this mechanism only benefits firms if they can persuade their own governments to invoke the procedure on their behalf.

The third type of dispute settlement takes place under chapter 19. Chapter 19 applies only to disputes over the manner in which members' administrative agencies interpret and apply domestic trade-remedy law. As mentioned in the preceding discussion of trade-remedy laws, this mechanism replaces judicial review in the domestic courts of NAFTA countries with respect to NAFTA companies. Both private parties and governments can request the review by a chapter 19 panel of an agency's ADD and CVD decisions.

Chapter 19

NAFTA parties were unable to agree to a common set of rules governing subsidies and dumping when they negotiated the agreement. When CUSFTA was negotiated, the parties compromised by creating chapter 19. This same compromise was extended to Mexico under NAFTA. Rather than harmonize their trade-remedy laws, they replaced judicial review of agency decisions in domestic courts with binational panels in chapter 19.

Canadian negotiators pushed for chapter 19 because of a perception that the administrative agencies in the United States charged with deciding CVD and ADD cases were biased in favor of domestic complainants. The concern was that the International Trade Administration (ITA) and the International Trade Commission (ITC) made decisions based on political factors rather than economic analysis, thereby creating a form of administered protection.[24] While the decisions of the ITA and ITC were subject to judicial review in U.S. courts, the process of seeking judicial review and appeals through the courts could take several years, with duties in place in the interim; justice delayed would indeed be justice denied. In addition to concerns about delays, judges would generally not have technical expertise in the area of trade law and would show considerable deference to the decisions of specialized government agencies. Chapter 19 was designed to address these issues by providing a procedure that took less than one year, provided no appeal from panel decisions, and had expert trade lawyers serving as panelists. With their greater expertise, the panels would show less deference to administrative agencies that had erred in their decision making.

Under chapter 19 of NAFTA, a dispute panel may overturn a CVD or ADD decision where the agency's decision is "unsupported by substantial evidence on the record, or otherwise not in accordance with law."[25] A NAFTA government or citizen has thirty days to request a panel, and the panel process takes 315 days. Each government that is a party in the dispute chooses two panelists; all agree on the fifth. The majority must be lawyers in good standing. The panelists elect the chair from among themselves.

Panel decisions are binding and cannot be appealed. However, an "extraordinary challenge" procedure is available in place of appeal. Extraordinary challenge committees are made up of three judges or former judges. Each party selects one, and the parties draw lots to select the third. The extraordinary challenge committee can overturn the chapter 19 panel's decision where there is a violation of the code of conduct (for example, bias or conflict); a serious procedural flaw; or the panel exceeded its powers or jurisdiction. However, the panel's error must have materially affected its decision and must threaten the integrity of the panel process. As the name suggests, governments should only invoke this procedure in extraordinary circumstances. Moreover, it is only in extraordinary cases that the committee will overturn a panel's decision.

Chapter 20

Government-to-government disputes over the interpretation of NAFTA follow a procedure that is similar to WTO dispute-settlement procedures. However, the WTO procedure is better than NAFTA chapter 20 procedure. Moreover, many of the principles and obligations contained in NAFTA and WTO agreements are the same. As a result, since the WTO agreement came into effect, NAFTA chapter 20 has only been used occasionally. NAFTA countries have tended to resort to chapter 20 in cases only where WTO does not apply, as in the trucking dispute between Mexico and the United States.

Before a panel is formed, the Free Trade Commission (that is, the three trade ministers) must conduct consultations to seek a negotiated resolution. Should negotiations fail, the complaining country (the plaintiff) can request the formation of a panel. The plaintiff chooses the forum (WTO or NAFTA) unless an environmental issue is raised and the defendant prefers NAFTA.

The procedure for choosing panelists is different from that under chapter 19. In chapter 20, the parties either agree on a chair or draw lots and choose a nonnational. There is a process of reverse selection for the other four panelists—each party chooses two panelists from the other party's country. The five panel members must have experience in law, international law, international trade law or dispute settlement. They must be independent (that is, not work for one of the parties) and must follow a code of conduct. The independence requirement has tended to exclude most practicing trade lawyers from acting as panelists, as they or their firms will have represented NAFTA governments in the past. Thus, most chapter 20 panels have been composed primarily of academics.

Once the panel makes its final report, the disputing governments normally agree to adopt the recommendation of the panel. However, they are not obliged to follow its recommendation to the letter and may agree to an alternative resolution. If possible, the resolution should be removal of the law that violates NAFTA. If not, the parties should agree on the payment of compensation.[26] If they cannot agree on a resolution within thirty days of receiving the panel report, the plaintiff may retaliate with trade sanctions, preferably in the same sector that was the subject of the dispute.[27]

WTO DISPUTE SETTLEMENT

WTO dispute-settlement rules prohibit unilateral action against violations of the trade rules.[28] Rather, WTO members must seek recourse in the multilateral dispute-settlement system and comply with its rulings. The WTO Dispute Settlement Body (DSB) has the sole authority to establish panels, adopt panel and appellate reports, maintain surveillance of implementation of rulings and recommendations, and authorize retaliatory measures in cases of nonimplementation of recommendations.

The Dispute Settlement Body

The WTO dispute-settlement process resembles NAFTA chapter 20 in many ways, but they are not identical. The first step consists of consultations between the governments. If consultations fail and both parties agree, the WTO director-general offers good offices, conciliation or mediation to settle the dispute. If consultations fail to arrive at a solution after sixty days, the complainant can ask the DSB to establish a panel to examine the case. The DSB must establish a panel unless there is a consensus against the decision. The WTO Secretariat will suggest the names of three potential panelists to the parties to the dispute, drawing as necessary on a list of qualified persons. If there is real difficulty in the choice, the director-general can appoint the panelists.

Each party to the dispute transmits to the panel a submission on the facts and arguments in the case, in advance of the first substantive meeting. At that first meeting, the complainant presents its case and the responding party its defense. Third parties that have notified WTO of their interest in the dispute may also present views. Formal rebuttals are made at the second substantive meeting. In cases where a party raises scientific or other technical matters, the panel may appoint an expert review group to provide an advisory report.

The panel submits to the parties sections of its report that outline the facts presented and the arguments made by the parties, giving them two weeks to comment. The panel then submits to the parties an interim report, including its findings and conclusions, giving them one week to request a review. The period of review is not to exceed two weeks, during which the panel may hold additional meetings with the parties. Next, a final report is submitted to the parties. Three weeks later, it is circulated to all WTO members.

Where the panel finds a measure to be in violation of a WTO agreement, the panel recommends that the member concerned bring the measure into conformity with the agreement in question. It may also suggest ways in which the member could implement the recommendation. Panel reports are adopted by the DSB within sixty days of issuance, unless one party notifies its decision to appeal or a consensus emerges against the adoption of the report.

Appeals must be limited to issues of law covered in the panel report and the legal interpretation developed by the panel. Appeals are heard by three members of the WTO Appellate Body. They can uphold, modify or reverse the legal findings and conclusions of the panel. As a general rule, the appeal proceedings are not to exceed sixty days, but in no case shall they exceed ninety days. Thirty days after it is issued, the DSB adopts the report of the Appellate Body. The decision must be unconditionally accepted by the parties to the dispute, unless there is a consensus against its adoption.

Within thirty days of the adoption of the panel or appellate report, the party concerned must state its intentions in respect of the implementation of the recommendations. If it is impractical to comply immediately, the member will be given a "reasonable period of time" (to be set by the DSB) to do so.[29] If WTO member fails to act within this period, it is obliged to enter into negotiations with the complainant in order to determine a mutually acceptable compensation (for instance, tariff reductions in areas of particular interest to the complainant). If after twenty days no satisfactory compensation has been agreed upon, the complainant may request authorization from the DSB to suspend concessions or obligations against the other party (that is, impose retaliatory trade sanctions). The DSB should grant this authorization within thirty days of the expiry of the "reasonable period of time" unless there is a consensus against the request.

In principle, concessions should be suspended in the same sector as that in issue in the panel case. If this is not practicable or effective, the suspension can be made in a different sector of the same agreement. In turn, if this is not effective or practicable and if the circumstances are serious enough, the suspension of concessions may be made under another agreement.

While the imposition of trade sanctions goes against the WTO goal to reduce trade barriers, there is no other mechanism in place to compel countries to comply with decisions against them. The logic behind imposing sanctions (as a last resort) is that the industries that are subject to the trade sanctions will put political pressure on their own governments to comply with WTO decision. While the risk of sanctions may seem high, in practice most members have complied with the decisions of WTO. Without such compliance, the dispute-resolution system would not work.

Waivers

Where the dispute-resolution process is not the appropriate way to resolve an important issue, a member may choose to seek a waiver. The WTO Ministerial Conference, composed of representatives of all the members, meets at least once every two years.[30] In exceptional circumstances, the Ministerial Conference may decide to waive an obligation imposed on a member by the WTO Agreement or any of the multilateral trade agreements, if three-fourths of the members agree. A request for a waiver must be submitted initially for consideration by the appropriate council, which then submits a report to the Ministerial Conference.[31]

The EU has resisted complying with DSB decisions regarding the preferential treatment it gives to banana imports from former colonies. Even after the DSU authorized trade sanctions against EU agricultural exports, the EU did not comply. At the Doha meeting, the EU was granted a waiver for its banana import regime.

CHOICE OF FORUM: NAFTA OR WTO?

Some dispute-resolution mechanisms are open to the private sector, while others are open only to governments. However, companies should understand which is the preferable forum even when they do not have direct access, because it is the private sector's interests that are usually at stake. Before considering the pros and cons of the different options, however, one must consider the rules that apply when choosing between treaties (NAFTA and WTO) and when choosing between the dispute-settlement forums those treaties provide. The key issues are (1) who may choose the forum, and (2) which forum is most appropriate. For example, either a NAFTA government or a NAFTA company can challenge the application of another NAFTA member's subsidies law under chapter 19 of NAFTA. However, a chapter 19 panel cannot rule on whether the substance of the law complies with WTO Subsidies Agreement. The panel would have to consider the application of the law as it is written.

Alternatively, the WTO dispute-resolution system may be used to challenge the substance of the law. However, only governments have access to the WTO system. In addition, the agreements contain rules regarding which system has jurisdiction in a given case and who gets to choose the forum.

Under NAFTA article 103, Canada, Mexico and the United States affirmed their existing rights and obligations with respect to each other under GATT. They also agreed that in the event of any inconsistency between NAFTA and "such other agreements," NAFTA would prevail as a general rule.[32] The prevailing view of public international law, as noted in the first chapter, is that a later treaty is presumed to supercede an earlier treaty as between parties to both[33] and that a specific provision prevails over a general provision.[34] One may view article 103 as a confirmation of the presumption that the later supercedes the earlier law; NAFTA prevails over the GATT because NAFTA was later in time. Depending on which interpretation of article 103 prevails, NAFTA may or may not prevail over WTO agreements, which were not yet "existing" at the time NAFTA came into force.[35] The phrase "such other agreements" could be interpreted as referring to (1) existing agreements, (2) trade agreements in general, including future trade agreements, or (3) existing trade agreements. The presumption should be that WTO agreements prevail in the event of a conflict, being later in time.

The general conflicts rule in article 103 and the presumptions of international law may be superseded by more specific provisions in either agreement. Article 802 provides a good example of a specific provision that takes precedence over article 103. Article 802 explicitly states that "each Party retains its rights and obligations under Article XIX of the GATT or any safeguard agreement pursuant thereto." Article 802 goes on to require that NAFTA members exclude each other from such global safeguard actions, as a general rule, before detailing the circumstances in which NAFTA members may include each other in such actions. Article 802's detailed rules regarding the relationship between the safeguard provisions of NAFTA and the safeguard provisions of the GATT stand in sharp contrast to the broader wording of article 103. The words "or any safeguard agreement pursuant thereto" appear to anticipate the entry into force of WTO Agreement on Safeguards, bringing it under NAFTA conflicts provision. The absence of the qualifier "existing" before the rights and obligations confirms that the parties intended NAFTA article 802 to govern future safeguard obligations. All of this lends support to the view that article 103, in contrast, was not intended to require that NAFTA rights and obligations prevail over WTO agreements, as a general rule. As a result, in the absence of a specific NAFTA provision such as article 802, WTO agreements must be presumed to prevail over NAFTA in the event of a conflict.

NAFTA chapter 20 contains specific, detailed rules regarding the choice of forum between the NAFTA and WTO dispute-settlement systems, and it expressly provides that the choice-of-forum rules of NAFTA govern not only the GATT but any successor agreement as well. The general rule is that disputes involving both agreements may be settled in either forum at the discretion of the complaining party.[36] This general rule governs all choice-of-forum issues that arise between NAFTA and WTO agreements in matters of interpretation. However, the dispute-settlement provisions of chapter 20 do not apply to chapter 19.[37]

Chapter 19 is silent as to choice of forum between NAFTA and WTO agreements. However, the WTO has the exclusive authority to adopt interpretations of WTO agreements. [38] The end result is that only WTO can serve as a forum to resolve trade-remedy law issues that are governed by WTO agreements. Chapter 19 should only be used to provide judicial review of ADD and CVD decisions, which is required by both the subsidies and dumping agreements. However, conflicts may arise, because chapter 19 leaves open the possibility of pursuing different aspects of the same dispute in different forums.

CONCLUSION

Dispute-settlement mechanisms in international trade agreements provide international business strategists with an international forum in which to challenge laws that hamper business activities. Many laws may also be challenged in domestic courts using a variety of legal arguments. In effect, the international agreements add additional layers of litigation options.

Some of the international mechanisms are available directly to the affected companies, such as NAFTA chapter 11. Other mechanisms, such as NAFTA chapter 20 and the WTO dispute-resolution system, are available only to governments and thus only indirectly available to the firms whose interests they are ultimately designed to protect. Even though the governments are the ones using these systems, firms whose interests are at stake need to understand how they work and actively participate in the process.

There are also nonlitigious means for firms to use trade laws to their advantage. Firms can and should influence the content of the agreements during negotiations. In some cases their goal will be to seek protection in their domestic market. In other cases their goal may be to open foreign markets to their products. Outside of trade negotiations, firms can use trade-remedy laws to seek protection from foreign competitors. While seeking protection may not be the best competitive strategy over the long term, it may be a necessary evil for some firms.

Firms that rely on trade-remedy laws to maintain their competitive position should be aware of the new trend to eliminate the use of such laws (especially antidumping laws) in free trade agreements. They should follow such developments closely, as should firms whose exports are impeded by trade-remedy laws. Both types of firms will want to influence future negotiations on trade-remedy laws and dispute settlement. Legal disputes will probably always require a great deal of time and money to reach uncertain and imperfect outcomes. However, there is always room for improvement to the systems that are in place. Efforts to achieve deeper economic integration in North America must go hand in hand with efforts to improve the resolution of disputes.

NOTES

1. For example, Drucker argues that firms should be as accountable to their customers as they are to their shareholders. See Peter Drucker, *Management Challenges for the 21st Century* (New York: Harper Business, 1999). In the context of the softwood lumber dispute, it is interesting to note that the customers of the lumber companies, such as Home Depot, are opposed to the trade action taken. Others argue that a protectionist strategy may provide short-term benefits but that such strategies may prove detrimental in the long term. See, for example, Alan Rugman and Alain Verbeke, *Global Corporate Strategy and Trade Policy* (New York: Routledge, 1990).

2. Rugman and Verbeke, 9.

3. Ibid.

4. Drucker.

5. NAFTA article 1802.

6. "Agreement on Subsidies and Countervailing Measures, Final Act Embodying the Results of the Uruguay Round of Multilateral Trade Negotiations," April 15, 1994, *Legal Instruments—Results of the Uruguay Round*, annex 1A, vol. I, 33 ILM 1125 (1994), article 3 [hereafter "Agreement on Subsidies and Countervailing Measures"].

7. There are no WTO definitions of "developed" and "developing" countries. Members can announce for themselves whether they are developing countries. However, other members can challenge the announcement. For countries that negotiated to join WTO after 1995, their status depends on the terms agreed in the accession negotiations. WTO recognizes as least-developed countries those countries that have been designated as such by the United Nations. See also, "Agreement on Subsidies and Countervailing Measures," annex VII.

8. See "Agreement on Subsidies and Countervailing Measures," article 27. Export competitiveness in a product exists if the developing country's exports of that product have reached a share of at least 3.25 percent in world trade of that product for two consecutive calendar years. See article 27.5.

9. See, for example, Michael Porter, "The Competitive Advantage of Nations," *Harvard Business Review* 2 (1990), 73–95, and Michael Fairbanks and Stace Lindsay, *Plowing the Sea: Nurturing the Hidden Sources of Growth in the Developing World* (Cambridge, Mass.: Harvard Business School Press, 1997).

10. "Agreement on Subsidies and Countervailing Measures," article 4.

11. "Agreement on Subsidies and Countervailing Measures," article 8.

12. "Agreement on Subsidies and Countervailing Measures," articles 1 and 5. Subsidies on agricultural products are not governed by article 5 but rather are governed by the Agreement on Agriculture.

13. "Agreement on Subsidies and Countervailing Measures," articles 5–7.

14. "Agreement on Subsidies and Countervailing Measures," articles 10–11.

15. "Agreement on Subsidies and Countervailing Measures," article 23.

16. "Agreement on Implementation of article VI of the General Agreement on Tariffs and Trade 1994, Final Act Embodying the Results of the Uruguay Round of Multilateral Trade Negotiations," April 15, 1994, *Legal Instruments—Results of the Uruguay Round*, annex 1A, vol. I, 33 ILM 1125 (1994) [hereafter "Agreement on Dumping"], article 2.

17. "Agreement on Dumping," article 17.

18. For a more detailed explanation of trade-remedy laws in NAFTA countries, see North American Committee, *Trading Punches: Trade Remedy Law and Dispute Settlement under NAFTA*, ed. Beatriz Leycegui, William Robson and Dahlia Stein (Washington, D.C.: North American Committee, 1995).

19. For a discussion of competition laws in the Americas, see Moisés Naím and Joseph Tulchin, eds., *Competition Policy, Deregulation and Modernization in Latin America* (Boulder, Colo.: Lynne Rienner, 1999).

20. See Canada-Chile Free Trade Agreement, article M-01, available at http:/ /www. dfait-maeci.gc.ca/tna-nac/cda-chile/menu.asp. The agreement also establishes a committee to consider eliminating domestic CVD measures on trade between them. See article M-05(a).

21. NAFTA article 1501.

22. Ian Jack, "North American Body Urged to Police Mergers," *National Post*, June 20, 2001, C9.

23. NAFTA article 2021.

24. See Rugman and Verbeke, 27.

25. *In the Matter of Certain Softwood Lumber Products from Canada, Decision of the Panel*, Q.L. [1993] F.T.A.D. No. 5, 78.

26. NAFTA article 2018.

27. NAFTA article 2019.

28. See "Understanding on Rules and Procedures Governing the Settlement of Disputes, Final Act Embodying the Results of the Uruguay Round of Multilateral Trade Negotiations," April 15, 1994, *Legal Instruments—Results of the Uruguay Round*, annex 2, vol. I, 33 ILM 1125 (1994) [hereafter DSU]. Also *see US— Sections 301–310 of the Trade Act of 1974, Report of the Panel*, WT/DS132/R (1999), available at http://www.wto.org.

29. The "reasonable period of time" should not exceed fifteen months. See DSU article 21.3(c). Also see *European Communities—Regime for the Importation, Sale and Distribution of Bananas, Arbitration under Article 21.3(c) of the Understanding on Rules*

and Procedures Governing the Settlement of Disputes, Award of the Arbitrator, WT/DS27/15 (1998), available at http://www.wto.org.

30. "Marrakesh Agreement Establishing the World Trade Organization, April 15, 1994, Final Act Embodying the Results of the Uruguay Round of Multilateral Trade Negotiations," *Legal Instruments—Results of the Uruguay Round,* vol. I, 33 ILM 1125 (1994) [hereafter WTO Agreement].

31. WTO Agreement article IX(3).

32. GATT article XXIV, regarding free trade areas, does not prohibit such inconsistencies.

33. See I. Brownlie, *Principles of Public International Law,* 2d ed. (Oxford: Clarendon Press, 1973), 603, and Lord McNair, *The Law of Treaties* (Oxford: Clarendon Press, 1961), 219. See also *Vienna Convention on the Law of Treaties,* articles 30 and 59.

34. See McNair, 219.

35. NAFTA entered into force on January 1, 1994 (article 2203). Most WTO agreements were scheduled to enter into force January 1, 1995. See "Final Act Embodying the Results of the Uruguay Round of Multilateral Trade Negotiations," April 15, 1994, *Legal Instruments—Results of the Uruguay Round,* vol. I, 33 ILM 1125 (1994), paragraph 3.

36. NAFTA article 2005(1).

37. NAFTA article 2004.

38. WTO Agreement article IX(2).

Chapter 7

How AIDS, Trade and Terrorism Affect Our Economic Future

INTRODUCTION

It is important for business leaders to watch trends in trade liberalization and to consider how future developments may affect current business strategies. Firms that count the use of cheap labor in Mexico among their key strategies must realistically assess how long such a strategy will work. Other firms that depend on Mexico's preferential access to the United States and Canadian markets to maintain their competitive edge over nonmembers must consider how the addition of other Latin American nations might affect this strategy. In addition to looking at regional trends, firms must consider whether global trade liberalization might outpace regional trade liberalization, bringing even greater competition from Asia.

This chapter looks at two likely directions NAFTA may head over the next twenty years. The first part looks at the prospects for the expansion of NAFTA membership. The second part looks at the possibility of a European-style common market between Canada, Mexico and the United States, with a particular focus on the free movement of labor. The third part considers how the aftermath of September 11 may affect economic integration and security in the NAFTA region. The fourth part considers how the Doha Round may play out, given North-South tensions.

WIDENING VERSUS DEEPENING

There are essentially two directions in which NAFTA may go. First, NAFTA may be widened to include other members. In the mid-1990s, it was expected that Chile would be the first country outside of North America to join NAFTA. However, Chile got cold feet when President

Clinton failed to secure fast-track authority (now known as "trade-promotion authority") from Congress to negotiate the agreement. Instead, Canada negotiated a bilateral free trade agreement with Chile, and Mexico negotiated improvements to its existing agreement with Chile. The George W. Bush administration, in an effort to move forward the negotiation of the Free Trade Agreement of the Americas (FTAA), announced plans to negotiate a bilateral agreement with Chile as well, even in the absence of fast track. Many view the negotiation of the FTAA as the ultimate goal in widening NAFTA to include other members. However, much stands in the way of progress along this route.

The second direction for NAFTA may be a deepening of the level of integration between Canada, Mexico and the United States. A deepening integration is already occurring, first through the ongoing fifteen-year implementation time frame and secondly through ongoing negotiations to reach new agreements to eliminate barriers to the movement of goods, services, capital and people in the region.

Many perceive the ultimate goal of the deepening process as moving NAFTA in the direction of the European Union. This could involve adopting a common external-trade policy with respect to nonmembers, replacing trade-remedy laws with some form of harmonized competition law, moving toward free movement of labor in the region, creation of permanent supranational institutions and even the adoption of a common currency.

Widening and deepening are not mutually exclusive goals. If Canada, Mexico and the United States transform NAFTA into a customs union along the lines of the European Common Market, they could enter a FTAA as a single member. Indeed, MERCOSUR, the customs union between Argentina, Brazil, Paraguay and Uruguay, may enter the FTAA as a single member, just as the EU constitutes a single member of WTO. Alternatively, a North American Customs Union could negotiate free trade agreements with other countries, as the EU has done.

WIDENING: NAFTA EXPANSION AND THE FTAA

The addition of new members to NAFTA may take two different routes. Countries may join NAFTA by way of accession, or the negotiation of FTAA could join together all the countries of the hemisphere under a single trade agreement. Either route will require the granting of trade-promotion authority for the president of the United States.

U.S. Trade-Promotion Authority: Can the President and Congress Just Get Along?

With trade-promotion authority, the U.S. Congress authorizes the president to negotiate trade agreements that Congress cannot amend, but only approve or reject. This process also limits debate in Congress to sixty days.

Other countries are reluctant to negotiate with the United States without trade-promotion authority, because congressional participation in the negotiation process would make it very lengthy and difficult to reach agreement. After the president has negotiated a trade agreement, the Congress would seek a variety of changes to satisfy special interest groups, which the president would then have to take back to the other countries in the negotiation. This would require other countries to negotiate twice, something they are not inclined to do.

President Clinton's fast-track authority expired in 1994. He was unsuccessful in his subsequent efforts to persuade Congress to grant him trade-promotion authority. President George W. Bush narrowly secured a 215-214 vote for trade-promotion authority in December of 2001 in the House of Representatives. However, the Senate Finance Committee voted 18-3 to restrict the scope of the trade authority. The more restrictive the scope, the more difficult it will be for the president to negotiate trade agreements.

Republicans and Democrats in Congress disagree over the linkage between trade and nontrade issues, particularly environmental and labor issues. Some want trade sanctions used to change environmental and labor laws or practices in other countries. Others want environmental and labor laws regulated within trade agreements. Others are happy with the type of side agreements negotiated with NAFTA, agreements that primarily create mechanisms for cooperation on these issues and preserve the sovereignty of each country to make its own environmental and labor laws. Still others think discussions on environmental and labor issues should not be included in trade negotiations at all. Since Congress has been unable to agree on the approach to take on these issues, it has been difficult for the president to secure trade-promotion authority. Congress is also strongly opposed to the negotiation of trade-remedy laws in the Doha Round.

NAFTA Accessions Clause and Criteria for Accession

NAFTA article 2204 governs accession of new members to the agreement. It states:

1. Any country or group of countries may accede to this Agreement subject to such terms and conditions as may be agreed between such country or countries and the commission [cabinet-level representatives or their designates] and following approval in accordance with the applicable legal procedures of the country.

2. This Agreement shall not apply as between any Party and any acceding country or group of countries if, at the time of accession, either does not consent to such application.

This provision anticipates the accession of individual countries, such as Chile, or a group, such as the MERCOSUR countries. However, article 2204 does not specify conditions for eligibility.

The economic prerequisites for accession are likely to be that countries have inflation and fiscal deficits under control, adopt outward-looking and market-oriented domestic policies, set market-based exchange rates, fully implement WTO obligations, and make significant reductions in trade barriers. These reforms will be required in order to ensure that acceding countries are able to adjust to free trade and open competition without undue economic disruption. Mexico opened its economy rapidly and dramatically, before all of the necessary domestic reforms were in place. The lack of domestic savings, the reliance on foreign capital, and a government-controlled exchange rate contributed to the Mexican economic crisis of 1995, making adjustment to free trade more difficult and reducing the political acceptability of NAFTA in both Mexico and the United States.

Other advisable reforms would include the modernization of legal regimes, such as antidumping and countervailing duty laws, and the development of information and education programs to help domestic industry to adjust to changes in market conditions.

Article 2204 envisages the partial accession of countries to NAFTA, in the event that one or more existing members object to a particular candidate. Under this provision, Chile could have acceded to NAFTA only with respect to Canada and Mexico, given that the president of the United States was hobbled by his lack of fast-track negotiating authority. However, this route was not followed. Instead, Chile withdrew its request for accession, negotiated a bilateral trade and investment agreement with Canada, and entered into negotiations with Mexico to amend the bilateral trade agreement that already existed between the two. This reflects the economic reality that the U.S. market will be the main prize for any acceding country; no accession negotiations are likely to reach a successful conclusion without the participation of the United States.

The FTAA: From Alaska to Argentina without Fidel

In December of 1994, the leaders of the Western Hemisphere (minus Fidel Castro) met in Miami and announced plans to negotiate a FTAA by 2005. In 1998, the trade ministers of the participating countries agreed to an initial structure for the negotiations. They established nine negotiating groups: market access, investment, services, government procurement, dispute settlement, agriculture, intellectual property rights, competition policy, and subsidies and antidumping and countervailing duties.

At the Quebec City summit, leaders set the end of 2005 as the date for implementing the FTAA. They produced a 458-page document that reflected the progress made so far in the negotiations. The document contained many proposals but revealed little agreement. However, the leaders agreed to insert a "democracy clause" requiring consultations should one of the FTAA countries "interrupt" the "democratic order."[1]

No final agreement will likely be reached unless the United States President has adequate trade-promotion authority. Moreover, it remains unclear how quickly trade barriers will be phased out under this agreement. NAFTA phases out trade barriers over a period of fifteen years; if the FTAA chooses the same time frame, it would take until 2020.

The relevance of the FTAA will be affected by ongoing negotiations in WTO. If WTO negotiations are able to achieve the same degree of trade liberalization as the FTAA and in the same period of time, there will be no reason to have a FTAA, since the members of the proposed FTAA are also members of WTO.

A major challenge of the FTAA negotiations will be the coordination of the relationship between WTO and the FTAA, and their relationship to NAFTA and other existing trade agreements, such as MERCOSUR, the Group of Three (Colombia, Venezuela and Mexico) and the multitude of bilateral trade agreements that exist in the region. For example, Mexico has trade agreements with Costa Rica, Bolivia, Chile, and Nicaragua, El Salvador, Guatemala, Honduras and the EU.

While Mexico is officially in favor of the FTAA, it is not in Mexico's interest to see these negotiations proceed quickly. Mexico currently has preferential access to the U.S. market, which gives it an advantage over other Latin American countries. The FTAA would take away Mexico's advantage and open it up to greater competition from other Latin American countries that enjoy comparable advantages. Mexico has made a strategic move in this regard by seeking deeper integration with NAFTA countries. Should this result in a North American customs union, Mexico would maintain an advantage over Latin American countries that have only a free trade relationship with the United States and Canada. It is also possible to negotiate the accession of new NAFTA members at the same time countries are negotiating the FTAA. Indeed, should the U.S. president secure trade-promotion authority, some Latin American countries may choose this path, since it would provide improved access to the American market more quickly than the FTAA negotiations would.

THE PROSPECT OF A NORTH AMERICAN CUSTOMS UNION

Mexico has become one of the major trading nations of the world in a relatively short period of time.[2] The vast majority of Mexico's trade takes place with the United States. In an effort to diversify trade partners and attract foreign investment, Mexico has signed many free trade agreements since NAFTA, most notably with the EU. Underlying the free trade policy of the Mexican government has been a desire to generate economic growth through trade and foreign direct investment.

However, it is the individual firm that must exploit international trade and investment opportunities, using business strategies that will allow it to succeed in the global business environment against a backdrop of appropriate national government policies.[3] Business strategy and prosperity in Mexico will be affected by demographic trends and the prospects for the creation of a customs union between NAFTA countries.

Free Movement of Labor in NAFTA Is Attainable in the Long Run

The election of President Vicente Fox in Mexico in 2000 ushered in a new era in United States–Mexico relations. President Fox is the first president in seventy-one years who is not a member of the PRI, the party that ruled Mexico during that time. His democratic credentials, his warm relationship with President Bush in Washington, and his background as a business executive have given him tremendous credibility in the eyes of U.S. political leaders.

President Fox has made it clear not only that his administration will continue to pursue an economic policy of trade liberalization but that his vision includes a much closer economic integration in North America that would include the free movement of labor. While this goal has been described as highly controversial by the press and was rejected initially by political leaders in the United States and Canada,[4] demographic and economic realities make it a highly desirable and realistic goal for Mexico to pursue.

Presidents Bush and Fox, at their first meeting as presidents on February 16, 2001, said they would seek to "consolidate a North American economic community."[5] They appointed a working group to explore new policies to address illegal immigration from Mexico to the United States and to improve protection for Mexican migrants, including proposals to expand guest worker programs in the United States.[6]

The Elements of a Common Market: Money and Migrants

President Fox has proposed that NAFTA evolve into a European-style common market. A common market removes trade barriers, adopts a common external trade policy, and permits the free movement of labor and capital. The removal of trade barriers is already in progress under NAFTA. Capital movements are basically free between the member countries.[7]

There is a common external trade policy for some products, such as computers, but it would be challenging politically to adopt a common trade policy generally.

U.S. trade embargoes imposed on the grounds of national security, such as those against Cuba and Iran, could complicate negotiating a common external trade policy. The countries would have to agree on a common security policy in trade-related matters. This may be easier to achieve in the wake of the terrorist attacks of September 11.

Another issue that would have to be addressed is the relationship between the customs union and the free trade agreements that exist between NAFTA members and other countries. One option would be to renegotiate these agreements so as to be between the customs union and outside countries rather than with individual NAFTA members. This would require agreement on the part of each outside country involved and all three NAFTA members. In some cases this may be relatively easy to achieve. For example, all three NAFTA countries currently have individual free trade agreements with Israel; these three bilateral agreements could be folded into a single agreement between the customs union and Israel. Other cases may prove more difficult. For example, Mexico has a free trade agreement with the EU, but Canada and the United States do not. The negotiation of a free trade agreement between the EU and a North American Customs Union would be more complex.

There has also been some discussion of a European-style monetary union among NAFTA countries. Unlike in Europe, however, this would probably entail the adoption of the U.S. dollar in Canada and Mexico rather than the creation of a new currency. Such a move would prove difficult to manage politically. Nevertheless, Jim Jones, a former U.S. ambassador to Mexico, foresees a "de facto monetary union" between the United States and Mexico in ten to fifteen years. He predicted that "people and events will run ahead of the politicians," citing a poll taken in Mexico on "dollarizing" the Mexican economy. The poll showed that about 80 percent of the Mexican people favored using the U.S. dollar as their currency. Jones said the poll indicates the Mexican peso, which has long been one of the major symbols of Mexican sovereignty, "is no longer an important issue." However, he doubted that Canada would join such a monetary union, because Canadians attach much more importance to the Canadian dollar than Mexicans do to their peso.[8] While it is difficult to predict political sentiments, exchange rates probably influence Mexican attitudes to dollarization. Decades of devaluation may have weakened political support for the currency. However, the peso has been much stronger in recent years, and that may increase Mexicans' desire to retain it.

Economists are divided on the issue of dollarization. Some argue that such a move would reduce transaction costs and reflect what are already the bookkeeping practices of many North American firms. Others argue that the structure of the Canadian and Mexican economies are sufficiently different from that of the United States to require independent monetary policies.[9] However, the three economies are becoming increasingly integrated as a result of NAFTA, particularly in key sectors such as manufacturing and financial services.

Demographics and Free Movement of Labor

Demographics in the NAFTA countries will help to resolve the issue of free movement of labor in the region. Declining birthrates in the developed countries are shaping demand for labor. In the United States and Canada, the so-called baby-boom generation has had a profound impact on investment and consumption patterns for several years. The "baby boom" is the generation of people born between 1945 and 1963, when birthrates in Anglo America spiked between the end of the Second World War and the introduction of the pill.

The post-1963 generation is known as the "baby bust," because the pill led to a dramatic decrease in the birthrate. It has remained relatively low ever since. What this means is that Canada and the United States will experience labor shortages in many areas once the baby boomers retire. Declining birthrates in Mexico will reduce the number of people entering the labor market. Together with rising incomes in Mexico, this should reduce the flow of undocumented Mexican workers to the United States. Tables 7.1 and 7.2 show the age structure and fertility rates in NAFTA countries, respectively.

Demand for Mexico's Youth Will Rise

Mexico's population is relatively young. This means that Mexico will have a relatively abundant supply of labor when Canada and the United States are experiencing labor shortages. Under this scenario, free movement of labor would benefit all three NAFTA countries. Anglo-American businesses would gain access to the labor they need, and Mexicans would gain access to the jobs they need. However, as noted, Mexican birthrates are declining, and the growth in the supply of labor in Mexico will slow down.

One implication is that labor costs in Mexico will rise, for two reasons. First, the growth in the Mexican economy through free trade and international investment will raise the standard of living, and hence labor costs, over time. Secondly, the increased demand for Mexican labor in Anglo America, which will coincide with lower growth rates in Mexico's labor force, will put further upward pressure on the cost of labor. It is unlikely that the productivity of Mexican workers will rise as quickly as labor costs

Table 7.1
Age Structure in NAFTA Countries (% of Total Population)

Under 15	Canada	USA	Mexico
1960	33.7	31.0	. . .
1998	19.8	22.2	34.4
Over 65	Canada	USA	Mexico
1998	12.3	11.9	5.1
2020	16.7	16.3	7.2

Source: OECD and UN Population Division.

under these circumstances. The result will be that other low-wage countries will soon have a significant labor-cost advantage over Mexico.

The implication is that NAFTA firms that rely on low-cost Mexican labor to maintain a competitive advantage will experience declining competitiveness. This trend is likely to be further exacerbated by further trade-barrier reductions under WTO and other trade agreements, particularly with the accession of China to WTO. As a result of these trends, NAFTA firms that depend on cheap Mexican labor to compete must change their strategy.

Current programs cover workers at opposite ends of the spectrum. On one end, there are programs for unskilled agricultural workers. At the other end are agreements to facilitate the mobility of highly educated technical and professional workers. In the middle lies the most challenging category to address—semiskilled workers with no more than high school educations. This is precisely the constituency of workers in the United States and Canada that labor unions most want to protect from lower-wage Mexican competition. For these reasons, the pursuit of such an

Table 7.2
NAFTA Fertility Rates (2.08 is necessary to maintain a stable population)

Years	Canada	USA	Mexico
1950–1955	3.7	3.45	6.75
1985–1990	1.7	1.92	3.0

Source: OECD, *Maintaining Prosperity in an Aging Society* (Paris: 1998).

agreement will be a long-term project that will require a narrowing of the wage gap in order to overcome union opposition.

Greater labor mobility will dramatically change North American labor markets. It is likely to have a particularly strong impact on firms with operations in Mexico that now rely on cheap labor to remain competitive. However, the availability of labor will also affect the competitive strategies of firms located in Canada and the United States. The demographic clouds on the horizon suggest that labor-intensive industries in Canada and the United States will either need Mexico's labor to come to them or will have to go to Mexico, or elsewhere. It will be necessary for firms to take these demographic trends into account in the development of their competitive strategies.

THE WARMTH OF THE NORTH AND THE CHILL OF THE SOUTH: AMERICAN BORDERS AFTER SEPTEMBER 11

> Good fences don't make good neighbors. Good neighbors make good neighbors.
>
> William Graham, member of the Canadian Parliament, chairman of the Parliamentary Committee on Foreign Affairs and International Trade, speaking at the Instituto Tecnológico Autónomo de México, Mexico City, on October 10, 2001.

The terrorist attacks of September 11 brought the issue of border security to the forefront in the NAFTA countries.[10] In the weeks following the attacks, heightened security caused serious delays on the southern and northern borders of the United States, with longer delays on the southern. These delays created a serious disruption of auto production in the United States, as that industry depends on just-in-time delivery. The attacks have motivated politicians to dedicate greater resources to border security on the continent. After all, Los Angeles is not far from Tijuana, and neither is Seattle from Vancouver.

Herein lies the dilemma. Higher security will raise the cost of business in NAFTA countries, but lower security might raise the risk of an attack launched from somewhere in North America. Security resources will have to be deployed in a way that minimizes the economic costs of doing business across the borders of an increasingly integrated North American economy.

Border Talks before September 11: On the CUSP of Deeper Integration

During his visit to Washington in early September 2001, as we have seen, President Fox raised the issue of legalizing the status of Mexico's illegal migrants in the United States—through some form of guest worker permits, within a year. For President Fox, legalization would provide a way to protect citizens making a dangerous migration that killed over four hundred in the year 2000 alone (although the numbers have fallen since then).

For U.S. President Bush, such a policy had its own charm—it would appeal to Mexican-American voters. According to the 2000 census of the United States, 12 percent of Americans are of Hispanic origin, and at least 65 percent of these are of Mexican origin. By 2010, the United States will have the second-largest Spanish-speaking population in the world—with forty-three million native Spanish speakers, second only to Mexico. In the 2000 presidential election, only 35 percent of Hispanics voted for Bush (and that was the best showing by a Republican among Hispanic voters since Ronald Reagan in 1984). In Texas, Mr. Bush got 43 percent of the Hispanic vote in 2000, and in Florida, where Hispanics include traditionally Republican Cuban-Americans, he received 49 percent. But in California, Mr. Bush polled 29 percent. In New York, where Puerto Ricans are a major component, he got only 18 percent.

On his first visit to the United States after the September 11 attack, President Fox made a very clear statement of his vision of a trilateral cooperation on October 5: "We have to share information about intelligence, share control of migratory movements, customs issues, information about airports and aircraft in our territories."

Prior to the attacks, the notion of a common security perimeter was widely discussed in Washington and Ottawa, amid security concerns and growing cross-border traffic. In Ottawa, Paul Cellucci, the American ambassador to Canada, suggested a European-style "perimeter" within which Canada, the United States and Mexico would jointly manage North America's external border entry points while dismantling internal borders. In Detroit, the Canadian ambassador to the United States, Michael Kergin, pointed out that the average nontariff border cost had reached about 5 percent of the price of products, 10–13 percent in trade-sensitive industries. Somewhat prophetically, he asked whether Canada and U.S. customs and immigrations rules should be aligned, while improving controls "to keep undesirable elements away from our common North American space."

The Canada–United States Partnership (CUSP), an advisory group created by Prime Minister Jean Chrétien and President Clinton in 1999, has called for policy harmonization on visa requirements, immigration, and security operations between the two countries. The Canadian cochair of CUSP has warned that businesses are being hurt by the potential for border gridlock. However, he acknowledged the need to reassure citizens in both countries that their security would not be compromised.

To be sure, there are conflicting views about the common-perimeter idea. Canada's minister for international trade supports the idea of reducing border frictions, but his comments have focused on the Canadian-U.S. border. The Canadian minister of foreign affairs has rejected outright the idea of a common perimeter that would include Mexico, preferring to focus on the Canadian-U.S. border. Canada's minister of immigration has objected to the notion of harmonizing immigration policies, voicing concerns over the independence of Canadian policy. Similarly, the deputy prime minister of Canada has challenged the idea of a common perimeter, because of the implications for Canadian sovereignty.

Essentially, a common perimeter between Canada and the United States would mean that people or goods entering either country from other countries would gain entry to both simultaneously. As one commentator has pointed out, that would require "a lot of sharing . . . and a lot of trust." Among NAFTA countries the relationship that enjoys the least amount of mutual trust is that of the United States and Mexico.

Perceptions after September 11: The "Staunch Ally" versus the "Fair Weather Friend"

The day after the attack, the U.S. ambassador to Canada reiterated his support for a North American perimeter and suggested that Canada and the United States consider harmonizing immigration policies to reduce such threats in the future. In the weeks following, some of the U.S. media advocated reinforced patrols and inspections on the Canadian border, while others supported the views of the ambassador. The United States had only 334 Border Patrol agents and 498 inspectors on the Canadian border, compared with 8,893 on the Mexican border, over 1,400 in Arizona alone. On the northern border, there is one border guard for every four thousand legal crossings; on the southern side, there is one border guard for every 1,100 legal crossings. Clearly, most of the border guards on the southern side are deployed to catch the illegal crossings.

The U.S. customs service stationed one hundred extra officers on the Canadian border in order to staff all crossing points twenty-four hours a day following the attack. The United States decided to end the practice of simply placing orange cones in the middle of the road to indicate that a particular border crossing with Canada was closed at night. The crossings would be on the highest level of alert for the foreseeable future. Initially, wait times to enter the United States increased dramatically. On September 13, the United States–bound commercial flow faced lineups ten to twenty kilometers long at some points and wait times as high twelve hours. At the Windsor Ambassador Bridge, a major crossing point for North America's integrated automobile industry, the backup was so extreme that it was impossible to estimate wait times. Those times were reduced to near normal within one week (in part due to a sharp drop in freight volumes).

The story was very different on the southern border of the United States. On the busiest border in the world, trucks formed long lines on the Mexican side of the border. In some cases, they were delayed by days—upsetting production schedules of U.S. manufacturing companies that depended on intermediate goods for just-in-time production processes.

The Northern Exposure: From Cold War Allies to Terror War Allies

When the United States and Britain launched attacks against Afghanistan, the president of the United States asked Canada to provide military assistance. Canada agreed to send ships, planes and troops to support the United States. Canada made the third-largest military contribution, after the United States and Britain, to the Bush government's operation in Afghanistan.

Canada and the United States have a long history of military and security cooperation, most recently in the Persian Gulf War, but also including World Wars I and II, the Korean War, and the Cold War. The two continue this tradition through the North American Aerospace Defense Command (NORAD) and the North Atlantic Treaty Organization (NATO). The Canada–United States Joint Defense Board, which reports to the prime minister and the president, has existed for over fifty years. There is a high level of trust between these culturally close countries. Together with the extensive cooperation links that already exist, such trust makes even greater cooperation likely in the wake of the September 11 attacks. Indeed, a recent survey found that 85 percent of Canadians generally favor making the changes necessary to create a North American security perimeter. Another poll found that 59 percent of Canadians "don't mind giving up some of our national sovereignty if it increases the overall security of North America."

Despite the public protests of some politicians, Canada has already begun the process of harmonizing some of its laws with those of the United States. Recently introduced draft legislation on terrorism, border operations and immigration procedures resemble their equivalents in the United States and Britain. Canadian-landed immigrants will get new identification cards that are similar to the U.S. green card, with photographs and magnetic information strips. In addition, three hundred new officers are to be hired to screen refugees and immigrants more rigorously.

The Southern Blues: Hard Cases Need Better Policies

Mexico has had an uneasy relationship with the United States ever since it lost about half of its territory to the United States some 150 years ago.

With a long history of foreign invasions by both the United States and European powers, Mexico adopted a "live and let live" foreign policy. It was formally enshrined in the so-called Estrada Doctrine of 1930 (named after the then-foreign minister of Mexico, Genero Estrada). President Fox is seeking to change this and to involve Mexico in world affairs to a greater extent. This stance may be facilitated by Mexico's new seat on the United Nations Security Council. However, the initial reaction of many in Mexico was to not get involved in the aftermath of the attacks of September 11. Polls in Mexico showed 62 percent of Mexicans think that Mexico should be neutral.

Against the backdrop of Monroe Doctrine (which stipulated that the United States has the right to intervene anywhere in the Americas if it finds itself threatened), the relationship between Mexico and the United States has been fraught with mistrust. Most Mexicans are vividly aware of their losses to the United States in the 1846–48 war. Corruption under the PRI regime caused the United States to have little trust for Mexico. In the past, efforts to cooperate on drugs have been complicated when corrupt officials in Mexico passed on information to the traffickers. Mexican customs officials also have a bad reputation for corruption. It hit a nadir when an elephant was smuggled into Mexico from Texas in 2000 and no record was ever found of its entry. Police corruption makes most people in Mexico unwilling to report crime; a survey by the Fundación Rosenblueth in 2000 found that less than 20 percent of people from Mexico City are willing to report criminal activities. This attitude may hamper the flagging of terrorist activities by the general public, such as store owners who sell products that may be used by terrorists.

Corruption will not be eliminated overnight, and it will likely continue to complicate the information sharing and trust required to cooperate closely on security issues. The relationship improved with the election of Vicente Fox in 2000. The U.S. Foreign Relations Committee, headed by Senator Jesse Helms, held its first-ever meeting outside of the United States in Mexico in May 2001. In a letter published in the influential Mexico City daily *La Reforma,* Helms wrote, "The US recognizes Fox as a genuinely democratic leader and a true reformer—and US leaders of all stripes are more than disposed to work with him." But the reaction to the September attacks of the "man in the street" in Mexico demonstrated that the relationship needs to improve much more than it has. A mutual lack of trust endures.

Ironically, Mexico is one of the countries that will be hardest hit by the repercussions of the terrorist attacks of September 11, despite the initial indifference of the Mexican people. Extra security on the border has slowed the passage of goods and people. The economic impact on the U.S. economy has echoed across the border in Mexico. Almost 90 percent of

Mexican exports are destined for the United States, and roughly one-third of the Mexican economy depends on trade.

Manufacturing in Mexico had been growing at the rate of 10 percent a year between 1996 and 2000. Much of manufacturing growth in Mexico came from the export of durable goods. In September 2001, U.S. consumption of durable goods was down by 8 percent, the single biggest monthly drop ever recorded. Although the effect of this drop is not yet available in the form of hard data in Mexico, it is sure to be considerable. The tourism industry has suffered, with American tourists reluctant to drive across the border for lineups and fearful of flying. In the first month after the attack, big tourist resorts in Cancun and Acapulco reported a reduction in the number of tourists of at least 50 percent.

Hundreds of thousands of poor Mexicans cross the border illegally each year in search of jobs in the United States and send money back to their families in Mexico. They now have a harder time going across the border, for which the indirect evidence is that the number of people deported by the U.S. Immigration and Naturalization Service fell by 40 percent during the first month after the attack. Moreover, efforts by the United States to legalize this flow of Mexican migrants will likely be delayed by the heightened concern over border security.

Criticism leveled at Mexico for its lukewarm response to the tragedy, together with the realization that the attacks have caused economic damage in Mexico, has provoked some soul searching on the Mexican side of the border that may ultimately improve the relationship. Moreover, Mexican authorities cooperated fully with their American counterparts to monitor the flow of people from the United States to Mexico in the days following the attacks. Mexican airlines also cooperated with the Federal Aviation Administration, working with American officials to ensure that they meet U.S. security standards. Two largest Mexican carriers, Mexicana and AeroMexico, already have code-sharing agreements with two U.S. carriers, United Airlines and Delta Airlines. Regardless of past difficulties, there really is no choice for Mexico but to work more closely with the United States on security issues.

Rivers of People: Cross-Border Movement in North America

The exact implications of September 11 for the movement of people remain unclear. On the northern border, roughly five million Canadians and six million Americans cross the border each month. An estimated twenty-five million people cross the southern border each month.

On the northern border, the United States continues to press for a common security perimeter. Official statements from Canadian leaders suggest that they will resist harmonizing Canada's immigration policies with those of the United States. However, as noted above, the Canadian people appear to be ahead of the politicians on this issue, and the actions taken by the government appear to contradict the statements of reluctant political leaders.

On the southern border, the politicians may be ahead of the people in terms of the degree of policy harmonization they would be willing to accept. The United States may encounter more resistance among the Mexican people than among Canadians to the notion of giving up a degree of national sovereignty to ensure the security of the region. However, the Fox administration has improved cooperation on many fronts, including immigration policies, in order to reduce the attractiveness of Mexico as a gateway for "people smugglers" whose destination is the United States. However, many U.S. lawmakers have resisted the Mexican push for some form of legalization for the estimated three million undocumented Mexicans working in the United States.

With respect to visa requirements, the United States has a visa requirement for Mexicans, but Canada does not. Given the flows of illegal migration, harmonization with the United States would require Canada to introduce such a requirement. While this would ruffle feathers in Mexico, there would be little political cost in Canada, where there are few voters of Mexican heritage. Moreover, abuse of Canada's refugee system has been much publicized in the press, creating widespread political support for tightening it. That will mean screening refugees before they come, which in turn means visas will likely be required from countries that are significant sources of bogus refugee claims. The number of such claims coming from Mexico increased after the passage of NAFTA, so Canada may not be unwilling to impose a visa requirement on Mexicans. The alternative would be for the United States to eliminate its visa requirement and proceed with some form of legalization program for the three hundred thousand undocumented workers that cross the border each year from Mexico.

The harmonization of immigration policy is a different matter. The three NAFTA countries have different needs and policies with respect to immigration. The United States follows a "quota by country system"; Canada uses a "points system" that does not take account of the origin of the would-be immigrant. However, security screening of immigrants can be improved in all three countries without requiring the complete harmonization of their policies. Immigration to Mexico is a long and complicated process. Most immigrants to Mexico have to demonstrate that they have jobs in Mexico that cannot be filled by Mexicans. Achieving residency is a decade-long process.

Must a more open border between Canada and the United States be accompanied by labor mobility? The short answer is no. To be legally employed in the United States, workers require social security numbers in the United States, or in Canada, a social insurance number. Since most of the economic activity in both countries takes place in the formal sector and the two countries have similar employment markets and standards of living, there is less risk of open borders leading to flows of illegal workers. Indeed, the border is already sufficiently open for that to have occurred, and it has not been a significant problem for either country. It is, rather, a problem specifically between the United States and Mexico.

Illegal immigration from Mexico represents both a blessing and a curse for the United States. On the one hand, the American economy benefits from a supply of much-needed labor (especially for the types of jobs no U.S. resident wants). On the other hand, the illegal nature of this flow of people promotes more illegal activities, such as people smuggling and the abuse of undocumented workers' rights.

In the long run, the problem will sort itself out. Demographic trends in the United States over the next thirty years will lead to increasing shortages of labor and a significant change in the makeup of the population pyramid in Mexico. Economic trends in Mexico will likely raise incomes sufficiently over the same period of time so that the same degree of openness can be achieved for Mexicans as for Canadians.

In the meantime, however, border issues related to the mobility of people will probably not be addressed on a trilateral basis between the members of NAFTA, even though President Fox (through the foreign minister, Jorge Castañeda) is trying to include Mexico in such discussions. Most border issues have not been addressed on a trilateral basis in the past, primarily due to the dramatic differences in standards of living. For instance, the United States has a visa requirement (as noted) for Mexicans but not for Canadians; it imposes a limit of 5,500 NAFTA visas for Mexican professionals but no limit for Canadians; U.S. customs officers are stationed at airports in Canada but not at airports in Mexico; the United States continued to resist the entry of Mexican trucks long after they allowed Canadian trucks to operate in the country. Many border issues are handled on a bilateral basis rather than on a trilateral basis, and that format may continue. For example, Canada and the United States formalized cooperation under a 1995 bilateral border accord that has since been enhanced by several bilateral initiatives. These include the CUSP, USINC-CIC Border Vision (a strategic planning initiative of the immigration authorities to deal with illegal immigration), and the Cross-Border Crime Forum (cooperation and information sharing on transnational crime). These initiatives are designed to help the two countries improve the passage of commercial traffic on the border while facing the common external threats of international terrorism, transnational crime, and drug and people smuggling.

The impact of September 11 may be to perpetuate the existing asymmetries in the bilateral border relationships in North America with respect to the movement of people. National security takes precedence over trade under the trade agreements that apply, and it is perhaps the broadest exception contained in those agreements. Despite recent advances in the relationship between Mexico and the United States, the Canadian border remains more open to the movement of people than the Mexican border, and it can be policed with fewer personnel. However, even the tighter security on the Mexican border is insufficient to stop the passage of three hundred thousand illegal migrants each year, making it a less than optimal solution over the long term.

Capital Movements: Doing the Laundry

On the surface, free capital movement already occurs among NAFTA countries. More than 70 percent of banking capital in Mexico is under foreign control. The largest bank in Mexico, Banamex, was taken over by Citigroup in mid-2001. Citigroup took the unprecedented step of listing itself on the Mexican stock exchange—the first foreign company ever to do so. More than half of the insurance industry in Mexico is under foreign control.

Canada is the largest foreign real estate owner in the United States. The United States is the largest source of foreign investment in Canada. Recently, there has been a flurry of cross-border mergers and acquisitions in the financial sectors of the United States and Canada, further blurring financial borders. For example, the Canadian firm TD Waterhouse handles investments in both countries. For security purposes, each of the three governments may exercise considerable discretionary power in the financial sector, using the security exception under NAFTA and WTO.

NAFTA has done much to break down barriers to cross-border capital flows. A company from outside NAFTA region that is able to meet the requirements for incorporation (or other forms of business organization) and complies with foreign investment laws may become a NAFTA company. However, companies that are controlled by investors from outside NAFTA countries may be denied NAFTA benefits if they have no substantial business activities in the territory of the countries under whose laws they are constituted. Benefits may also be denied if a NAFTA country does not maintain diplomatic relations with the investor's home country or prohibits business transactions with enterprises from that country.

NAFTA prohibits restrictions on transfers of profits, proceeds or payments unless the restrictions are due to the application of laws relating to bankruptcy, securities, criminal offenses, currency transfer reporting or enforcement of judgments. Governments therefore remain free to restrict transfers under such laws as those relating to money laundering. Following the September 2001 attacks, NAFTA governments used money-laundering laws to deal with terrorist funds.

NAFTA also contains a more general national-security exception that applies to all of its provisions, including the treatment of foreign investors. This exception could be used to restrict capital movements whenever one of the governments considers such restrictions necessary for the protection of its essential security interests in a time of war or other emergency in international relations. Capital restrictions placed on terrorist funds in the context of the September 11 attacks would very likely qualify under this exception. In the case of restrictions on terrorist funds, the measures would clearly be related to security interests, not commercial purposes.

Movement of Goods: The Goods, the Bads and the Uglies

Higher security efforts will increase the cost of movement of goods across the border. This will impose a higher cost of producing goods across borders. This might slow the process of integration among the three countries. With technology and large-scale movement of goods, NAFTA countries should be able to exploit economies of scale. Thus, the additional long-run marginal cost may be negligible. An instructive example can be drawn from the seizure of illegal drugs—a barometer of the drug trade between Mexico and the United States. For the first two weeks after the attacks, seizures across the border were down by half. By early October, they were back to the pre-attack level. That is, the traffickers quickly found alternative ways of keeping up their supply. The same could be true of the movement of legal goods. However, to eliminate border delays, manufacturers will incur costs associated with the extra security measures they have to implement to get preferred treatment at the border.

Three's Company: The Importance of Including Mexico

The movements of illegal goods and illegal migrants also point to the importance of Mexico. Ignoring Mexico leaves a large hole in the U.S. security perimeter. If it is so easy for goods (even elephants), capital, and people to move across the border, how can the United States expect to improve security without Mexican cooperation? Unless the United States sets up an impenetrable fence along its southern border, it will need to make Mexico a part of its security strategy. If Washington fails to bring Mexico on board, the United States might regret it in the future. Of course, given the level of corruption, apathy and downright hostility toward the "gringos" on the Mexican side, involving Mexico substantively will not be an easy task. But it is absolutely essential. After all, the biggest foreign "invasion" of the United States before the attack on September 11, 2001, was launched by the famous Mexican general Pancho Villa (on March 6, 1916, against the tiny village of Columbus, New Mexico).

The events of September 11 show how unexpected events can affect the process of economic integration in unforeseeable ways. Despite political rhetoric regarding the importance of Mexico to the United States, Canada remains a more trusted and reliable ally in matters of national security. Thus, the events of September 11 may accelerate the integration of Canada and the United States and slow that of Mexico and the United States on border and security issues. National security takes precedence over trade. However, the two are not unrelated.

THE WTO DOHA ROUND: A CONVERGENCE OF AIDS, TRADE AND TERRORISM

2001 saw an extraordinary convergence of three apparently unrelated events. First, the North-South battle over patent protections versus access to AIDS drugs came to a head in Africa and Brazil, following the declaration by the UN of AIDS as a global security issue in 2000. Second, terrorists attacked the United States, further slowing the global economy and forever shattering the illusion that North Americans were somehow insulated from such turmoil. Third, the WTO held a meeting of trade ministers in Doha to launch a new round of global trade negotiations, counter the economic slowdown and show unity in the face of the terrorist threat. The fact that the Doha meeting almost failed over the issue of patents and AIDS drugs vividly displayed the connection between AIDS, trade and terrorism.

The success or failure of the Doha Round has enormous implications for global prosperity, security and the ability of the world to work together to resolve issues of global importance. At Doha, had an agreement not been reached to facilitate access to American and European patented drugs in poor countries ravaged by AIDS, there would have been no Doha Round. If the Doha Round fails, the world will be a less prosperous and more dangerous place than if it succeeds.

The aftermath of September 11 did not just affect the process of economic integration in the NAFTA region; it also heightened the importance of launching a new round of global WTO negotiations at the Doha meeting, for both economic and security reasons. WTO leaders felt the need to send a positive message to markets, particularly after the failure of the Seattle meeting of 1999. The United States wanted to send a message that the terrorist attacks, which exacerbated the preexisting economic slowdown, would not prevent the world from carrying on. It was also important to show unity among the nations of the world. As a result, the United States showed renewed leadership at the Doha meeting.

When the Uruguay Round negotiations bogged down and it appeared that they might fail, there was talk of the world's breaking down into regional trading blocs. The terms "Fortress Europe" and "Fortress North

America" entered the lexicon. The concern was that countries (and firms) would either be in or out and that disparities would grow accordingly in the wealth of nations. Following the failure of the OECD Multilateral Agreement on Investment negotiations and of the Seattle WTO meeting, these concerns were raised again. Thus for this reason as well, there was great political pressure to launch a new round at Doha, and in particular to ensure that developing countries captured a greater share of the economic benefits of trade and investment liberalization.

The new round of negotiations began in January 2002 and is set to conclude by January 2005. However, the Doha agreement on the negotiation agenda cleared only the first hurdle. The WTO members must now reach agreements on such difficult issues as agricultural subsidies, environmental protection, competition policy, trade-remedy laws and foreign investment. Even if the negotiations produce agreement on these issues, the resulting instrument will have to be approved by many legislatures, including the U.S. Congress, which is strongly opposed to negotiations on trade-remedy laws. However, failure to achieve further liberalization at the global level could divide the world into regional trading blocs, as seemed possible during the Uruguay Round, at the expense of countries that remain outside of such blocs.

The World Bank has calculated that launching a new trade round, together with related market reforms, could add $2.8 trillion to global income by 2015. Of that, $1.5 trillion would go to developing countries and potentially raise 320 million people out of poverty.[11] Developing countries have the majority of votes among the 144 members of the WTO. The Seattle ministerial meeting of 1999 failed to launch a new round of global trade negotiations because developed and developing countries were unable to agree on the agenda. At the Doha meeting the resolution of the patents issue created a climate in which compromises could be reached on other issues.

However, the September 11 attacks demonstrate that there is more at stake than negotiating new WTO agreements. Should the Doha Round fail, there will be serious implications for global security, not just the global economy. The WTO would be seriously wounded. The failure of global trade talks would add impetus to the negotiation of more manageable regional agreements wherein liberalization could proceed more quickly. The most successful trade blocs would coalesce around the EU, NAFTA and East Asia.

The EU is expanding to incorporate members from Eastern Europe, but it is unlikely to include Russia in the foreseeable future. Turkey is likely to join relatively soon. If WTO negotiations fail, NAFTA will be more likely to expand to include other countries of the Americas, probably through the vehicle of the FTAA. The economic problems experienced by Japan have left the Japanese more open to negotiating trade agreements outside the multilateral framework. A trade bloc could take shape in East Asia in the form of a free trade agreement with Japan at its center, or through Asia Pacific Economic Co-operation (APEC) negotiations. APEC trade negotiations would provide a link between the Americas and East Asia, given the membership of Canada, the United States, Mexico and Chile. Should this occur, a transatlantic free trade agreement would be more likely between Europe and the Americas.

This consolidation of trade blocs would primarily exclude Russia, Africa and (aside from Turkey and Israel) the Middle East. The further marginalization of these regions in the global economy would be a recipe for disaster. Between them these regions contain the majority of the world's Muslims, and Russia retains a large arsenal of nuclear, biological and chemical weapons. Marginalization of these regions could sow the seeds of a far more serious global security problem than currently exists. For this reason, if for no other, there is much at stake in the Doha Round negotiations.

CONCLUSION

NAFTA has not yet been fully implemented, but it has already led to greater economic integration between the three members, particularly with respect to manufacturing, but also with respect to services. Negotiations on labor mobility in the NAFTA region will likely move Canada, Mexico and the United States toward increasingly free movement of labor. Demographic trends in the three countries and the needs of firms in the region will spur movement in this direction. However, security concerns may either slow or speed up the process.

Economic integration under NAFTA will deepen over time, and this will spur a further deepening of NAFTA rules. The likelihood of the widening of NAFTA remains uncertain. Much will depend on the position taken by the U.S. Congress and on the progress made in the Doha Round. If the Doha Round fails, the FTAA negotiations will be given greater impetus.

The course of global economic growth and global security issues will affect the outcome of the Doha negotiations. The worse the state of the global economy and the more severe the global security problems, the more pressure there will be on negotiators to succeed. Notwithstanding the visibility of globalization protesters, the real issue will be whether the developed and developing country members are able to find effective compromises on the issues that divide them.

NOTES

1. Tony Smith, "Leaders Sign Trade-Pact Agreement," *The News*, April 23, 2001, 25.

2. Excluding intra-EU trade, Mexico ranked eighth in merchandise exports and seventh in merchandise imports in 1999. International Trade Statistics 2000. World Trade Organization, Geneva.

3. See Michael E. Porter, "The Competitive Advantage of Nations," *Harvard Business Review* 68 (March/April, 1990), 73–95; Thomas Hout, Michael E. Porter, and Eileen Rudden, "How Global Companies Win Out," *Harvard Business Review* 60 (Sept/Oct,1982), 98–108; C.K. Prahalad and Gary Hamel, "Strategic Intent, *Harvard Business Review* 67 (May/June 1989), 63–76; C.K. Prahalad and Gary Hamel, "The Core Competence of the Corporation," *Harvard Business Review* 68 (May/June,1990), 79–93.

4. "Breaking Foreign Policy Taboos," *The Economist*, August 26, 2000, 25; Tim Weiner, "Mexican President-Elect Warmly Greeted in Washington," *New York Times*, August 25, 2000; José Luis Ruiz y Claudia Mendoza, "Respetaré libertades: Fox," *El Universal*, August 23, 2000, 1.

5. Paul Knox, "Leaders Talk Oil and Gas in Mexico," *Globe and Mail*, February 17, 2001.

6. Tim Weiner and Ginger Thompson, "Bush Gives Mexico Backing on Drive against Narcotics," *New York Times*, February 17, 2001.

7. There are few remaining impediments to capital flows. Tax regulations may impede capital flows, such as withholding taxes on payments to non-residents. Subsidiaries may not be able to claim full tax deductions for payments made to a foreign parent, under rules designed to prevent using transfer pricing to avoid taxes. See International Bureau of Fiscal Documentation, *Taxation and Investment in Canada*, June 21, 1999, available on Lexis-Nexis.

8. Eric Green, "De Facto Monetary Union Predicted between US and Mexico," *Washington File*, December 7, 2000, www.mac.doc.gov/nafta/ar-dec7 percent231.htm.

9. See Thomas J. Courchene and Richard G. Harris, *From Fixing to Monetary Union: Options for North American Currency Integration*, C.D. Howe Institute Commentary 127 (June 1999); and David Laidler and Finn Poschmann, *Leaving Well Enough Alone: Canada's Monetary Order in a Changing International Environment*, C.D. Howe Institute Commentary 142 (May 2000); both available at http://www.cdhowe.org.

10. Tapen Sinha coauthored this section of the chapter.

11. "World Trade Talks Go Down to the Wire," Reuters, November 13, 2001.

Chapter 8

Conclusion

INTRODUCTION

The globalization of the world economy has increased international trade in goods, services and foreign investment. This has coincided with a proliferation of international trade and investment agreements. This book has analyzed and compared NAFTA and WTO rules on trade in goods and services, foreign investment and intellectual property rights and how these rules affect global business strategy. It has also explored the link between trade and security issues. On the one hand, trade barriers contribute to the economic marginalization of the developing world, which could sow the seeds of terrorism and war. On the other hand, the liberalization of flows of goods, services, capital and people can facilitate the flow of weapons and of both terrorists and the money needed to support their activities.

Global environmental issues are also affected by international trade. The shrimp case, discussed in chapter 2, shows how the general rules and general exceptions of trade agreements may interact with domestic politics and international law. Countries can pass laws governing activities inside their territorial limits and governing the activities of their own citizens. However, they have no jurisdiction to regulate noncitizens outside their territory. Without trade agreements, countries would be free to ban all imports if they wished. Once they enter trade agreements, however, governments are bound by rules that limit the use of trade barriers to achieve extraterritorial environmental goals.

Sovereign nations can either negotiate international agreements governing the regulation of international affairs or maintain their independence by refusing to enter such agreements. There is no alternative that respects the principle of national sovereignty, and we have yet to discover an alternative method of regulating international relations. Most countries of the world have entered trade agreements because they recognize the economic benefits of trade liberalization for their citizens.

However, the process of trade liberalization is not always politically smooth. In the case of WTO, the diversity and size of the membership generally makes for slower progress than under regional trade agreements like NAFTA. The trucking and insurance case, discussed in chapter 3, illustrates how regional trade agreements may interact with global trade agreements. It shows how national constitutional law can complicate domestic implementation of international commitments. The case also provides an example of how domestic industry groups can influence international trade policy.

BUSINESS STRATEGY AND WTO/NAFTA
RULES ON GOODS

The main issues facing firms under both NAFTA and WTO is how to minimize duties and eliminate import and export restrictions. There are fewer barriers under NAFTA than under WTO. Thus, these trade barriers have a greater impact on global strategies than on regional strategies.

Duties and import restrictions increase the cost of importing inputs in manufacturing, the cost of products in export markets, and access to markets. These trade barriers thus affect the price competitiveness of a firm's products, the location of manufacturing facilities and the choice of export markets. The availability of such trade barriers also affects the strategies available to firms to protect home markets against foreign competitors. In this regard, trade remedy laws are particularly relevant.

The lumber case, discussed in chapter 2, provides a good example of the protectionist ends that may be served by trade-remedy laws. It also reveals how the impact of trade barriers on consumers can be used to organize opposition to trade barriers within the target market. The lumber case also shows how exporters may have to choose between negotiating a predictable level of trade barriers and using international dispute settlement mechanisms to eliminate trade barriers.

With respect to customs, the major issues facing firms are to minimize import duties and ensure predictability in how imports and exports will be treated. Predicting duties on shipments of goods is an essential part of the business planning process, particularly with respect to setting prices. Import duties protect domestic industry from foreign competition on the basis of price. Exporters that choose to absorb the cost of duties by charging a lower price in the export market run the risk of antidumping duties. Import duties may thus influence whether the firm chooses to compete on price or on other product characteristics, such as the quality or image of the product.

Product standards affect the choice a firm has between a strategy of product standardization and a strategy of adaptation to local market demands. If standards are harmonized, the choice of strategy can be based on whether consumers require adaptation. Without harmonized standards, the cost of products rises, because firms cannot achieve economies of scale in the production of "global" products. Standards may influence the policies of firms where the target market is important enough and access to the market depends on accepting the cost of adapting production runs to different standards.

Trade barriers also influence whether a firm chooses to enter foreign markets with an export strategy or a foreign direct investment (FDI) strategy. Where the trade barriers in the target market make exporting impractical, the firm may have to invest in manufacturing facilities inside the country.

There is considerable overlap between WTO and NAFTA agreements in relation to trade in goods. The rules tend to cover the same issues, but NAFTA has made more progress in liberalizing trade in goods than has WTO. The general rules and the general exceptions are essentially the same. However, NAFTA generally eliminates tariffs much more quickly than WTO. With respect to rules of origin, NAFTA has an agreement in place, while the relevant WTO agreement remains under negotiation. However, with respect to customs valuation, NAFTA simply adopts the WTO agreement. With respect to standards, the two agreements provide essentially the same rules. However, in the area of government procurement, NAFTA is more advanced. Table 8.1 compares the progress made under NAFTA and WTO in six categories of rules relating to trade in goods.

Table 8.1
Comparison of Coverage of NAFTA and WTO Rules on Goods

Agreement	Tariffs	Standards	Valuation	Origin	Procurement	CVD/ADD
NAFTA	Eliminate	Similar	No	Yes	Yes	No
WTO	Reduces	Similar	Yes	No	No	Yes

BUSINESS STRATEGY AND WTO/NAFTA RULES
ON SERVICES

The strategies service firms adopt vary with the nature of the service and the barriers to market access. When the customer travels to the service provider's country to purchase the service, there may be limits on the provision of services to nonresidents. The firm's strategy to gain access to nonresident clients may thus have to take the form of FDI in foreign subsidiaries. Denying the firm the right to serve nonresidents also restricts the cross-border sale of services by telephone, fax and Internet.

The availability of entry visas for natural persons affects both market-entry strategy and decisions regarding the nationality of employees. This also affects the firm's ability to transfer personnel to, and hence the transmission of knowledge and expertise between operations in, different countries.

Foreign investment restrictions affect the control a firm has over foreign operations. Joint venture and merger strategies will vary with equity restrictions. Market entry may be available only through a minority equity stake in a joint venture with a local firm. Thus, a joint venture may be a necessity rather than a strategic choice.

The Mexican telecommunications case, discussed in chapter 3, provides an example of foreign investment restrictions that force companies to enter joint ventures in order to enter the market. The case demonstrates the importance of foreign investment as a market-entry strategy in certain service industries. The case also shows how firms can enhance market access by lobbying their own governments to use international dispute-resolution systems. However, it also shows how the lack of effective domestic competition regulations can impede market access. This demonstrates the importance to global service firms of placing foreign investment and competition laws on the negotiating agenda for the WTO Doha Round.

GATS and NAFTA operate very differently in the ways they liberalize trade in services. While NAFTA provides a comprehensive set of rules with which members must comply, GATS is primarily a framework for further negotiation. The GATS negotiations that began in 2000 have been folded into the Doha Round. GATS sets out some of the same general principles as NAFTA, such as most-favored nation (MFN) treatment and transparency. However, in contrast to NAFTA, the general obligations of GATS do not include market access or national treatment.

NAFTA uses a "negative list" of reservations, listing specific measures that do *not* comply with the general rules. This prevents governments from creating new restrictions, except where such restrictions qualify under exceptions. The creation of these negative lists enhances transparency and simplifies future negotiations. GATS uses the opposite approach; whereas

Table 8.2
Commitments by Mode of Supply under NAFTA and WTO

Mode of Supply	NAFTA	Canada (WTO)	USA (WTO)	Mexico (WTO)
Cross-border Supply	YES	YES	YES	NO
Consumption Abroad	YES	YES	YES	NO
Commercial Presence	YES	YES	YES	YES
Natural Persons	YES	YES	NO	NO

it sets out country-specific lists of services that are *liberalized*. Thus, if a WTO member does not make a specific commitment, it has no obligation to grant market access. Even when a commitment is made, the country in question may submit lengthy lists of reservations for measures that contradict the commitment. Table 8.2 compares the market access commitments of Canada, the United States and Mexico under NAFTA and WTO.

Table 8.3 compares the applicability of NAFTA and WTO rules in each of the three countries by mode of supply.

BUSINESS STRATEGY AND FOREIGN INVESTMENT RULES

FDI and international trade provide different strategies for firms to enter foreign markets. The choice between these entry strategies is influenced generally by factors such as market size, geographic location, the firm's penetration of the market and legal restrictions. In the case of services, FDI

Table 8.3
Comparison of NAFTA and WTO by Mode of Supply

Mode of Supply	Canada	United States	Mexico
Cross-border Supply	NAFTA/ WTO	NAFTA/ WTO	NAFTA
Consumption Abroad	NAFTA/ WTO	NAFTA/ WTO	NAFTA
Natural Persons	NAFTA/ WTO	NAFTA	NAFTA
Commercial Presence	NAFTA/ WTO	NAFTA/ WTO	NAFTA/ WTO

may be the only viable strategy where the firm needs a commercial presence in order to sell its service. However, FDI and international trade can also be complementary strategies, in that FDI often implies importing inputs and exporting final products in manufacturing industries. In addition, a prior strategy of exports establishes a foothold that later facilitates FDI once sales volumes justify a longer-term commitment to the market. However, FDI can achieve strategic goals that a simple export strategy does not—such as adapting the product to the needs of the local market, incorporating local inputs and gathering more sophisticated market intelligence.

The strategic goals served by FDI vary considerably depending on the sector, the target client, and the strategic purpose of the investment. In the services sector, firms that provide support services to multinationals may use FDI to enhance services for those clients. For other services firms, the purpose may be to compete against local firms for customers in the host country. In manufacturing, the strategic purpose of the investment may be to secure resources or to serve the host market. In both manufacturing and services, an investment in a joint venture may provide a vehicle to gain market access or to acquire the partner's technology or market intelligence.

The presence or absence of trade and investment barriers has become an important consideration in the FDI decisions of firms that base location of manufacturing on worldwide or regionwide sourcing of inputs and export of finished products. Where there are low barriers to trade in goods, manufacturers no longer have to set up factories to serve each market. Instead, they can export from a single location that is most cost effective. The nature of the country's foreign investment laws will likely determine whether FDI in manufacturing constitutes a market-entry strategy or is meant to produce goods for export.

NAFTA has liberalized foreign investment far more than has WTO. NAFTA provides protection, which WTO lacks, against expropriation and other government measures. TRIMS merely clarifies the application of GATT rules on trade in goods. However, there exists between many WTO members an extensive network of bilateral investment treaties that provide similar protection. In addition, some agreements under GATS liberalize FDI on a selective basis. Progress in this area has been difficult to achieve politically, as evidenced by the failure of the OECD negotiations. It remains to be seen how much progress will be achieved in the Doha Round on foreign investment and how that progress will in turn affect the global investment strategies of firms. Table 8.4 compares the coverage of NAFTA and WTO foreign investment rules.

The Metalclad case, discussed in chapter 5, shows how NAFTA provisions on expropriation and dispute settlement work. It confirms that federal governments are responsible to investors for the actions of states. The

Table 8.4
Comparison of NAFTA and WTO Foreign Investment Rules

Agreement	Market Access	Intell. Property	Protection	Investor Arbitration
NAFTA	Broad	Comparable	Yes	Yes
WTO	Limited	Comparable	No	No

case also clarifies the relationship between environmental law and foreign investors' rights. Finally, it provides a good example of the potential impact of legal protection for foreign investors on investment decisions, in a way that highlights the importance of WTO negotiations in this area.

BUSINESS STRATEGY AND INTELLECTUAL PROPERTY RIGHTS

Intellectual property laws may influence the kind of technology a firm chooses to bring to a foreign operation. Since most forms of intellectual property are easily copied, it is difficult to protect, even with adequate laws. However, right holders can lobby their governments to put pressure on foreign governments to enforce intellectual-property laws more vigorously. Industry associations can also lobby foreign governments in conjunction with the efforts of their own government.

Legal enforcement of intellectual property rights can be expensive and cause other business problems. Even with modern intellectual-property laws on the books, many countries still lack the financial and human resources needed to enforce them. In the case of the pharmaceutical industry, legal enforcement of patent rights in Africa proved damaging to its public image and fueled political opposition to patent holders that ultimately contributed to the dilution of patent rights in the Doha Declaration on TRIPS.

Despite the potential problems, however, it is in the interest of right holders to enjoy legal protection for intellectual property. Having strong laws in place improves the bargaining position of companies in negotiations over compensation when their rights are violated. Most importantly, it keeps the option of formal legal action available.

The pharmaceutical industry provides a good example of how proactive efforts can influence the negotiation of international trade agreements. Through lobbying efforts, the industry influenced the Uruguay Round negotiations. Those efforts continue to seek further development of the law that would enhance the protection of their patent rights. For the Doha meeting, the industry put pressure on the United States and other countries to resist any dilution of TRIPS obligations. While the industry did not entirely succeed, these efforts probably minimized the degree to which those obligations were diminished.

NAFTA chapter 17 and TRIPS both oblige governments to protect and enforce intellectual property rights on a nondiscriminatory basis. Both provide protection for copyright, trademarks, patents, trade secrets and industrial designs. Like TRIPS, NAFTA incorporates preexisting intellectual property treaties.

An important difference between NAFTA and TRIPS is that NAFTA does not expressly exclude the issue of exhaustion of intellectual property rights from dispute settlement. NAFTA is not entirely clear on the exhaustion issue; however, right holders may seek enforcement at the border when there is an infringement of intellectual property rights under the laws of the importing country. Patent owners are provided the right to prevent others from making, using or selling the subject matter of their patents without their consent. However, unlike TRIPS, this right does not cover importation. As a result, the issue of exhaustion is left to the domestic legislation of each country. Differential-pricing strategies in the NAFTA region therefore need to take national laws into account.

A major difference between WTO and NAFTA is that NAFTA provides protection for foreign investors, including investments in intellectual property. However, the requirement to pay compensation for expropriation excludes compulsory licenses issued on patents. Nevertheless, governments may be liable to pay compensation where their actions otherwise violate NAFTA chapter 17 obligations on intellectual property.

BUSINESS STRATEGY AND RULES ENFORCEMENT

International business people have an important role to play in the enforcement of trade agreements. Under WTO, governments pursue dispute settlement to enhance the ability of their firms to expand internationally. Under NAFTA, firms have direct access to dispute settlement to protect their foreign investments and to challenge the application of trade-remedy laws.

Trade-remedy laws can have a tremendous impact on international business strategy, as illustrated by the lumber case. Where firms receive financial support from government, the subsidies should be structured to fit exceptions in the WTO rules. Firms also need to assess the effect of dumping laws on differential pricing strategies. Competitors may use trade-remedy laws to seek protection against foreign competition.

Where NAFTA and WTO rules overlap, the WTO may be the better forum in which to settle disputes, for both legal and strategic reasons. A

WTO decision carries more weight than a NAFTA decision, due to the size of the WTO membership. For Canada and Mexico, the disproportionate bargaining power of the United States is offset by other influential WTO members, increasing the likelihood that a decisions will be implemented by the United States. Moreover, the WTO has established both a permanent roster of arbitrators and an appellate body to review their decisions. NAFTA chapter 20 lacks both. WTO decisions thus enjoy greater credibility than decisions made by chapter 20 panels.

CONCLUSION

National trade and investment policies can either facilitate or impede international business strategies. The deeper integration achieved in regional trade and investment blocs helps to explain the regional orientations of many firms. Trade agreements provide greater predictability and transparency in domestic laws that affect international business strategy. Market-entry strategies are influenced by foreign investment restrictions, trade barriers and the ability to transfer personnel between countries. The reduction of barriers to the movement of goods, services and people, along with laws protecting foreign investments and intellectual property, expands the strategic options available to firms.

Since World War II, policy makers have recognized that trade liberalization contributes to wealth creation and that economic interdependence enhances international security. In the aftermath of September 11, these twin issues have crystallized in the minds of world leaders and underlined the importance of global trade negotiations. Multinational enterprises are major beneficiaries of trade liberalization and therefore have a big stake in future negotiations. Firms can and should help to shape the rules that are negotiated in trade agreements, by lobbying their governments to take specific negotiating positions in the Doha Round and future NAFTA negotiations.

The "big picture" allows us to see the links between AIDS, trade, terrorism and global business strategy and to understand the economic, historical and political context in which trade negotiations take place. In the details, we see how trade agreements work, what they contain, how regional and global agreements compare, and where the intersections of NAFTA, WTO and global business strategy lie. In formulating appropriate strategies and negotiating positions, one must see the big picture but remember that the devil is in the details.

Selected Bibliography

BOOKS AND MONOGRAPHS

Aulakh, Preet S., and Michael G. Schecter, eds. "Rethinking Globalization(s): From Corporate Transnationalism to Local Interventions." New York: St. Martin's Press, 2000.

Brownlie, Ian. *Principles of Public International Law*. 2d ed. Oxford: Clarendon Press, 1973.

Drucker, Peter. *Management Challenges for the 21st Century*. New York: Harper Business, 1999.

Dunning, John ed. *Globalization, Trade and Foreign Direct Investment*. Oxford: Elsevier, 1998.

Fairbanks, Michael, and Stace Lindsay. *Plowing the Sea: Nurturing the Hidden Sources of Growth in the Developing World*. Cambridge, Mass.: Harvard Business School Press, 1997.

Leycegui, Beatriz, William Robson and Dahlia Stein, eds. *Trading Punches: Trade Remedy Law and Dispute Settlement under NAFTA*. Washington, D.C.: North American Committee, 1995.

Lipsey, Richard, Daniel Schwanen and Ronald Wonnacott. *The NAFTA: What's In, What's Out, What's Next*. Toronto: C.D. Howe Institute, 1994.

Mailander, Christopher J. *Reshaping North American Banking: The Transforming Effects of Regional Market and Policy Shifts*. Washington, D.C.: Center for Strategic and International Studies, 1999.

McNair, Lord. *The Law of Treaties*. Oxford: Clarendon Press, 1961.

Naím, Moisés, and Joseph Tulchin, eds. *Competition Policy, Deregulation and Modernization in Latin America*. Boulder, Colo.: Lynne Rienner, 1999.

OECD. *Liberalization of Insurance Operations: Cross-Border Trade and Establishment of Foreign Branches*. Paris: OECD, 1999.

———. *Survey of OECD Work on International Investment*. Paris: OECD, 1998.

Riggs, A.R., and Tom Velk, eds. *Beyond NAFTA: An Economic, Political and Socio-logical Perspective.* Vancouver: Fraser Institute, 1993.

Rugman, Alan, and Alain Verbeke. *Global Corporate Strategy and Trade Policy.* New York: Routledge, 1990.

Rugman, Alan. *The End of Globalization: Why Global Strategy Is a Myth and How to Profit from the Realities of Regional Markets.* New York: Amacom, 2001.

Sauvé, Pierre, and Daniel Schwanen, eds. *Investment Rules for the Global Economy: Enhancing Access to Markets.* Toronto: C.D. Howe Institute, 1996.

WTO. *Guide to GATT Law and Practice.* 6th ed. Geneva: Bernan Press, 1995.

CASES

Canada—Patent Protection of Pharmaceutical Products, Report of the Panel, WT/DS114/R (2000).

Canada—Term of Patent Protection, Report of the Panel, WT/DS170/R (2000).

European Communities—Regime for the Importation, Sale and Distribution of Bananas, Report of the Panel, WT/DS27 (1997).

European Communities—Regime for the Importation, Sale and Distribution of Bananas, Award of the Arbitrator, WT/DS27/15 (1998).

Indonesia—Certain Measures Affecting the Automobile Industry, Report of the Panel, WT/DS55 (1998).

In the Matter of Certain Softwood Lumber Products from Canada, Decision of the Panel, Q.L. [1993] F.T.A.D. No. 5.

In the Matter of Cross-Border Trucking Services, Final Report of the Panel, USA-MEX-98-2008-01, February 6, 2001

Metalclad Corporation v. The United Mexican States, ICSID Case No. ARB(AF)/97/1, 40 ILM 36 (2001); 13 *World Trade and Arbitration Materials* 47 (2001).

Pope & Talbot Inc. v. Government of Canada (April 10,2001).

Robert Azinian, Kenneth Davitian, & Ellen Baca v. The United Mexican States, 14 ICSID Rev.-FILJ 538 (1999); 39 ILM 537 (2000).

S.D. Myers Inc. v. Government of Canada (November 13, 2000).

The United Mexican States v. Metalclad Corporation, May 2, 2001, B.C.S.C. 664.

US—Import Prohibition of Certain Shrimp and Shrimp Products, Report of the Appellate Body, AB-1998-4 (1998).

US—Measures Treating Export Restraints as Subsidies, Complaint by Canada, Report of the Panel, DS194/R (2001).

Waste Management Inc. v. United Mexican States, 15 ICSID Rev.—FILJ 214 (2000); 40 ILM 56 (2001).

Index

About the Author

BRADLY J. CONDON is Professor of International Law and Business at the Instituto Tecnologico Autonomo de Mexico. He is the author of two books and numerous articles and conference papers, and, in 2001, he won the Lumina Award for Pioneering Research in Law and Regulation.